T0319948

North American Freight Transportation

TRANSPORT ECONOMICS, MANAGEMENT AND POLICY

Series Editor: Kenneth Button, *University Professor, School of Public Policy, George Mason University, USA*

Transport is a critical input for economic development and for optimising social and political interaction. Recent years have seen significant new developments in the way that transport is perceived by private industry and governments, and in the way academics look at it.

The aim of this series is to provide original material and up-to-date synthesis of the state of modern transport analysis. The coverage embraces all conventional modes of transport but also includes contributions from important related fields such as urban and regional planning and telecommunications where they interface with transport. The books draw from many disciplines and some cross disciplinary boundaries. They are concerned with economics, planning, sociology, geography, management science, psychology and public policy. They are intended to help improve the understanding of transport, the policy needs of the most economically advanced countries and the problems of resource-poor developing economies. The authors come from around the world and represent some of the outstanding young scholars as well as established names.

Titles in the series include:

The Future of Automated Freight Transport
Concepts, Design and Implementation
Edited by Rob Konings, Hugo Priemus and Peter Nijkamp

Telecommunications, Transportation and Location
Kenneth Button and Roger Stough and Michelle Bragg and Samantha Taylor

Competition in the Railway Industry
An International Comparative Analysis
Edited by José A. Gómez-Ibáñez and Ginés de Rus

Globalized Freight Transport
Intermodality, E-Commerce, Logistics and Sustainability
Edited by Thomas R. Leinbach and Cristina Capineri

Decision-Making on Mega-Projects
Cost–Benefit Analysis, Planning and Innovation
Edited by Hugo Priemus, Bent Flyvbjerg and Bert van Wee

Port Privatisation
The Asia-Pacific Experience
Edited by James Reveley and Malcolm Tull

The Future of Intermodal Freight Transport
Operations, Design and Policy
Edited by Rob Konings, Hugo Priemus and Peter Nijkamp

North American Freight Transportation
The Road to Security and Prosperity
Mary R. Brooks

North American Freight Transportation

The Road to Security and Prosperity

Mary R. Brooks

Dalhousie University, Canada

TRANSPORT ECONOMICS, MANAGEMENT AND POLICY

Edward Elgar

Cheltenham, UK • Northampton, MA, USA

Published by
Edward Elgar Publishing Limited
Glensanda House
Montpellier Parade
Cheltenham
Glos GL50 1UA
UK

Edward Elgar Publishing, Inc.
William Pratt House
9 Dewey Court
Northampton
Massachusetts 01060
USA

A catalogue record for this book
is available from the British Library

Library of Congress Control Number: 2008926562

ISBN 978 1 84720 799 9

Printed and bound in Great Britain by MPG Books Ltd, Bodmin, Cornwall

Contents

Preface

I would very much like to begin at the beginning – with the research assistance of Michael J. Siltala, MBA/LLB class of 1993 (Dalhousie University) for his work in analysing the North American Free Trade Agreement on a line-by-line basis, and helping me begin this 15-year journey. If it had not been for his diligence and then-Dean Jim McNiven's challenge to examine the impacts of the agreement on an industry I had been researching for many years, this entire journey would never have begun. It opened my eyes to more than the narrow worlds of shipping and air cargo – to the broader fields of surface transport, and the importance of transportation to the North American economy. I had never been much of a student of Canada–US relations, but my trip to Washington and the Transportation Research Board Annual Meeting to present my first efforts at looking at the impact of *NAFTA* on the industry was a milestone in this life-changing journey.

Once on the road to thinking continentally, there were a number of people instrumental in shaping the direction in which this research has gone. Rob Harrison of the University of Texas at Austin served as more of a sounding board than he was possibly aware, Joedy Cambridge of the Transportation Research Board encouraged me to continue my interest in observing the key issues, and Stephen Blank (then of Pace University) encouraged me to apply to the Canada–US Fulbright Program to study the matter further. The Foundation for Educational Exchange between Canada and the United States (Canada–US Fulbright Program) provided the funding to undertake a five-month stay in the US, and my colleague Ken Button arranged for a welcome reception at George Mason University's School of Public Policy.

Once in the greater Washington area, but 'outside the beltway', everyone in the US government and its many departments were open and available. I wished I had more than five months to understand the issues of transportation and security and, of course, American public policy-making. There were so many people I met, whose ideas are sometimes found between the lines of this book. There are a few I will take time to recognize in particular.

I would like to thank Michael Sprung, of the US Department of Transportation, for his help in understanding the structure and content of the databases of the US Department of Transportation Research and Innovative Technology Administration, and Henry Vega, Ph.D. candidate at George Mason University, for his adept ability at making the data understandable. Jennifer Milne of Dalhousie University's GIS Department turned the data into the maps in Figures 3.1 to 3.5 and created Figure 2.3 for me; her successor, Ian Bryson, re-created Figure 6.1 with the permission of the Atlantic Institute for Market Studies. A picture really is worth a thousand words. Without their efforts, the book would have had much less meaning for those of us who relate better to maps.

Without the research assistance of Denise Napoliello and Marc Thibault of George Mason University, the compiling of all of the content analysis of the interviews for Chapters 3 and 4 would have been so much more difficult. The research assistance of Diana Dennis, Dalhousie MBA 2005 graduate, helped me get ready to go to the US. Monica Weshler, Dalhousie MBA 2006 graduate, assisted in the development of the air section of Chapter 5, and Veronica Ford, Dalhousie MBA/LLB 2007 collected the material on regionalism and perimeter security for Chapter 6. These efforts all made the task easier.

The collegial support of Dick Hodgson of the Dalhousie Marine Affairs Program was invaluable in shaping my thoughts of marine regulation in North America over the past five years; he has been a pleasure to work with, and a friend as well. The research on short sea shipping undertaken at Dalhousie – financially supported by the Strategic Highway Infrastructure Program (Transport Canada), the Halifax Port Authority and the Centre for International Business Studies (Dalhousie University) – shaped much of my current thinking on North American shipping. I continue to believe that no amount of rhetoric will switch traffic from truck to the more environmentally-preferable mode of short sea shipping without Americans coming to grips with the 'soft' but very 'hard' issue of the Jones Act.

Every book has a person or two without whom its writing would not have been completed. In this case, Margaret Sweet of the School of Business Administration provided that invaluable second set of eyes on the manuscript, but the end product is totally my responsibility. Finally, without the support of my husband and two children, this project would never have been completed. To them, I owe everything.

MRB
15 September, 2007

Acknowledgement

Statistics Canada information is used with the permission of Statistics Canada. Users are forbidden to copy this material and/or redisseminate the data, in an original or modified form, for commercial purposes, without the expressed permission of Statistics Canada. Information on the availability of the wide range of data from Statistics Canada can be obtained from Statistics Canada's Regional Offices, its World Wide Web site at www.statcan.ca, and its toll-free access number 001-800-263-1136.

1. *NAFTA*: A history and post-9/11 assessment

INTRODUCTION

It is a delicate balancing act to ensure security without compromising operational effectiveness in transborder shipments. Without a timely and efficient goods movement network, the benefits of a liberalized trading relationship may be lost. This concern, that the economic benefits that have grown from the *Canada–US Trade Agreement* (*CUSTA*) and the *North American Free Trade Agreement* (*NAFTA*)[1] may have been diminished by the current security-focus of American officials, is a key reason why this book has been written. Heightened awareness of North America's vulnerability to terrorism and subversion in the post-9/11 era has precipitated a crisis for transport suppliers, one that threatens to compromise the economic prosperity of Canada and the United States of America (US). The primary priority of the US government has been to protect its citizens and commerce by increasing security in an effort to manage risk. The implementation of security measures is, for the most part, overriding US considerations of trade facilitation and economic growth, and at a cost and with consequences that are not fully understood. It is no longer possible to assume that the future of the North American economic relationship will continue to evolve in the direction it has in the past, or that the spillover effects from further economic integration will mean greater efficiency in the North American market in the short to medium term.

This book is about the transportation system in North America, primarily from a Canadian and US perspective, and the impact of security on the transport suppliers and traders using the system. This chapter sets the scene. It begins with a primer about the three countries and their economic situation relative to the world in order to provide context for the book. It then explores the general historical relationship between Canada, the US and Mexico to provide additional context, as part of the trading relationship is driven by the cultural and historical one. The chapter then discusses the negotiating history for both the *Canada–US Trade Agreement* and the *North American Free Trade Agreement*, so that the relative perspectives of the three countries come into focus. Using secondary data sources, the trading and investing patterns within the NAFTA region are examined, and conclusions about the nature of economic integration are discussed. The chapter closes with a synopsis of the structure of the remainder of the book.

NORTH AMERICA IN THE WORLD

At the time the *NAFTA* was signed, the region was a key player in the global economy, accounting for almost 18 per cent of global trade (Table 1.1 and Figure 1.1). Over the period 1993–2000, the benefits that NAFTA brought were invariably assessed as dramatic gains arising from the liberalization of trade. Hills (1999) reported that Canada/Mexico and US/Mexico trade growth from 1994 to 1998 was twice that of world trade growth. The total trilateral volume of trade (in value terms) expanded at a faster rate than the growth in total world trade, but peaked in 2000. Intra-NAFTA exports as a percentage of global exports rose from 1995 to 2000 (7.9 per cent to 10.9 per cent) and then dropped by 2003 to 8.9 per cent (WTO, 2004) and to 8.3 per cent in 2004 (WTO, 2005). By 2005, intra-NAFTA imports had returned in share terms to 1990 levels (WTO, 2007, Table I.10). This implies that from 1993 to 2000, *NAFTA* was a success in generating trade growth within the region, but the gains have since been eroded.

The data in Table 1.1 are expanded and better illustrated by Figure 1.1. The share of global exports from the NAFTA region rose from the mid-1990s (after the Mexican peso crisis) to a high of 19.0 per cent in 2000 before falling steadily since; in 2005, the region's share of global exports was less than it had been in 1993 or 1995 (its lowest point in the 1990s) to a mere 14.2 per cent in 2005. The decline in the region's share of global

Table 1.1 NAFTA's share of global exports (in millions of US dollars at current prices)

World exports from	1993	1996	1999	2002	2005
NAFTA	661 837	922 706	1 070 634	1 106 179	1 477 578
Canada	145 178	201 633	238 446	252 394	359 578
Mexico	51 886	96 000	136 391	160 682	213 711
United States	464 773	625 073	695 797	693 103	904 289
World	3 781 000	5 401 000	5 713 000	6 484 000	10 393 000

Source: Merchandise trade statistics from World Trade Organization (2006).

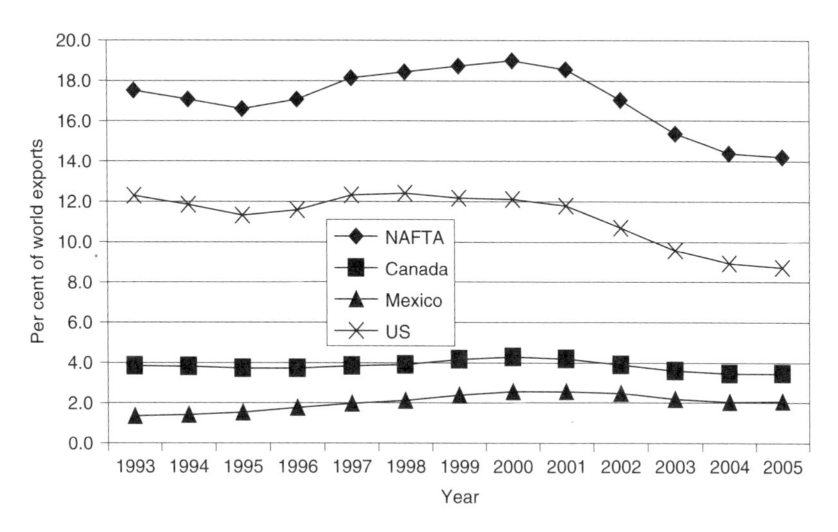

Source: Merchandise trade statistics from World Trade Organization (2006).

Figure 1.1 NAFTA's share of global exports

trade since 2001 is worrisome, and raises questions that cannot really be answered given the data available: is this decline due to security concerns or other factors, such as the changing currency exchange rates? Has it come from the outsourcing of Canadian and US manufacturing to non-NAFTA countries? Would the decline have been worse without the agreement?

Hilsenrath and Buckman (2003) reported that manufacturing jobs decreased in the US by 11 per cent between 1995 and 2002, but that these losses were less severe than losses in China (15 per cent), Japan (16 per cent) and Brazil (19.9 per cent), and comparable to those in the United Kingdom (12 per cent) and Korea (12 per cent). In the same period, countries experiencing growth in manufacturing employment included Canada with 22 per cent and Mexico with 1 per cent. The Mexican stability was attributed to the currency devaluation the country experienced in 1994, while the Canadian situation reflected the weakened Canadian dollar through this period. This growth in manufacturing in Canada and Mexico suggests that the overall decline could have been much worse than it was.

Of the three countries, Canada is the most trade-dependent (Figure 1.2). That trade dependence has grown since long before the signing of both agreements. In the early 1980s, approximately 60 per cent of Canada's exports were bound for the US; since the signing of both agreements, US markets have become the foundation for the Canadian economy. Throughout the

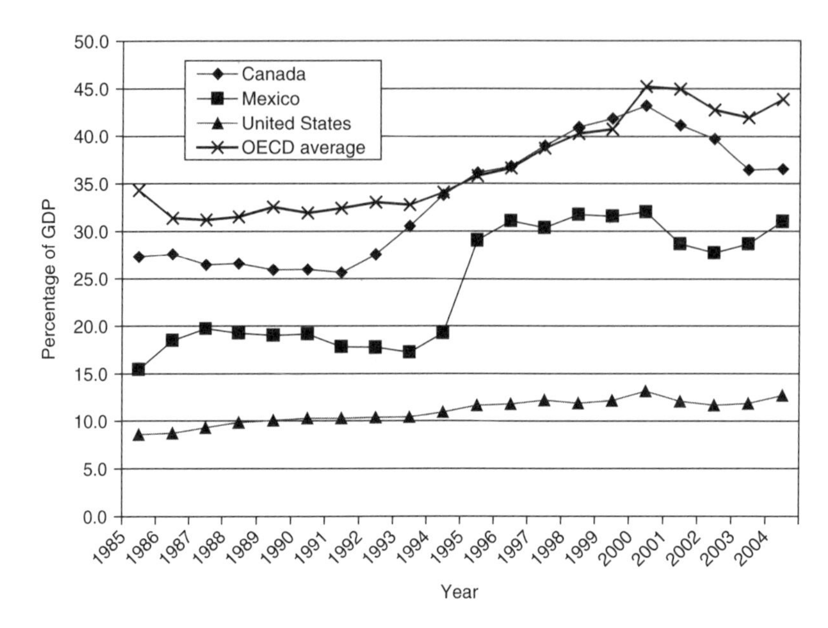

Source: Adapted from macroeconomic trends – gross domestic product (GDP) – national income per capita, *OECD Factbook 2006: Economic, Environmental and Social Statistics*, © OECD 2006. Used with permission.

Figure 1.2 Trade as a percentage of GDP (for the three NAFTA countries)

1980s and early 1990s, Canada reduced its trade diversification so much that its future became irrevocably tied to that of the US.

In the period immediately after the signing of the *NAFTA*, Mexico grew to be Canada's third largest import source (after the US and Japan) by 1999, but was bumped to fourth by China in 2001. In 2004, Mexico was Canada's fifth largest export market, with Japan, the United Kingdom and China in second, third and fourth place (Industry Canada, 2006). Mexico's trade with Canada peaked in 2002 and also seems to have stalled, while its trade with the US peaked earlier in 2000 (North American Transportation Statistics, 2006), (see Table 1.2). However, as Figure 1.1 clearly indicates, the global trading relationships enjoyed by Canada and Mexico pale in comparison to the size and clout that the US represents in the world economy.

Since the signing of the *NAFTA*, Mexico increased its trade dependence on the US market as well, and the boost in the importance of trade to its GDP is quite obvious in Figure 1.2. Its pattern of dependence is quite similar to that of Canada while the US is much less export-oriented. The

Table 1.2 NAFTA trade by value (millions of Canadian dollars)

Route/Year	1990	1995	1998	2000	2002	2004
Canadian imports from the US	87 865	150 683	203 578	229 644	218 329	208 553
Canadian exports to the US	108 586	207 752	269 908	359 289	345 366	347 933
US exports to Mexico	33 108	63 557	117 211	165 917	153 159	144 176
US imports from Mexico	35 205	84 684	140 501	201 842	211 578	202 833
Canadian exports to Mexico	656	1 161	1 467	2 035	2 420	2 975
Canadian imports from Mexico	1 749	5 352	7 682	12 066	12 732	13 398

Note: Because each country defines and collects merchandise trade data differently, these numbers should be treated as approximate only. Detailed use should rely on the original data available at the NATS website. This table is an amalgam of Tables 6-1a and 6-1c. It is expanded by mode in Table 2.1, Chapter 2 of this book.

Source: Selected data from North American Transportation Statistics (NATS) database, January 2006.

large size of the US domestic market and the smaller role of exports in its economy means the US is simply not as trade-dependent as the other two NAFTA partners.

RELATIONSHIPS IN THE NAFTA REGION

As Condon and Sinha (2003, pp. 4–5) pointed out, a deep historical distrust framed the early years of the Canada–US relationship. The War of Independence provided the seeds of not one nation but two. Canada became the place of refuge for British loyalists and, not satisfied with the British retreat, the Americans sought unsuccessfully to drive the British from the continent in the War of 1812. This second war was not a success for the US, as Canadian (British) forces overran Washington, burning both the White House and the Capitol. The eventual development of Canada as a nation was partly forced by US aggression against Britain for supporting the South in the American Civil War; confederation of the first four colonies – Upper Canada (now Ontario), Lower Canada (now Quebec), Nova Scotia and New Brunswick – in 1867. Britain did not finally leave the continent until Newfoundland and Labrador joined Canada in 1949.

The same historical distrust is also found in Mexico's relationship with the US (Condon and Sinha, 2003, pp. 5–6), growing out of the US annexation of Texas in 1845, the US declaration of war against Mexico and the 1848 *Treaty of Guadalupe Hidalgo*. The treaty resulted in Mexico losing two-fifths of its territory to the US. As a result, distrust permeated the Mexico–US relationship until well into the twentieth century.

A third plank of history is relevant to understanding the relationship and the development of transport on the continent. Both Canada and the US developed as nations from East to West, with settlement of the continent following the exploration routes and later its transportation networks. East–West networks were strengthened in both countries by the development of the railroads in the 1800s and transcontinental highway networks in the 1900s. The US interstate highway system was made a reality in 1956 by the signing of the *Federal-Aid Highway Act of 1956*, creating the US network used today. In 1949, Canada passed the *Trans Canada Highway Act* with the aim of building a network to rival the transcontinental rail system by 1967, the centennial of Canada's Confederation. Today, the nature of the continental trade and transport networks reflects these early East–West networks overlaid by strong regional corridors (North–South). The regional nature of the Canada–US relationship will be examined in more detail in Chapter 6.

As a former interest of Spain, Mexican culture is closer to that of Central America than the former British colonies. Canada and the US differ significantly in their cultural values. While Canada and the US share a history of nation-building through immigration, the US has seen itself as a melting pot of migrants over the past two centuries, with a focus on assimilation. Canadians boast of their cultural mosaic or multicultural society where diversity is celebrated. This divergence in cultural development has left a wide philosophical gap between Canadians and Americans about the role of government in the economy, how immigration should be managed, and the rights of citizens. The two, however, remain 'best friends' and 'close neighbours in time of need'. As a result of both history and culture, Mexico and the southern US look north and see wide cultural differences between the South and the North. The original 'Yankee' North looks south and does not always see Mexico as part of North America, but as part of the 'south' that is Central and South America. In spite of a European perception that 'America' is culturally similar, the reality is that it faces cultural divergence not dissimilar to that seen within the European Union. North America is not a homogeneous region.[2]

In both Canada and the US today, citizens question what their governments have done for (or to) them as of late. While both Canada and the US were former British colonies, their tolerance of government developed radically differently. Canada is somewhat further to the left, with its citizens expecting a 'cradle to grave' safety net of social services and prepared to accept higher tax rates for it; when its government pension plan became unsustainable, there was no outrage over the increase in premiums. The US has been unable to deal with its failing Medicare or old age pension programs because of the fractious nature of its political process. Perhaps the differences can be all summed up by comparing the two national 'brands': Americans believe wholeheartedly in 'Life, Liberty and the Pursuit of Happiness', while Canadians are seldom likely to repeat their mantra – 'Peace, Order and Good Government' – in more than a whisper. Both continue to view Mexico more as part of Latin America than North America; it has been a struggle for the citizen of each to think more broadly about the continent.

The Three Amigos

Today, the NAFTA trading region is still quite diverse. Canada and Mexico track similarly in population size, while the US is not only more populous but has economic clout that overwhelms its two neighbours (Table 1.3). Over the last decade, US GDP per capita has risen more sharply than that of either Mexico or Canada (Figure 1.3).

The asymmetrical nature of the relationship is also illustrated by the basic size of the transport sectors, with that of the US clearly dominant in sheer volume carried (Table 1.4). Only in pipelines is the Canadian network significantly larger than would be suggested by the relative population size. Little is really known about Mexican transport infrastructure, with the exception of its road network, which is on a similar scale to the network in Canada but must serve a population three times as large. It would appear in terms of sheer volume and network scale that the US would have little to fear

Table 1.3 Population and GDP of the NAFTA countries

Country	Population (in 000s)			GDP (in billions of US dollars)		
	1996	2000	2005	1996	2000	2004
Canada	29 447	30 529	32 107	679.9	860.2	1 003.0
Mexico	93 182	100 349	106 719	672.1	897.6	1 046.1
United States	265 502	275 306	287 716	7 762.3	9 764.8	11 679.2

Sources: Population data from US Census Bureau (2006). GDP data adapted from Macroeconomic trends – gross domestic product (GDP) – national income per capita, *OECD Factbook 2006: Economic, Environmental and Social Statistics*, © OECD 2006. Used with permission.

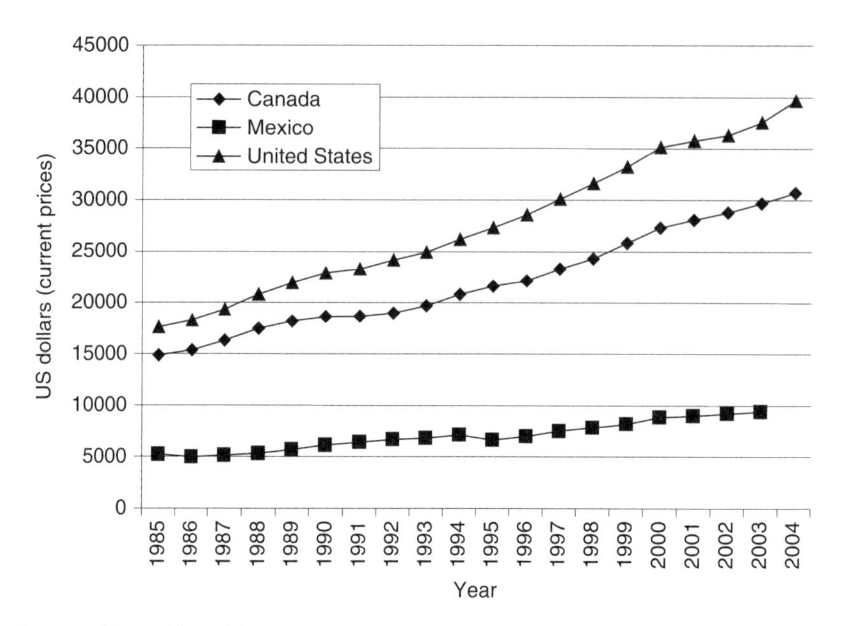

Source: Adapted from Macroeconomic trends – gross domestic product (GDP) – national income per capita, *OECD Factbook 2006: Economic, Environmental and Social Statistics*, © OECD 2006. Used with permission.

Figure 1.3 GDP per capita for the three NAFTA countries

Table 1.4 Freight transport (billion tonne-kilometres) 2003

	Rail	Roads	Inland waterways	Pipe-lines	Total inland freight	Coastal shipping
Canada	317.9	185.0	24.7	303.5	831.1	17.5[a]
Mexico	23.7	195.2	*	..	..	22.2
United States	2 200.2[c]	1 534.4[a]	506.7[c]	855.8[c]	5 464.4[a]	384.9[c]

Notes: .. = not available; * = not applicable; a. 2001; b. 1998; c. 2002; d. 1999; e. 2000.

Sources: *Trends in the Transport Sector*, ECMT, Paris 2005 and IRTAD: www.irtad.net as cited by *OECD in Figures 2005:* a supplement to the OECD Observer (OECD, 2005). © OECD 2005. Used with permission.

from greater liberalization in transportation services, and that the potential to exploit its position in terms of size and experience, as well as geographical centrality in a hub and spoke world, would have been seen by the most entrepreneurial and capital rich of the three countries as an opportunity to be welcomed. Why this was not the case is only a matter for speculation.

Table 1.5 The Human Development Index for NAFTA countries

Data	Canada	Mexico	United States
2000 Report			
HDI rank	1	55	3
HDI value	0.935	0.784	0.929
Life expectancy	79.1	72.3	76.8
Education index	0.99	0.84	0.97
GDP index	0.91	0.73	0.95
2005 Report			
HDI rank	5	53	10
HDI value	0.949	0.814	0.944
Life expectancy	80	75.1	77.4
Education index	0.97	0.85	0.97
GDP index	0.96	0.75	0.99

Note: The 2000 report is based on 1998 data and the 2005 report on 2003 data.

Source: Extracts from p. 219, Table 1, The Human Development Index: Monitoring Human Development: Enlarging People's Choices from the *Human Development Report 2005*, edited by UNHDR (United Nations, 2005), and from pp. 157–8, Table 1, The Human Development Index: Enlarging People's Choices from the *Human Development Report 2000*, edited by UNHDR (United Nations, 2000). By permission of Oxford University Press, Inc.

Finally, the asymmetrical nature of the trilateral relationship is also evident from economic development data. Canada and the US are clearly in the club of developed economies while Mexico is trying very hard to become a member. This is most obvious from the ranking of Mexico in the Human Development Index undertaken annually by the United Nations Development Program (Table 1.5). While Canada and the US jockey for position in the top 10 countries, Mexico barely makes it into the category of high human development, and it has been surpassed by Costa Rica, for example, over the past five years. Mexico's inability to dramatically improve its situation from 1998 to 2003 speaks volumes about the failure of the other two NAFTA countries to pull up Mexico's fortunes. Table 1.5 also suggests that the fortunes of Canada and the US are in decline, and that there is an imperative to address those of their less fortunate partner.

Table 1.6 indicates that the NAFTA relationship became stronger over the 1990s and then scaled back somewhat since 2000. While the US trade to GDP share grew in these earlier NAFTA years, the three largest markets for each country remained remarkably stable and the dependence of each

Table 1.6 The NAFTA relationship over time

	Canada	Mexico	United States
1993 data			
Trade to GDP (%)	30.6%	17.2%	10.4%
GDP in USD billions	585.0	614.5	6286.8
Exports (1)	187515	51832	464858
Imports (1)	169953	65367	580469
Three largest markets	US, Japan, United Kingdom	US, Canada, Spain	Canada, Japan, Mexico
Importance of largest market (%)	80%	83%	22%
2000 data			
Trade to GDP (%)	43.2%	32.0%	13.2%
GDP in USD millions	860.2	897.6	9764.8
Exports (1)	413215	166455	780419
Imports (1)	356922	174458	1216888
Three largest markets	US, Japan, United Kingdom	US, Canada, Germany	Canada, Mexico, Japan
Importance of largest market (%)	84%	89%	23%
2004 data			
Trade to GDP (%)	36.4% (2004)	27.8% (2002)	11.7% (2002)
GDP in USD millions	1003.0	1046.1	11679.2
Exports (1)	411802	189200	817936
Imports (1)	355711	197303	1469670
Three largest markets	US, Japan, United Kingdom	US, Canada, Germany	Canada, Mexico, Japan
Importance of largest market (%)	85%	87%	23%

Note: (1) Canadian data are in millions of Canadian dollars (except where specified); US and Mexican data are in millions of US dollars.

Sources: Trade to GDP and GDP data are adapted from Macroeconomic trends – gross domestic product (GDP) – national income per capita, *OECD Factbook 2006: Economic, Environmental and Social Statistics*, © OECD 2006. Used with permission. The remaining data are from Strategis (http://strategis.gc.ca), from TradeStats Express (http://tse.export.gov/) and the Mexican data are from the Government of Mexico (http://www.economia.gob.mx/index.jsp?P=2261&NLang=en#).

on their largest trading partner (which was invariably within NAFTA) grew. It is clear from Figure 1.4 that trade with NAFTA countries grew increasingly important to the US throughout the 1990s, but it appears that the US has, since 2000, grown less dependent on *NAFTA*.

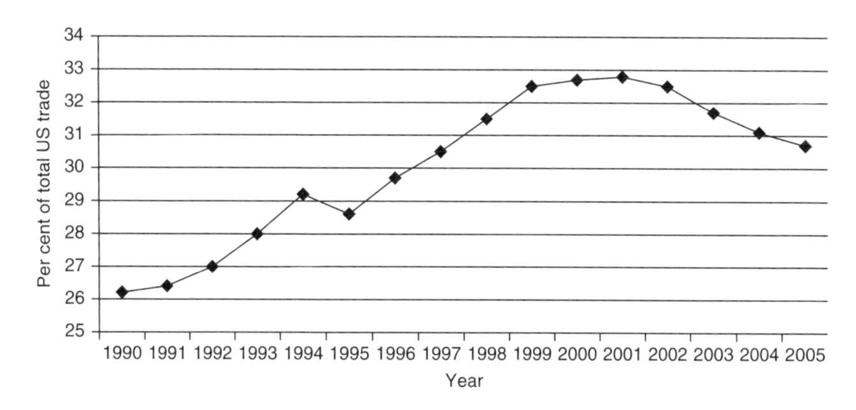

Source: Created from data in US Department of Transportation Research and Innovative Technology Administration (2006), Table 1, p. 4. The 1990–1993 data are from the earlier equivalent document in US Department of Transportation Research and Innovative Technology Administration (2005), Table 1, p. 2.

Figure 1.4 Percentage NAFTA trade of total US trade (all countries)

The Northern Border as Illustration

Since World War II, Canada has periodically refreshed its 'special trading status' with the US. Free trade discussions in the late 1940s, 'special status' for Canada in the 1950s, the *Auto Pact* in the 1960s, *CUSTA* in the 1980s, and *NAFTA* in the 1990s are all high-profile examples of this continuing effort. Furthermore, global liberalization has gradually removed many of the old tariff issues, but deeper institutional barriers within North America remain to be resolved.

For most industries, the *CUSTA* was the key platform in improved Canada–US trade, but for the most important industry – the automobile industry – the development process really began with the Auto Pact, signed in 1965.[3] Since 1992, the sector has continued to integrate across all three NAFTA countries, and the relationship, as noted by Sawchuk and Sydor (2003), is a complementary rather than competing one. Table 1.7 also reveals the importance of Canadian imports of this product. Automobiles are the clearest example of industry integration as they are simply 'made together'.

The importance of paper products and lumber is also not to be forgotten, and the data show why the long-running softwood lumber dispute between the two countries was and is so critical to the trading relationship. In recent years, Canadian oil and gas exports to the US have become increasingly important; while not a well-known fact in the US, Canada is

Table 1.7 Top 10 exports between the US and Canada (2005, 1998, and 1992) (in millions of Canadian dollars)

Product type (NAICS Code)	1992	1998	2005
Canadian exports to the US			
Oil and Gas	11 464	17 707	65 223
Automobile and Light-duty Motor Vehicles	25 880	49 408	53 500
Petroleum Products	2 766		14 018
Products Produced at Paper Mills	2 262	10 456	10 033
Sawmill and Wood Derived Products	4 737	10 071	9 326
Aerospace Products and Parts	2 339	6 259	8 283
Aluminum Products	2 350	5 215	7 408
Resin and Synthetic Rubber	1 147	3 555	6 206
Veneer, Plywood and Engineered Wood Products			6 146
Other Plastic Products		6 199	5 164
Computer and Peripheral Equipment	3 201	5 556	
Semiconductor and Electronic Components	2 939	4 739	
Pulp	2 262		
Heavy Duty Trucks		4 828	
Subtotal of the above	**61 347**	**123 993**	**185 307**
Total of all industries	**125 670**	**269 909**	**365 741**
US exports to Canada			
Automobile and Light-duty Motor Vehicles	8 681	16 276	19 385
Other Motor Vehicle Parts	4 180	10 326	10 181
Motor Vehicle Gasoline Engine and Engine Parts	2 876	7975	7 086
Motor Vehicle Transmission and Power Train Parts	2 873	6 319	5 822
Resin and Synthetic Rubber	1 625	4 114	5 747
Aerospace Products and Parts	2 352	4 607	5 207
Computer and Peripheral Equipment	4 151	6 804	4 763
Heavy-duty Trucks	855	3 104	4 696
Navigational, Measuring, Medical and Control Instruments	1 971	4 910	4 518
Oil and Gas	94	1 060	4 477
Subtotal of the above	**29 658**	**65 495**	**71 882**
Total of all industries	**96 470**	**203 578**	**215 109**

Source: Based on Statistics Canada data. Industry Canada (2006), www.strategis.gc.ca/sc_mrkti/tdst/engdoc/tr_homep.html, last accessed 3 August, 2006. Reproduced with the permission of the Minister of Public Works and Government Services, 2007.

Table 1.8 Canada's international service trade with the US (in millions of Canadian dollars)

	1998	2000	2002	2004	2005
Canada with the US					
Total receipts (Exports)	29 258	36 601	36 647	36 013	35 868
Travel	8 606	9 449	10 334	9 869	9 003
Transportation	4 977	6 027	5 864	5 349	6 155
Commercial services	15 426	20 813	20 134	20 388	20 710
Government services (1)	249	311	315	407	
Canada with the US					
Total payments (Imports)	35 142	41 686	41 819	42 797	45 293
Travel	9 951	11 517	10 852	11 639	12 417
Transportation	5 238	5 782	5 911	5 965	6 785
Commercial services	19 784	24 187	24 755	24 952	26 091
Government services (1)	170	199	302	242	

Note: Beginning in 2005, government services are included in transportation services.

Source: Adapted from Statistics Canada CANSIM database http://cansim2.statcan.ca/, Table 376-0003, extracted 15 January, 2007.

the most important import energy source for the US (not Saudi Arabia, Venezuela or Mexico as assumed by many Americans). The increasing specialization of a few Canadian industries underscores Canadian concerns about its dependence on the US economy; the top 10 products traded between Canada and the US have accounted for a larger share of trade in both directions since the early 1990s.

In examining the Canada–US trading relationship, Trefler (1999) argued that tariff cuts explain the success of liberalized trade for the most impacted industries; not all of that success, however, can be attributed to the removal of tariffs. Factors such as currency depreciation in Canada and the Peso crises in Mexico, as well as a restructuring of foreign direct investment through the period, also contributed to the changing Canada–US trading relationship in the 1990s.[4] Schwanen (1997), in his assessment of *CUSTA*, noted that between 1988 and 1995, Canadian exports to the US grew by 139 per cent in goods that were liberalized, compared with 65 per cent in those that were not. On the import side, trade in liberalized goods grew 103 per cent, and in non-liberalized only 38 per cent. He concluded that trade with other countries in the same liberalized goods did not keep pace with the growth within the CUSTA region.

In spite of this growth in merchandise trade, services trade – particularly in transportation services – do not appear to have kept pace (Table 1.8).

Canada's trade in transportation services from 1990 to 1999 grew by only an average annual growth rate of 7.4 per cent, less than anticipated given the phenomenal trade growth. Exports of transportation services in 2003 were about 18 per cent of all service exports, although transportation service exports averaged 32 per cent of Canada's service exports from 1989–94 (International Trade Canada, annual). In terms of Canada–US transborder trucking, 57 per cent of loaded one-way trips is carried in Canadian for-hire trucking (DAMF, 2005).

ECONOMIC INTEGRATION, TRANSPORTATION AND CONTINENTALISM

When the concept of economic integration is discussed, Europe is the commonly referenced example. For Europe, the development of the Single European Market was not built on 'theology or appearance, but the hard practical fact that the maintenance of any internal frontier controls will perpetuate the costs and disadvantages of a divided market' (Commission of the European Communities, 1985, Para. 12). The premise underpinning the European approach was the belief that as the need for controls diminishes, the costs to be borne for the remaining activities become disproportionate. The European Commission particularly wanted to increase the scale of the market to enable industries to garner the benefits of economies of scale and so become more competitive. In North America, the three governments focused not on the greater endeavour of customs union or political union but took just the first step of a free trade area, and then a goods-focused free trade area, leaving the thornier questions of trade-facilitating services, for the most part, to one side. So while technical standards have been minimized or eliminated throughout Europe in transportation services, they continue to hamper efficiency and competitiveness within North America. The European Commission addressed much of the discrepancy through mutual recognition, something not adopted within the NAFTA framework for road transportation services. The rail sector, with fewer, larger companies and private infrastructure, worked cooperatively to introduce interoperability and hence strengthen the total rail network.

Clearly, removal or harmonization of regulatory barriers is only part of the challenge; the other part is to prevent the creation of new technical non-tariff barriers. The Europeans addressed this, while the North Americans did not. 'In order to prevent the erection of new barriers, Directive 83/189/EEC now obliges Member States to notify the Commission in advance of all draft regulations and standards concerning technical specifications that they intend to introduce on their own territory' (Commission of the European Communities, 1985, Para. 75).

The European Commission particularly noted common safety standards as an important component of transport efficiency and the elimination of internal borders (Commission of the European Communities, 1985, Para. 44). The practice of using technical standards as a barrier encouraged the Commission to delegate responsibility for technical standards to Comité Européan de la Normalisation (CEN) or sectoral standards groups. As will be seen in Chapter 2, *NAFTA* offloaded the transportation standards issue to a tri-national subcommittee with mixed results.

The critical divergence between the European approach in promulgating its single market and the trade agreement signed in North America was the freedom of access acquired by transportation companies. The right to provide transportation services freely within the region was a key tenet (Paragraph 108) of Europe's Common Transport Policy.

In addition to eliminating border checks on road haulage, the completion of the internal market required Member States to phase out quantitative restrictions, and the establishment of conditions under which non-resident carriers may be able to provide services (Commission of the European Communities, 1985, Para. 109). This paragraph also referenced important changes to the cabotage provisions of maritime and air transport services, and that these changes would be addressed through Council decisions. There was also a fallback position articulated in Paragraph 111 that if Council failed to take the decisions necessary for the liberalization of air and maritime sectors, the Commission would authorize Member States within its authority under Article 89 of the *Treaty of Rome*.[5] History has since shown that the Council did indeed introduce reform packages in both air and maritime sectors to liberalize these sectors.

In addition to dealing with existing non-tariff barriers, new technical standards, safety regulations, and market access (cabotage reform), the Europeans saw state aid regulation, taxation and common competition policy as integral to the development of a free-flowing single market. State aids were seen to distort competition and undermine efforts to increase Community-wide competitiveness through conferring artificial advantage to some firms over others; Commission of the European Communities (1985, Para. 158) notes the importance that 'community discipline on state aids be rigorously enforced'. It would be 'necessary to ensure that anti-competitive practices do not engender new forms of local protectionism which would only lead to a re-partitioning of the market' (Commission of the European Communities, 1985, Para. 157). These were not addressed in the North American context and their relative importance to and impact upon North American transport companies is not clear. One of the issues this book addresses is the relative importance of these issues to transportation companies in their search for competitive advantage within NAFTA.

At the time of the *NAFTA* negotiations, greater integration in the automotive sector was anticipated as a result of the investment framework incorporated into the Agreement. The 1990s witnessed considerable global integration in automobile manufacture, with autos and parts accounting for the largest single product category traded between Canada and the US. Studer (2004) noted that the integration of the North American automotive industry, which began with the Auto Pact, was expanded continentally by investment in Mexico by the US Big Three a considerable time before the passage of *NAFTA*. It was her conclusion that *NAFTA* facilitated the deepening of the existing integration in the auto industry. It is now estimated that an automobile crosses the border at least five times in its production and assembly. Since the WTO forced the removal of Auto Pact benefits in 2000, expectations of future deeper integration in this sector have been curbed.

The extent of integration in the energy sector is also extremely high (Dukert, 2004), and it is not just about sales in petroleum and natural gas. The true nature of the integration of the electrical grid was evident in the transborder nature of the blackout of August 2003. The two countries ensure that electricity is available through a continental system, with three distinct regional grids, managed by the North American Electric Reliability Council. The Council is tasked with ensuring reliable electricity to North American customers (US–Canada Power System Outage Task Force, 2004). While the system ensures that areas that cannot meet their electricity demands can purchase electricity from areas that have a surplus of electricity, as electricity cannot be stored economically, the availability is accompanied by the risk that a problem originating in one area can quickly spread, causing power outages over a wider geographical area. Such was the case on 14 August 2003, when a blackout originating in Ohio affected more than 50 million people in Eastern US and Canada (US–Canada Power System Outage Task Force, 2004) on the Eastern Interconnection grid. The Task Force recommended (Recommendation 3, p. 139) that governments and industry work together to effect improvements to the energy system, recognizing how deeply interwoven the electricity grid has become. Like Studer (2004), Dukert (2004) argued that energy integration was a pre-existing integration rather than a product of the *NAFTA*. Wilson (2003) would have agreed with Dukert's assessment; she concluded that the impact was very small, as Canada–US trade was largely free of tariffs before the *NAFTA* went into effect. 'In the case of U.S.–Canadian trade, however, where intraindustry trade in manufactured goods plays a large role, the gains from specialization are based far more on economies of scale than on comparative advantage' (Wilson, 2003, p. 199).

Furthermore, throughout the 1990s, a number of companies began to institute world product mandates, developing intra-firm bidding processes for the granting of these mandates (Blank and Haar, 1998, pp. 56–61); this was not just a factor within *NAFTA*, but it occurred globally. As almost half of Canada–US trade is intra-firm trade, Blank and Haar's (1998) premise that, in *NAFTA*, 'we make things together' is a substantiated one.

There is a long-standing relationship of bilateral cooperation between Canada and the US. Perhaps none is stronger than the commitment to joint defense of their airspace through the North American Aerospace Defense Command (NORAD). NORAD was established in 1958 by the two governments to address the potential threat of nuclear war and their common security requirements, and this commitment continues today. Likewise, the two countries formed the St Lawrence Seaway Authority to jointly manage the Seaway through the Great Lakes in 1954, and even earlier, in 1909, formed the International Joint Commission (IJC) to resolve disputes between the United States and Canada under the *1909 Boundary Waters Treaty*. The IJC serves as an independent advisor to the two governments on issues associated with water management, including the implementation of the *Canada–US Great Lakes Water Quality Agreement*, and more recently transborder air quality.

Before we can assess the importance of the institutions of the *NAFTA* on the transport system, and look forward as will be done in this book, it would be useful to understand the history of the two deals from a transport perspective. The next section does just that.

THE HISTORY OF THE DEALS FROM A TRANSPORT PERSPECTIVE

Canada–US Trade Agreement

Baker (2000), Porter (2000b) and Hart et al. (1994), in combination, provide a rich insight into the negotiations that shaped the modern North American trade psyche – the *Canada–US Trade Agreement*. While Baker set the larger scene from an American perspective, Porter interviewed those close to the process long after the event, and Hart et al. provided a detailed chronology of the policy positions, the Canadian strategies behind the negotiations, and the details of what happened on a day-by-day basis.

Baker (2000) noted the particular importance of leadership to the successful conclusion of the deal. Only the President and the Prime Minister, he believed, were able to provide the necessary vision and commitment to bringing public opinion onside and making the deal happen. Baker concluded that pragmatism was also a critical ingredient to the successful outcome; without what he called 'proactive policy making', he believed the two would have failed to find agreement. '[C]omplexity is particularly acute in the United States, where in contrast with the parliamentary system such as Canada's, party discipline is weak and authority is shared by the executive and legislative branches of government. . . . [T]here is a tendency, regrettable but real, for Americans to take their northern neighbors for granted' (Baker, 2000, p. 4).

Porter (2000b) traced the difficulties of the negotiations back to the challenges of process and organization in addition to the priority attached to the negotiation:

> Despite their geographical proximity, the U.S. and Canada could hardly have organized for the negotiations more differently. The Canadian approach reflected the priority attached to the effort by the Prime Minister and the Cabinet. A special negotiator, not tied to a departmental or ministerial bureaucracy, was appointed and given frequent, direct access to the Prime Minister. . . . [Simon] Reisman quickly assembled a staff of roughly 110 of whom forty were professionals, demonstrating early the depth of the Canadian commitment to the effort (Porter, 2000b, p. xv).

Porter noted that only four staff were assigned to the US side, and there was no seasoned negotiator to lead the team; this conveyed to the Canadians 'that the U.S. did not take the negotiations seriously' (Porter, 2000b, p. xv).

Furthermore, Porter (2000a, p. 26) reported on the differences in what each negotiating team wanted to accomplish and how they approached the issues; quoting Derek Burney and Charles Roh:[6]

> Derek Burney: The point here is that there were different perceptions on both sides about the goal. The U.S. came at it with a laundry list of irritants, wanting to get as much political cover as it could. We were coming at it from the top, saying, 'let's not talk about irritants, let's blaze a new trail, new rules-broad-based negotiation.' . . . there was a mismatch from the very beginning.
>
> Charles Roh: . . . Our negotiating style tended to focus on irritants, which led to many an aimless debate, but in the end what we got was a big agreement. . . . It always amuses me that the United States of 250 million people and the world's largest economic power seems to be terrified of entering into agreements with small countries for fear that they steal its sovereignty.

Porter (2000b) drew several conclusions about the overall deal. First, he noted that it strengthened the largest trading arrangement in the world. Second, it did more than just compromise on issues of concern; it represented a novel approach to addressing disputes between countries. Third, and most important from a Canadian perspective, it reflected a Canadian attitude, not so much one of vulnerability and dependency, as had been the case in the past, but one of seeing the opportunities for a strong economic future. He concluded that the Canadian team believed that if the agreement was satisfactory, it would be supported in Canada. From an American perspective, he also noted that the deal represented an activist approach to trade policy, where 'senior officials sought to maintain control and guide the direction of policy' and engaged in relationship management with Congress and building support (Porter, 2000b, p. xiv).

As in any negotiations, it is the end game that delivers the vision. Porter's recollections of the end game were not that dissimilar to those of Hart et al. (1994). Both focused on the critical fact that the congressional grant of authority for the US negotiators focused the minds of the Americans in the final days, while it had a discouraging impact on the Canadians. From Porter's storyline:

> At a crucial moment in the negotiations on 23 September 1987, . . . the talks reached an impasse prompting Reisman to seek and gain approval from his Canadian masters to walk out of the negotiations leaving the next steps in doubt. In the end, the event signaled an elevation of the negotiations. When the talks resumed they actively engaged Mulroney's chief of staff, Derek Burney, and U.S. Treasury Secretary James Baker.
>
> Reisman's role, now diminished, was not extinguished. His reputation and extended visibility combined with the divisions within the Canadian electorate on the issue left him with a de facto veto. Close observers of the process on both sides of the border have suggested that had Reisman opposed the agreement as finally negotiated, it would have been virtually impossible for the Mulroney government to secure the approval of Parliament and the country. His support for the final agreement proved crucial (Porter, 2000b, pp. xvii–viii).

Hart et al. (1994) saw the end game as beginning somewhat earlier, in the summer of 1987, with the realization by the Canadian team that the US negotiators had developed policy positions without testing them at home (Hart et al., 1994, p. 268). One particular example they use is that neither the US Department of Transportation nor US industry endorsed the principles of non-discrimination that had been introduced. As a result, Canada decided it was time to take negotiations out of the public eye and get down to the business of securing a dispute resolution system that Canada felt it needed to gain stability in the trading relationship. The Canadian team had decided where it would draw the line as to what was necessary for Canada to agree to the deal.

Both Porter (2000b) and Hart et al. (1994) noted that, by mid-September 1987, it was looking more likely that failure to achieve an agreement would be the outcome. Hart et al. (1994) completed the story, noting that the US continued to talk in terms of specific irritants while Canada was looking for agreement on principles with respect to subsidies and dispute resolution. Canadian enthusiasm was diminished and word of the death of the negotiations began to appear in the Canadian media (Hart et al., 1994, p. 324). It appeared that the US negotiators did not seem to understand that Canada was ready to walk away from the deal and, when they realized it, it seemed to be too late. Senator Bradley and Canadian Ambassador to Washington Alan Gotlieb continued efforts on 30 September, garnering support for a bilateral approach to trade remedies. Hart et al. concluded that the deal was indeed a 'decision at midnight' because the US did not want to fail, and Canada needed to have an agreement that made long-term economic sense.

The *North American Free Trade Agreement*

Once the deal with Canada was done, the US turned its attention to a deal with Mexico and that bilateral relationship. While a number of bilateral agreements had been reached between the two countries on textiles, steel, beer and wine, and civil aviation, there was considerable interest in a broader relationship by the time of the Salinas–Bush summit in October of 1989.

> NAFTA . . . had the effect of restructuring basic property rules and state–society relations in each of the three countries, but especially in Mexico. It was also an effort to 'lock in' the reforms the Salinas government had already undertaken or was planning, and it was a way of providing investors with the same risks and guarantees in their operations throughout North America that they enjoyed in the United States and Canada (Cameron and Tomlin, 2000, p. 232).

Canada did not wish to lose the gains made in its bilateral with the US by seeing a US–Mexico deal in which it was not a participant; the Canadian position was that it needed to build on the *Canada–US Trade Agreement* and extend the gains to Mexico. Canada had three objectives in the *NAFTA* negotiations. These were to: (1) secure better market access to the Mexican market; (2) improve the gains made in the *Canada–US Trade Agreement*; and (3) maintain Canada as an attractive investment location (Government of Canada, 1992a). According to Brooks (1994), it was the first of these that was the primary driver of the Canadian strategy at the negotiating table. Without participating in the process, Canada could not be sure of meeting either the second or the third objective, as the outcome would have been a Mexico–US bilateral trade agreement. Furthermore, Canada also hoped to resolve a number of specific trade irritants in its trading relationship with the US while ensuring no reduction in benefits and obligations of the existing trade agreement, *CUSTA*. Canada believed that fair market access requires ultimately balanced and mutually advantageous rules, coupled with equitable and expeditious procedures for resolving problems (Government of Canada, 1992b).

As already discussed (with respect to the previous negotiations), the Government of Canada preferred a rules-based approach, while the United States took a more irritants-based approach. As explained by Cameron and Tomlin (2000, pp. 93–4):

> The negotiations on services encompassed a number of areas, including transportation . . . At the outset, Canada tried to put maritime transportation on the table. The United States responded by saying, 'If you bring in maritime transportation, we'll talk about culture!' . . . Neither Katz [Chief US negotiator] nor Weekes [Chief Canadian negotiator] attached great importance to the service negotiations.

The transportation talks focused mostly on the mode of trucking. This was much more important to the Mexicans than the Canadians, as the Canadians had achieved what they expected to get from the US in the earlier agreement but wanted to ensure that if the Mexicans got more, they would get it too. The transportation-specific discussions, therefore, predominantly concentrated on dealing with the Southern Border. Again, Cameron and Tomlin (2000, p. 94) provide excellent insight:

> In the transportation working group, the negotiators agreed to break apart land, sea, and air. Once the United States had set aside maritime issues, the Canadians and Americans had little to talk about. With their open-skies agreement in place and a long-standing agreement on land transportation, there was little for Canada in the talks, except to get from Mexico whatever benefits the United States might negotiate. . . . The United States opened the negotiations with a request for access to Mexican truck and bus operations, liberalization in rail transportation, and opening in ports and civil aviation.

Chapter 5 of this book examines the state of the marine and air transport industries at the time of the negotiations. As in the case of the *CUSTA* negotiations, the marine mode was not on the table because of the opposition of the US marine industry and its unions. As air was dealt with under other institutional arrangements, the *NAFTA* negotiations focused predominantly on land transport, and did so through annexes to the service chapter. The Mexicans sought an asymmetrical deal reflecting Mexico's lower level of economic development; for the Mexicans, transportation was a sector where they wanted concessions (Cameron and Tomlin, 2000).

Canada acted more like an observer in this process, and the Canadian Chief Negotiator John Weekes, from the Department of External Affairs, did not appoint anyone specifically for transportation. Ultimately, Jules Katz and the Working Group Head Land Transportation (for the US), Nancy MacRae, agreed to an asymmetrical deal with Alejandro Peniche, Working Group Head, Transportation (for Mexico), with phased-in milestones on access and investment (discussed in greater detail in Chapter 2). Agreement on the transportation elements was reached in May 1992, three months before the negotiations closed and the deal was signed.

THE IMPACT OF THE TWO AGREEMENTS

There is no doubt that all three countries experienced substantial improvement in trade growth throughout the 1990s within the NAFTA region, and Hejazi and Safarian (2005) noted that trade gains from *NAFTA* accrued mostly to Mexico. Beyond the initial broad statement, there is considerable disagreement among economists and trade analysts as to what really happened. Debates about trade creation or trade diversion are still being published, and there remains some question about benefits, given the decline in NAFTA's share of global trade since the turn of the millennium.

Sawchuk and Sydor (2003), for example, reported that the noticeable growth in intra-NAFTA trade strongly indicated the possibility of trade diversion taking place. However, they reported that the NAFTA trade with non-NAFTA countries also grew. Citing the example that Mexico's trade in manufactured goods with the US grew by more than two times the rate of its growth in trade with Canada (between 1990 and 1998), which itself was larger than the rate of growth with the rest of the world, they concluded that there was no evidence against trade diversion and so whatever trade diversion there had been must be modest.

Clausing (2001) concluded, from data at the commodity level, that the *CUSTA* had substantial trade creation effects, with little evidence of trade diversion. It may be argued that this supports the initial findings by Taylor and Closs (1993) that firms would be unlikely to fully integrate manufacturing operations within Canada and the US by trading off production efficiencies against larger logistics (primarily transport) costs until such time as transport regulations became more harmonized. They concluded that the response of manufacturers to the *CUSTA* would be an integrated manufacturing and logistics strategy, with efficiencies resulting only from realignment of existing manufacturing and logistics systems.

Some studies on the impact of the agreements have decomposed trade growth to understand its source (including Hillberry and McDaniel, 2002). Others (such as Clausing, 2001; and Karemera and Koo, 1994) have discussed the trade creation or trade diversion effects but eventually agreed that 'border issues' would continue because transportation and immigration regulations were not liberalized to the extent necessary for true economic integration to take place. In their study of the importance of imports for the creation of products to export, Ghanem and Cross (2003) sparked considerable discussion in the circles of NAFTA observers. In their analysis of provincial input/output data for 1999 in 21 major commodity groups, they found significant evidence of integration in manufacturing. For example, they discovered that over one-half of Ontario's auto exports is attributed to embedded imports, with machinery and electronics not far behind. As expected, they found less import embeddedness in provinces with raw commodity exports or oil and gas exports.

While Canada indicated that it was interested in a place at the table for the NAFTA negotiations, its primary concern was to protect Canada as a destination country for inward foreign investment. Canada wanted to preserve its position as a destination country for Foreign Direct Investment (FDI). An examination of Figure 1.5 makes it quite clear that Canada managed to achieve continuing inflows throughout the 1990s, as did the US, with inflows of FDI exceeding the rate seen as an OECD average. After the softening economy of 2001, both Canada and the US failed to maintain the volume of inflows. However, in share terms, the US remained a stable source of inward FDI to Canada (Table 1.9); Canadian outbound investments to

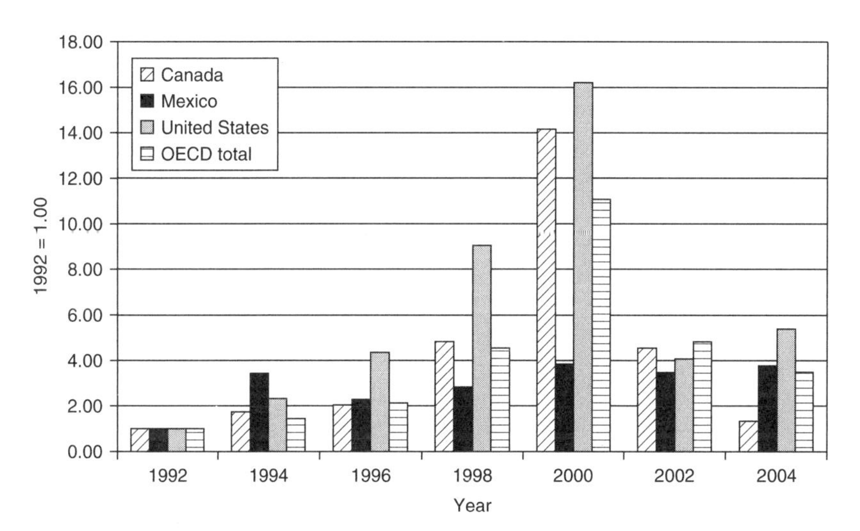

Source: Adapted from Economic globalisation – foreign direct investment (FDI) – FDI flows and stocks, *OECD Factbook 2006: Economic, Environmental and Social Statistics*, © OECD 2006. Used with permission.

Figure 1.5 NAFTA FDI inflows 1992–2004 (indexed to 1992=1.00)

Table 1.9 Canadian Foreign Direct Investment: outbound and inward (1993, 2000 and 2005)

	1993	2000	2005
Country of Direct Investment (outbound FDI)			
Mexico	neg	1.1%	neg
United States	55.3%	49.9%	46.0%
EU	19.9%	21.1%	23.7%
Investor Country (inward FDI)			
Mexico	neg	neg	neg
United States	64.0%	60.7%	64.1%
EU	22.3%	30.1%	25.1%

Note: Neg = less than 1 per cent.

Source: Adapted from Statistics Canada CANSIM database http://cansim2.statcan.ca/, Table 376-0051, extracted 15 May, 2006.

the US diminished and tended to favour Europe more. Only Canada was able to grow non-NAFTA inward share (Table 1.10); both the US and Mexico lost ground as non-NAFTA countries invested in NAFTA. It must be said, however, that Canada's investment offshore continued to grow as both the US and Canada sought to locate cheaper inputs for their own manufacturing enterprises.

Using the same technique, but setting 1998 FDI inflow to equal 1.00[7] and using the OECD total as the index, Figure 1.6 clearly shows that those with capital to invest moved that investment to other destinations, following the offshoring and outsourcing agendas of the global supply chain philosophy that was taking hold during the time. Interest in China, Brazil, India and the Russian Federation for Foreign Direct Investment took off, with China as the primary focus in 2000 and the others also seeking their place in the sun. While the volumes interested in the Russian Federation are still quite small by comparison with those for China, the growth is a harbinger of a possible diminishing interest in investing in the NAFTA region and, in particular, in Mexico. Mexico only engages in attracting inward flows as outward FDI is almost non-existent. On the other hand, Canada has become a foreign investor over time and FDI outflows exceed inflows significantly. Investment in Canada has diminished in concert with its rapidly appreciating currency. Today, Canada is no longer a cheap way to access the US market.

As for the service sector, there has been considerable examination of financial services and telecommunications within the Canada–US

Table 1.10 FDI and NAFTA 1992 and 2002 (in millions)

	Originating country									
	Canada		**US**		**Mexico**		**Non-NAFTA**		**Total**	
To	**FDI**	**%**	**FDI**	**%**	**FDI**	**%**	**FDI**	**%**	**FDI**	**%**
1992										
Canada (1)			3 218.0	36.2	neg	neg	3 640.0	63.8	5 708.0	100.0
US (2)	2 002.0	10.4			647.0	3.4	16 573.0	86.2	19 222.0	100.0
Mexico (3)	740.7	4.9	4 961.5	33.0			9 343.0	62.1	15 045.2	100.0
2002										
Canada (1)			11 534.0	34.9	neg	neg	21 492.0	65.1	33 026.0	100.0
US (2)	15 444.0	24.6			1 281.0	2.0	46 145.0	73.4	62 870.0	100.0
Mexico (3)	neg	neg	5 171.0	53.3			4 525.4	46.7	9 696.4	100.0

Note: Currency in US Dollars.

Source: UNCTAD (undated), The FDI/TNC database, accessed 28 April 2005.

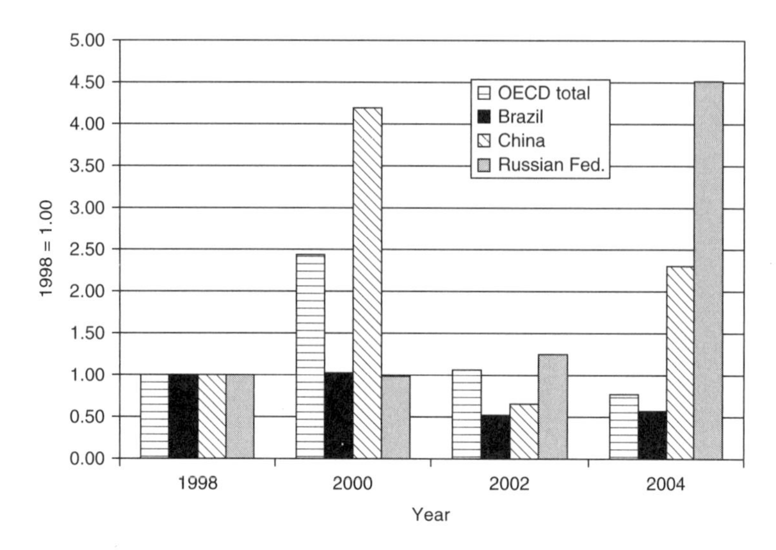

Source: Adapted from Economic globalisation – foreign direct investment (FDI) – FDI flows and stocks, *OECD Factbook 2006: Economic, Environmental and Social Statistics*, © OECD 2006. Used with permission.

Figure 1.6 New FDI targets 1998–2004 (indexed to 1992=1.00)

economic space. As the *NAFTA* was more about trade liberalization but limited the liberalization of many of the services supporting trading activities, the process of structural integration could stall, and may have already stalled, unless a more holistic view, incorporating the supporting and facilitating services that support trade, is taken. With the added security concerns (Flynn, 2003; Biersteker, 2003), this issue warrants a closer look.

Economic integration across the border between Canada and the US has taken place to quite a substantial degree in some sectors.[8] Three high-profile incidents in 2003 illustrate this point. In addition to the electric power blackout of August 2003 that shut down much of the eastern seaboard in the US and most of Ontario (previously discussed), both the beef industry and the pharmaceutical industry came to dominate diplomatic relations. The 2003 BSE (bovine spongiform encephalopathy, or 'mad cow disease') crisis in the cattle industry clearly demonstrated the integration of cattle feed and beef supply chains between the two countries. Second, in spite of regulatory barriers, the problem of cross-border pharmaceutical sales facing the American pharmaceutical industry from both Canadian and Mexican sources also became highly publicized in 2003, with an influx of bargain-seeking Americans shopping at Canadian pharmacies and Internet pharmaceutical websites (Thompson, 2003).

Both of these are briefly discussed next as they illustrate the problems of regulatory divergence.

Prior to the implementation of *NAFTA*, the beef industries of Canada, Mexico and the United States operated independently of each other, protected by tariffs and with little incentive to integrate (Sparling and Caswell, 2006). After *NAFTA* was implemented, the industries of Canada, the US and, to a lesser extent, Mexico became more integrated as producers realized the benefits of exploiting the competitive advantages offered by each of the NAFTA countries. In 1990, only 12 per cent of Canada's total beef production was exported to the United States for slaughter but, by 2002, this share had grown to 48 per cent (Sparling and Caswell, 2006). After the implementation of *NAFTA*, it became common for a cow to be born and raised in Canada, exported live to the US where it would be slaughtered and packaged and then exported back to Canada or to major US beef importers like Japan and Korea. By 2002, Canada was supplying 68 per cent of live beef imports to the US, with Mexico supplying the rest. In turn, the US became the major NAFTA partner to grow its beef exports to non-NAFTA countries. The sub-sectors of the beef industry became highly specialized and, as noted by *The Economist* (anonymous, 2005b), when the crisis hit, the US had too many slaughterhouses and Canada had only six meat packers and far too much product 'on the hoof'. Sparling and Caswell (2006) concluded that the rapid economic integration that occurred in the industry outpaced the integration of agricultural regulations.

Another industry with market issues that has become highly visible and an irritant in Canada–US relations is the pharmaceutical industry. While pharmaceutical products sold in North America are identical in composition, they differ in pricing, distribution and regulatory approval processes. Because a drug is approved for sale in the US does not mean it is approved for sale in Canada. Canadians seeking US-approved products have been known to engage in cross-border shopping, just as the reverse situation came to a head in 2003. Because many medicines are sold to government health care facilities, and there is a vibrant market in generic products in Canada, both factors tend to impose downward pressure on prices that the market is willing to pay; in 2001, the 'average price' gap was reported to be 69 per cent (Rosson, 2004). Thompson (2003) noted that the price discrepancy could be as high as 400 per cent. As a result, a brand name medicine sold in Canada is often sold at a far cheaper price than the exact same product is sold for in the US. This price discrepancy, coupled with the availability of the Internet as a distribution mechanism, resulted in an influx of bargain-seeking American customers shopping at Canadian pharmacies and on Canadian pharmaceutical websites. The US Food and Drug Administration permits American citizens to import Canadian drugs as long as they are for personal use and the supply is for 90 days or fewer (Arnold and Dickinson, 2003). The incidence of cross-border shopping in pharmaceuticals was also supported by a very advantageous exchange rate. The rise in Internet sales of prescription drugs by Canadian pharmacies to US patients in the 2000 to 2003 period, reported by Carlisle (2003) to be from $50 million (in 2000) to $800 million in 2003, provides another example of how the demands of the marketplace can highlight areas of international divergence and where transportation can play a role in securing new opportunities for those seeking to take advantage of the difference.

In fact, the Canadian and US markets are seen as so integrated that a number of options – customs union, monetary union, and others – have been mooted as the next logical step for the Canada–US relationship. Throughout the 1990s, fiscal policies in Canada and the US were converging sufficiently, it was argued, that a common currency with the US could make sense, given Canada's dependence on the US market. Coiteux (2004) examined the case for monetary union. He noted that, while both Canada and the US had, over the years, achieved convergence in interest and inflation rates, there were large fluctuations in the exchange rates. Coiteux (2004, p. 189):

> In a framework that emphasizes the exchange rate over output and prices fluctuations, the asymmetry in fiscal policies has been identified as the key factor that would have made living with the U.S. dollar difficult for Canada in the recent past. . . . However, current fiscal and political developments in the U.S. inhibit and possibly revert convergence. . . . [I]t is unlikely that NAFTA will evolve in the near future towards more than what it currently is, a free trade area.

Since the Bush Administration came to power in 2000, the divergence of fiscal policies between the two countries quieted talk of monetary union in Canada. With the subsequent dramatic rise in the value of the Canadian dollar, the interest in and opportunity for this type of integration has simply disappeared.

Blank and Coiteux (2003) examined the state of North American economic integration, concluding that levels of economic integration in North America exceed those in Europe by a considerable degree. They use the term 'structural' integration to suggest a North American economy integrated not only by trade flows but also more 'deeply' by complex cross-border production chains. Pursuing this line of research, Coiteux (2004) developed a regional dependence index that shows that Canada depends more on the North American market for its economic well-being than Belgium and Luxembourg depend on the European Union market. At the same time, *NAFTA* has transformed the US economy into a more regionally dependent country than large European economies like that of Germany and France. He then asked why such a strong level of regional dependence had not yet led to the type of convergence that would support the adoption of a single currency; the same question could be raised with respect to transportation. Why does a highly fragmented regulatory climate exist when efficient and effective transportation networks are so critical to continental manufacturing competitiveness?

In contrast to Blank and Coiteux (2003), Helliwell's (1998) study of border effects showed that trade integration had not proceeded as far in North America as in the European Union, although there had been some change. Corporate policy and attitudes among transnational corporations in NAFTA seemed to indicate that integration would continue to deepen. However, the record at the operations level of companies is rather mixed. Technology is eroding some distinctions between Canada and the US, as the Internet pharmacy issue attests, but in many other areas, practices seem as far apart as ever. Transportation practices, as will be seen in Chapters 2, 4 and 5, are highly fragmented and therefore are possible barriers to continuing economic integration of the North American market.

While there are differences of opinion about the impact of the two trade agreements, the pattern of possibilities and conclusions emerging from the above examples suggests that the *CUSTA* and *NAFTA* have led to considerable integration, but that further initiatives, both within trade sectors and at policy levels, must be taken if integration is to deepen. According to Hummels (2006), vertical specialization is very sensitive to transport inefficiency. Where imports are converted into exports, trade frictions are multiplicative for every border crossing. As North America becomes more specialized as a result of globalization, it is critical to minimize transport inefficiency.

> Data on non-tariff barriers are much harder to come by, but studies examining customs data consistently find that transportation costs pose a barrier to trade at least as large as and frequently larger than tariffs. For the typical good in US trade exporters pay $9 in shipping costs for every $1 they pay in tariffs (Hummels, 2006, p. 9).

Greater integration will also depend, to a large degree, on changes occurring in public policy concerning regulations on access to business lines, ownership barriers, and the like. Where the original impetus that led to the *CUSTA* and *NAFTA* was primarily aimed at reducing direct trade barriers, any future negotiations should focus more on the problems of 'plumbing', used by McNiven (1999) to express the institutional or policy fit between the three countries. Dobson (2002) suggested that, in order to proceed with shaping the economy, key sectors to analyse would be transportation, telecommunications and financial services – services that facilitate trade. This book focuses on the transportation sector.

THE STRUCTURE OF THE BOOK

Unlike Europe, North America has balked at mutual recognition in many industries and non-tariff barriers still exist. The policies and bureaucratic procedures that underlie *services that make trade happen*, such as transportation, financial services, retail marketing and selling, and professional services, have grown in importance. These services are far from the more high-profile trade dispute issues that typically capture headlines and, although some were included in *NAFTA*, they were not addressed fully. In fact, many of the annexes of the agreement focused on special exemptions for these. Yet these sectors affect the access accorded the goods traffic under *NAFTA*. The more than 10 years since the *NAFTA* established today's North American trading environment is long enough for many difficulties to become obvious.

Each of these service sectors has particular policy problems that affect the efficient movement of goods and services. Trucking regulations, airline ownership, cross-border pricing and marine transportation regulations all are affected by policies that inhibit effective and efficient movement. As Schwanen (2004) notes, there has been a structural shift in Canadian investments in the US in favour of service industries, concluding that service industries are seeking through investment what their manufacturing counterparts have achieved through trade. For instance, a corporate strategy one might expect to find within an integrating geographic region, if ownership restrictions do not prevent such moves, is mergers and acquisitions (M&As). Although Mexican trucking companies could not be acquired because ownership restriction milestones within *NAFTA* failed to be achieved, there were no national limits on trucking company ownership within Canada and the US. Ownership restrictions are not the only integration-limiting non-tariff barriers present in transportation services. What other barriers to access remain ten years after *NAFTA* was created? Even though trucking was the primary mode in which regulatory change occurred, this book will address marine, rail and air modes as well.

This book examines one sector of the Canada–US relationship, the transportation services sector, its past as seen from a Canadian perspective, and the present from the point of view of US transportation companies. It is based on previous research by the author, in-depth interviews with US transport suppliers undertaken in 2005 during a Canada–US Fulbright award at George Mason University, and then steps back to the larger view of the trilateral relationship in a security-minded future. In the course of writing this book, additional materials became available and shaped, to some extent, the concluding two chapters.

Given the perspective of the transportation sector concerned with making the flow of goods more seamless in modern global supply chains, the book examines the progress on liberalization in the transport sector in North America after the passing of the 1 January 2001 milestones. To do so, it begins in Chapter 2 with a review of the land transportation industry, both trucking and rail, in North America. It then proceeds to examine what the *Canada US Trade Agreement* and the *NAFTA* gave the transport sector and their customers in terms of a regulatory framework. This chapter also draws conclusions about key outstanding regulatory issues, and sets the scene for examining the Canada–US relationship from the perspective of transport suppliers, third party agents and the cargo owners, as well as their relevant industry associations. An appendix at the end of Chapter 2 provides a timeline of activities relevant to the transport sector.

As Chapter 3 is about the trading interests of cargo owners and their perspectives on transportation issues, it opens with an examination of the major trade flows by surface transportation from Canada to the US, northbound data by weight not being collected on a disaggregated basis. As part of the research for this book, a number of these companies and industry associations were approached to participate in a dialogue on what *NAFTA* did for them, and how they responded to the opportunity presented. They were also asked for their views on both the existing regulatory climate (both irritants and benefits) and what areas of regulatory convergence they believed to be priorities for future negotiation. Finally, they were asked about the impact of new security regulations on their businesses or members for further input into the discussion about Canada's future relationship with the US and potential for integration of the transport system.

Chapter 4 presents the views of those companies whose ability to supply transport services were most affected by *NAFTA* – the trucking and rail service providers. These companies were asked similar questions about *NAFTA*, the opportunity it presented and how the opportunity was exploited, as well as questions about the impact of security requirements on the company. This group also faced additional questions about what they required in terms of changes to the operating environment, including the need for changes in such broad-ranging areas as taxation and governance.

Chapter 5 examines two modes that were, by and large, left out of the *NAFTA* agreement – marine and air. As air has its own bilateral processes, the mode is addressed using only secondary sources. The marine mode, however, has been a rich field of study in recent years, and the chapter focuses on both the survey results and the secondary studies to explain the current regulatory climate that the industry faces.

While these three chapters (3–5) examine *NAFTA*, they also discuss the impact of security measures imposed in the post-2001 era, the age of terrorism. What becomes quite clear in these chapters is that security measures are still in a state of flux six years after the terrorist attacks of 11 September 2001 but that both service suppliers and cargo owners are working hard to comply and to optimize any benefits the new regimes have. The future of *NAFTA* seems to have been overtaken by other concerns, and these first five chapters set the stage for efforts to look forward and see what the future North American transportation network will look like.

Thinking continentally, although from a Canadian perspective, Chapter 6 examines, briefly, the concept of a security perimeter and explores further the nature of the Canada–US political relationship. The second half of the chapter looks at the rise of regional groupings and raises the question about whether regional groupings will be the way change is encouraged.

As the intention of the book is to explore areas where further liberalization, regulatory convergence or coordinated planning would deliver benefits to the continental transport system and hence the three economies involved, and to understand the key barriers to securing liberalization of transportation irritants, the final chapter (Chapter 7) examines these issues and draws conclusions about what needs to be on the political agenda next. For companies to rise to the strategic challenge of making North American transportation work, dialogue is needed. One of the critical questions in these two chapters is whether Mexico is at the discussion table or not, given its transport situation (and political position) vis-à-vis the other two countries. In the course of writing this final chapter, the Security and Prosperity Partnership dialogue was gaining traction and the North American Competitiveness Council was being formed. The impact of these is briefly touched upon.

This book reflects the duality within NAFTA. The funding for the research came from the Canada–US Fulbright Scholarship to look at Canada–US trade in transportation services. Yet the liberalizing mechanism for transportation services was seen by the US to be the *North America Free Trade Agreement*, and was seen by Canada to be the *Canada–US Trade Agreement*. The future, from a Canadian perspective, cannot be divorced morally from Canada's relationship with Mexico. However, by treating the region as two bilateral relationships, the US has chosen to signal that there is a pecking order in this tripartite relationship and that, with the exception of the marine mode (discussed in Chapter 5), the US will deal, by sheer dint of its economic clout, with each of its neighbours as it chooses.

Within the panoply of highly regarded books on the North American economic and political relationship (for example, Hart and Dymond, 2001; Hart, 2003; Pastor, 2001; and Hufbauer and Schott, 2004), there is very little said about transport services, and yet trade requires efficient and effective transportation. This book is intended to inform those interested in trade about the issues in North American transportation and the impact of regulatory gaps. It covers four modes, two of which (marine and air) were not addressed under the *CUSTA* or *NAFTA* umbrellas, as well as the views of the buyers of transport services. The views of large US multinationals, and what they want, will figure largely in political decisions on both security and infrastructure investment. The final two chapters step back to examine the larger picture about what needs to happen from a North American transport perspective if the continent is to maintain or improve its global competitiveness.

NOTES

1. Throughout this book, *NAFTA* is used to refer to the agreement. As it may also refer to the trade area, the term may be qualified by the addition of the word 'region' where the use is not completely clear from the context.
2. Adams (2003) has examined the 'tribes' of Canada and the US in his book *Fire and Ice*, and concluded that Canadians have increasingly rejected the traditional authority of religious institutions and are less deferential to patriarchal authority, while Americans have done the reverse, moving closer to religious fundamentalism and deference to a father as master of his house. More important is Adams' mapping of the socio-cultural characteristics of the regions of North America and the proximity of Pacific (US) and BC (Canada) cultures, for example, and their socio-cultural distance from the Deep South of the US.
3. The *Canada–United States Automobile Agreement* is more commonly called the Auto Pact. It removed tariffs on cars, trucks, buses, and automotive parts (including tires) and required that for every five cars sold in Canada, three would be made in Canada.
4. Wilson (2003) evaluated the sluggish Canadian economy in 1996 as a key issue in the situation in the mid-1990s, and concluded that it was economic conditions, not *NAFTA*, which had the greater impact on the trade relationship.
5. Treaty establishing the European Community, as Amended by Subsequent Treaties, Rome, 25 March 1957 (Treaty of Rome). The wording may be found at www.hri.org/MFA/foreign/treaties/Rome57/.
6. Derek Burney was the Chief of Staff to the Prime Minister of Canada and heavily involved at the end of negotiations. Charles Roh was responsible on the US side for the dispute settlement and integrating texts.
7. This is done because, while there are data for Brazil back to 1992, there are no data for either the Russian Federation or China before 1998 from this source.
8. Wilson (2003) would not agree. She concluded: 'The evidence suggests that the NAFTA itself did not significantly increase integration between the two economies.' (Wilson, 2003, p. 207). Globerman and Storer (2004) also argued that there is no evidence that these trade agreements had significant incremental impact. Therefore, what explains the mergers and acquisitions cross-border in the trucking industry after the agreement (Brooks and Ritchie, 2005) except that there were no barriers to prevent such investment (while there were to Mexican investment) and there were barriers to access through cabotage regulations?

2. The North American transport network: An economic and regulatory assessment

INTRODUCTION

The 1980s and 1990s were periods of massive change in the North American transportation industry. In the 1980s, deregulation in US trucking occurred with the *Motor Carrier Act of 1980* and in Canadian trucking with the *National Transportation Act of 1987*; these were followed by the *Canada–US Trade Agreement*, which liberalized Canada–US market access for international point-to-point cargoes. *CUSTA* also paved the way for cross-border investment by firms in the trucking industry. The 1990s was a period that saw many multinationals incorporate supply chain management principles into their global strategic plans, driven by a need to extract economies in distribution and the availability of new ways of doing business arising from deregulation, outsourcing, and inexpensive new information technologies. The march towards globalization was already under way when the *NAFTA* was signed. However, it really took flight with the widespread use of the Internet after 1996. There is no evidence indicating that *NAFTA* was a critical driver of this restructuring of North American transportation operations; that is, supply chain integration would likely have resulted without *NAFTA*, but *NAFTA* offered transport suppliers the opportunity to reconsider their business scope among other things. *NAFTA* was also supposed to extend investment access to Mexico, but the phased-in plan was not executed as negotiated. In sum, while there was liberalization occurring from a transport demand perspective, there remained a number of factors that dampened the liberalization of transport supply.

For both countries, road issues have been of primary importance. The same can be said of North American transport in general, as trucking is a vital dominant mode in Mexican transport. The US Department of Transportation's Freight Analysis Framework (Federal Highway Administration, 2005) paints a picture of US international truck traffic that looks positively 'arterial' with the 'heart' of the nation located somewhere in the congested northeast of the US and a second 'heart' in the southeast.

A truck crosses the Canada–US border every 2.5 seconds (DAMF Consultants et al., 2005). Truck shipments are the majority in value terms for Canada–US trade, accounting for 78.0 per cent of US exports to Canada and 52.7 per cent of US imports from Canada in 2004, versus 80.1 per cent and 57.5 per cent respectively in 1995 (Table 2.1). In Canada to US trade, pipeline has gained rapidly on rail, the key secondary mode,

Table 2.1 North American trade by value (millions of Canadian dollars)

Route/Year	1990	1995	1998	2000	2002	2004
Canadian imports from the US	87 865	150 683	203 578	229 644	218 329	208 553
Air	7 699	12 969	18 656	23 643	17 406	16 247
Water transport	2 045	2 189	3 158	3 270	3 337	2 753
Road	66 370	120 671	162 767	182 771	174 764	162 611
Rail	8 579	14 379	17 490	18 654	21 552	20 999
Pipeline and other	3 173	475	1 507	1 304	1 270	5 944
Canadian exports to the US	108 586	207 752	269 908	359 289	345 366	347 933
Air	4 041	9 804	13 981	23 845	18 906	15 769
Water transport	5 943	6 773	6 234	9 441	11 346	13 568
Road	69 556	119 485	169 135	200 310	196 868	183 451
Rail	20 691	52 107	56 211	75 593	75 632	77 300
Pipeline and other	8 357	19 583	24 349	50 100	42 615	57 845
US exports to Mexico	33 108	63 557	117 211	165 917	153 159	144 176
Air	1 608	2 436	6 817	11 596	9 587	7 826
Water transport	1 782	3 019	6 306	10 030	9 843	9 707
Road	N	N	89 651	122 356	111 378	103 274
Rail	N	N	9 181	15 588	15 928	17 744
Pipeline	N	N	108	449	892	113
US imports from Mexico	35 205	84 684	140 501	201 842	211 578	202 833
Air	667	1 897	4 406	8 412	5 097	4 498
Water transport	6 725	10 585	14 862	24 965	26 863	32 201
Road	N	N	97 739	131 682	142 265	136 587
Rail	N	N	17 846	31 270	32 649	26 269
Pipeline	N	N	3	18	2	0
Canadian exports to Mexico	656	1 161	1 467	2 035	2 420	2 975
Air	103	196	217	180	130	266
Water transport	103	399	626	650	671	742
Road	286	402	490	852	1 082	1 307
Rail	166	163	134	350	535	661
Pipeline and other	N	N	N	N	N	N

Table 2.1 (continued)

Route/Year	1990	1995	1998	2000	2002	2004
Canadian imports from Mexico	1749	5352	7682	12066	12732	13398
Air	68	317	378	873	707	1022
Water transport	147	67	266	535	148	312
Road	1038	3194	6398	8058	9052	9803
Rail	470	1672	630	2593	2546	2049
Pipeline and other	26	103	7	9	281	212

Notes:
Because each country defines and collects merchandise trade data differently, these numbers should be treated as approximate only. Detailed use should rely on the original data available at the NATS website. This table is an amalgam of Tables 6-1a and 6-1c.
N = Data are non-existent or unavailable. Data for 2005 are not provided as they are only available now in US dollars.

Source: Selected from North American Transportation Statistics (NATS) database, accessed January 2006.

in the past few years, reflecting the growing volume of energy sales to the US. In terms of tonnage, road's share takes second place to pipeline and the importance of oil in the trading relationship is even more apparent (Table 2.2). Air cargo developed strongly before the dot.com recession of early 2001 and declined after the attacks of September 11; it has not recovered the value share it had in 1995, although in tonnage terms there has been considerable growth in northbound air cargo. The share held by water transport between Canada and the US, whether by value or tonnage, is very small – smaller than air cargo – and has not changed significantly.

As for the Southern Border, road is also the dominant mode, by value, accounting for 67.3 per cent of imports to the US and 71.6 per cent of exports to Mexico. In value terms, rail and water play secondary roles in transporting trade between the two countries. In tonnage terms, there is a stronger role played by water transport than might be expected. The data gaps and the lack of mid-1990s information hamper deeper analysis of the changes that occurred along the Southern Border.

This chapter is intended to inform and educate those not familiar with the transport industry in North America, and to provide insights into what *NAFTA* did (and did not) do for the transport sector. It begins by examining the transportation network in place to deliver North American trade – the key modes, the major border crossings, and the issues faced by the suppliers of the transportation services. This sets the scene for discussing

Table 2.2 North American trade by mode (in 000 metric tonnes)

Route/Year	1990	1995	1998	2000	2002	2004
Canadian imports from the US	**U**	**87 758**	**131 836**	**122 814**	**128 865**	**167 481**
Air	U	1 527	1 765	1 796	1 814	4 988
Water transport	U	27 236	36 477	33 410	36 067	26 187
Road	U	45 734	72 291	67 847	68 918	94 721
Rail	U	12 180	14 067	17 624	18 103	19 974
Pipeline and other	U	1 080	7 236	2 136	3 963	21 613
Canadian exports to the US	**176 424**	**271 905**	**303 830**	**335 136**	**347 324**	**364 132**
Air	201	563	477	734	759	660
Water transport	40 060	45 273	49 084	53 191	60 585	66 273
Road	39 164	54 923	64 624	70 808	71 097	70 047
Rail	32 327	48 476	56 309	63 690	64 381	74 845
Pipeline and other	64 672	122 670	133 337	146 712	150 503	152 306
US exports to Mexico	**N**	**N**	**N**	**51 000**	**48 652**	**68 324**
Air	30	28	62	86	69	57
Water transport	9 027	8 632	18 553	25 157	23 061	20 267
Road	N	N	N	N	N	26 012
Rail	N	N	N	N	N	21 596
Pipeline	N	N	N	N	N	284
US imports from Mexico	**N**	**N**	**N**	**110 888**	**123 110**	**135 777**
Air	18	36	60	80	55	63
Water transport	43 115	63 719	81 734	83 232	93 606	101 633
Road	N	N	17 496	20 688	21 214	25 586
Rail	N	N	5 430	6 636	7 816	8 458
Pipeline	N	N	57	117	5	8
Canadian exports to Mexico	**698**	**2 278**	**2 781**	**3 653**	**2 766**	**4 182**
Air	8	32	11	13	20	63
Water transport	459	1 893	2 421	2 992	1 874	2 573
Road	83	176	183	302	400	481
Rail	149	176	166	346	472	1 066
Pipeline and other	N	N	N	N	N	N
Canadian imports from Mexico	**1 373**	**2 209**	**3 600**	**3 743**	**3 923**	**4 392**
Air	22	44	56	88	119	119
Water transport	846	617	1 863	2 141	786	1 320
Road	346	624	1 558	1 212	1 556	1 901
Rail	141	275	118	298	280	419
Pipeline and other	18	649	5	4	1 183	634

Notes:
Because each country defines and collects merchandise trade data differently, these numbers should be treated as approximate only. Detailed use should rely on the original data available at the NATS website. This table is an amalgam of Tables 6-2a and 6-2c.
N = Data are non-existent or unavailable.

Source: Selected from North American Transportation Statistics database, accessed January 2006.

the critical issues that the industry faces. As air and marine modes were for the most part excluded from the *NAFTA*, the balance of this chapter focuses on trucking and rail modes, leaving the discussion of marine and air modes to Chapter 5.

SURFACE TRANSPORTATION IN NORTH AMERICA

Land modes comprise the primary means of transport within North America (Figure 2.1). Of these, trucking is the dominant mode of freight transport, both domestically and continentally. This is particularly true when it comes to shipments of manufactured goods and component parts. In the trade between Canada and the US, more of the northbound cargo is carried by truck, with trucking handling 78 per cent of 2004 US exports to Canada compared with 53 per cent of US imports from Canada (Statistics Canada, 2006). The rail network has traditionally focused on the movement of commodities and raw materials, although rail intermodal has gained significant ground in the past two decades. The share held by land transport has deteriorated somewhat since the peak in the year after *NAFTA* was signed.

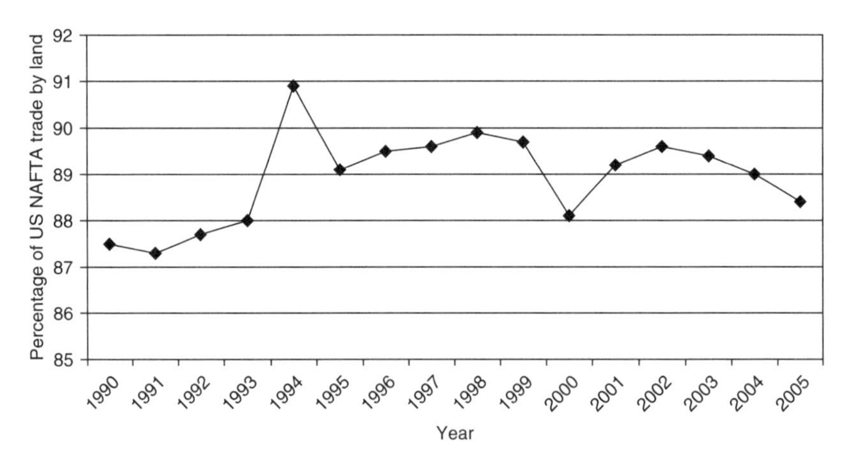

Source: Created from data in US Department of Transportation, Research and Innovative Technology Administration (2006), Table 1, p. 4. The 1990–1993 data are from the earlier equivalent document in US Department of Transportation, Research and Innovative Technology Administration (2005), Table 1, p. 2.

Figure 2.1 Percentage of US trade by land modes of all US NAFTA trade

The Trucking Market

The trucking market in both Canada and the US is highly fragmented. Deregulation of the interstate trucking industry in the US began in 1980, earlier than Canada's deregulation of inter-provincial trucking through the *Motor Vehicle Transport Act, 1987*. Following deregulation, the industry in both countries began a period of restructuring before the signing of *NAFTA*, a restructuring that continues today. Jones (1990) found that, in both countries, trucking productivity (as measured by revenue tonne-kilometers) had declined over the 10 years preceding *CUSTA*. Anecdotal evidence suggests the situation in Mexico was much worse.

Prior to deregulation, economic regulation of the trucking industry in both countries often took the form of entry restriction (Bonsor, 1995; Viscusi et al., 1996). Therefore, at the time of the *NAFTA* negotiations, the industry was still dealing with the effects of deregulation and inclined to be protectionist, particularly when it came to opening the market. While Corsi and Stowers (1991) noted that the US industry became much more strategic in its response post-deregulation, there was a significant concern, particularly among owner-operators, that the market would be flooded with cheap Mexican transport services. Canadian truckers were somewhat less concerned; Canada was a long way from Mexico. In Canada, the industry shrank from 1989 to 1991 as carriers shed unproductive assets (Barzyk, 1996); during that time, Canadian carriers expanded their share of the transborder market in order to gain the route densities required for efficient operations.

While reductions in transport costs fuelled continental trade developments and geographic market expansion by trucking companies, trucking remained fragmented. In Canada, there were 6040 small carriers (or 65 per cent of the companies) in the for-hire sector in 2000 in Canada (Nix, 2003), and 62.4 per cent of all 10 096 for-hire operators had less than C$1 million in revenue in 2004, down from 82.1 per cent in 1991 (Transport Canada, 2006, Table A7-3). While the share percentage of smaller operators dropped, the total number of for-hire companies grew, as did the number of carriers in the largest revenue category (over C$25 million in revenue). While measured differently, the same can be said of the US trucking market. By 2004, the number of US commercial motor carriers grew to more than 524 000; of these, 87 per cent operated six or fewer trucks and 96 per cent operated 20 or fewer trucks (American Trucking Associations, 2005). Ten years after *NAFTA* was signed, fully 70 per cent of US trucking companies still operated with seven or fewer vehicles (anonymous, 2003). Del Pilar Londoño (2006) noted that the Mexican trucking industry has 40 per cent of its trucks operated by owner-operators. The total number of motor carriers in all three countries grew in absolute numbers, not shrank, as would be expected had

NAFTA provided the impetus for consolidation of the motor carrier market. Because of the highly competitive nature of the market, many trucking companies survived through astute management of their assets and through asset utilization strategies such as triangulation.[1]

Currently, international trucking is provided by three sub-sectors of the trucking industry: the express package sector (which also, as will be noted in Chapter 5, competes in the air cargo market), the for-hire segment (offering both truckload (TL) and less-than-truckload (LTL) operations) and those who provide in-house trucking services for their owners. Drennen (2004) noted that these sub-sectors for the most part do not compete with each other, as they have different cost structures, types of customer, driver–employer relationships, and equipment and insurance issues. The transborder component (of these sub-sectors) is not an attractive one. Heads et al. (1991) noted that financial returns in the transborder market were low and expected to continue to decline throughout the 1990s. Since 2001, the transborder LTL market has been the most difficult one of all, as many security regulations penalize consolidated cargo operations (where multiple cargo owners use a single trailer).

Northbound truck crossings between Canada and the US grew 41 per cent between 1990 and 1995 (southbound data are unavailable). From 1995–2000, growth was 32 per cent northbound compared with southbound growth of 37 per cent (Figure 2.2). From 2000 to 2004, truck crossings on the Northern Border declined, reflecting the general stalling of trade in value terms.

While the total number of trucks crossing into the US on the Northern Border has stagnated, Ontario–Michigan traffic continues to grow (Table 2.3). However, when truck container data (both loaded and empty) is examined (Table 2.4), the growth in Ontario–Michigan traffic looks to be mostly a growth in tractor repositioning as the growth in trailers is small. Michigan crossings alone accounted for 36.7 per cent of the total in 1994 and this has grown to 40.8 per cent in 2005, and is expected to continue to grow. (The Ontario Chamber of Commerce (2003) projected that the truck traffic at the Detroit–Windsor border would grow 118 per cent over the next 30 years.) Ontario–Michigan and Ontario/Quebec–New York corridors dominate the Canada–US trading relationship. The decline in the trade across the Minnesota border with Canada is particularly striking, as it reflects a true trade decline.

Since the signing of *NAFTA*, growth in northbound truck traffic on the Southern Border reflected a similar pattern to that seen southbound on the Northern Border (Figure 2.2); southbound data being unavailable for the period. Tables 2.3 and 2.4 illustrate the sheer importance of Texas as an access point for Mexico–US trade, with California a distant second. Unlike the Northern Border, the growth in Mexico–Texas truck crossings in the

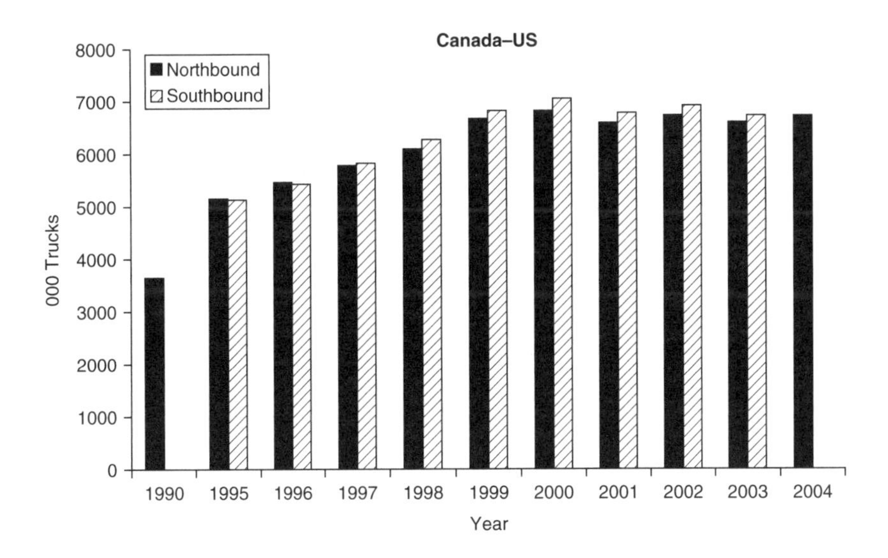

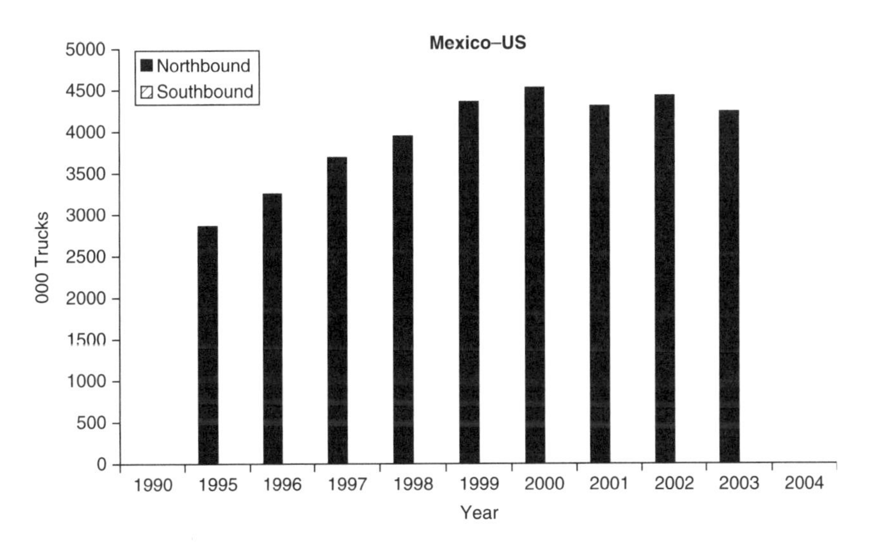

Note: Southbound data Canada–US for 1990 and 2004 were unavailable. No southbound data were available for Mexico–US. Truck crossing data are no longer supplied by this database.

Source: North American Transportation Statistics (2006), Table 12-6.

Figure 2.2 Border crossings by truck (in 000 trucks)

Table 2.3 Truck crossings from Canada and Mexico by US state (2001–2005)

State	2001	2002	2003	2004	2005*	% change 01–05
Northern Border total	**6776909**	**6915973**	**6728228**	**6903882**	**6703226**	**−1.1**
Alaska	11963	12323	11406	11134	10406	−13.0
Idaho	56478	58332	49794	49198	51804	−8.3
Maine	530485	511305	477906	520248	494704	−6.7
Michigan	2534370	2640808	2625761	2715757	2737154	8.0
Minnesota	127961	116971	109728	103065	86696	−32.2
Montana	198215	188195	156264	167678	164357	−17.1
New York	1902876	2011373	2000515	1987117	1902771	−0.0
North Dakota	360486	350409	330468	340862	335970	−6.8
Vermont	319700	319686	314181	334051	259241	−18.9
Washington	734375	706571	652205	674772	660123	−10.1
Southern Border total	**4304959**	**4426593**	**4238045**	**4503688**	**5028709**	**16.8**
Arizona	336090	311907	313250	323196	346444	3.1
California	1027815	1067411	1019908	1110758	1122784	9.2
New Mexico	34216	32603	33263	33716	38664	13.0
Texas	2906838	3014672	2871624	3036018	3520817	21.1

Note: * 2005 Border crossing data are preliminary.

Source: Selected data from US Department of Transportation, Research and Innovative Technology Administration (2006), Table A-3, p. 17.

past five years is substantial, but not the only growth area for truck traffic between Mexico and the US (Table 2.3). As with the Northern Border, there is a change in the mix of tractor and trailer repositioning over the period without an indication as to why.

The net result of these changes is severe stress on a few border crossing points; five border ports of entry for Canada–US trade bear 66.0 per cent of the burden of all truck container crossings (Table 2.5). Of these, traffic continues to grow at Port Huron, MI, but has eased substantially at Blaine, WA. On the Southern Border, traffic continues to grow at record pace at the smaller of the top five crossings, but appears to have pushed against capacity at the two largest access points (Laredo, TX and Otay Mesa/San Ysidro, CA). These five southern gateways account for 80.0 per cent of all Mexican-originating truck container crossings into the US. This consolidation of activity at a few access points on two long borders creates infrastructure

Table 2.4 Truck container crossings from Canada and Mexico by US state (2001–2005)

State	2001	2002	2003	2004	2005*	% change 01–05
Northern Border total	**6591357**	**6820052**	**6606187**	**6775329**	**6769051**	**2.7**
Alaska	9932	10009	9605	9771	8345	−16.0
Idaho	56577	58305	49967	48266	51157	−9.6
Maine	353068	468749	485682	509944	492542	39.5
Michigan	2605114	2650543	2589200	2661631	2674597	2.7
Minnesota	125457	118653	109289	102963	88031	−29.8
Montana	198084	189316	155603	165167	152397	−23.1
New York	1862948	1990530	1995820	1978035	1994093	7.0
North Dakota	365063	349059	328962	351968	357904	−2.0
Vermont	283441	292349	284606	281538	288486	1.8
Washington	731673	692539	597453	666046	661499	−9.6
Southern Border total	**4288332**	**4434441**	**4293226**	**4512900**	**4677562**	**9.1**
Arizona	327020	315086	310948	319872	344617	5.4
California	1014338	1076999	1091189	1135850	1128457	11.3
New Mexico	32882	31736	32039	32348	38868	18.2
Texas	2914092	3010620	2859050	3024830	3165620	8.6

Note: * 2005 data are preliminary.

Source: Selected data from US Department of Transportation, Research and Innovative Technology Administration (2006), Table A-3, p. 17.

stresses that require resolution at the highest political level. The largest border crossing points for both truck and rail are identified in Figure 2.3.

Before the negotiation of *NAFTA*, Chow and McRae (1990) examined the Canada–US trucking industry. They noted that earlier studies had shown that US transborder trucking rates were 30–60 per cent higher than published US domestic trucking rates, and that between 3 and 8 per cent of the transborder cost could be traced to interlining inefficiencies and customs administration. Therefore, they set out to examine the ability of Canadian carriers to compete in the transborder market, determining that the competitiveness of Canadian trucking companies in the US would be influenced by two factors: (1) each carrier's specific competitive advantages, which it could bring to bear on the situation; and (2) the advantages that would accrue from federal, state/provincial and/or local government involvement, altering the local competitive environment to the benefit of

Table 2.5 Top ports of entry for truck containers (loaded and empty) in number of crossings

Top 5 from Canada Northern Border port of entry	2001	2003	2005*	% change 01–05
Detroit, MI	1 722 185	1 588 769	1 678 177	−2.6
Buffalo-Niagara Falls, NY	1 123 481	1 162 950	1 142 274	1.7
Port Huron, MI	813 616	927 740	924 776	13.7
Champlain-Rouses Point, NY	369 194	378 783	374 524	1.4
Blaine, WA	482 611	338 762	346 691	−28.2

Top 5 from Mexico Southern Border port of entry	2001	2003	2005*	% change 01–05
Laredo, TX	1 404 683	1 345 099	1 455 504	3.6
Otay Mesa/San Ysidro, CA	715 847	711 526	744 278	4.0
El Paso, TX	667 155	665 422	734 851	10.1
Hidalgo, TX	364 138	405 238	494 572	35.8
Calexico East, CA	235 739	317 709	311 136	32.0

Note: * 2005 data are preliminary.

Source: Selected data from US Department of Transportation, Research and Innovative Technology Administration (2006), Table A-4, p. 19.

local carriers. The second category included immigration restrictions, duty on equipment, highway taxes, vehicle weight and dimension regulations, access to intrastate traffic, registration and licensing, and tax policy.[2] It was many of these issues that the *NAFTA* negotiators expected to address. What they actually achieved is discussed later in the chapter.

The Rail Market

The rail market in North America is predominantly freight-focused rather than passenger-oriented.[3] It is viewed as a highly successful transport sector that delivers products effectively.[4] About four times the tonnage goes from Canada into the US as moves north. In contrast with the trucking industry, the rail industry is a concentrated one, with a few large players – only seven Class 1 railroads[5] operating in the US, two in Mexico and two in Canada (Table 2.6). The sector, unlike other modes, operates a fixed network infrastructure that is privately owned. The American rail network is substantially denser than either Canadian or Mexican networks, and the US Class 1 network accounts for the majority

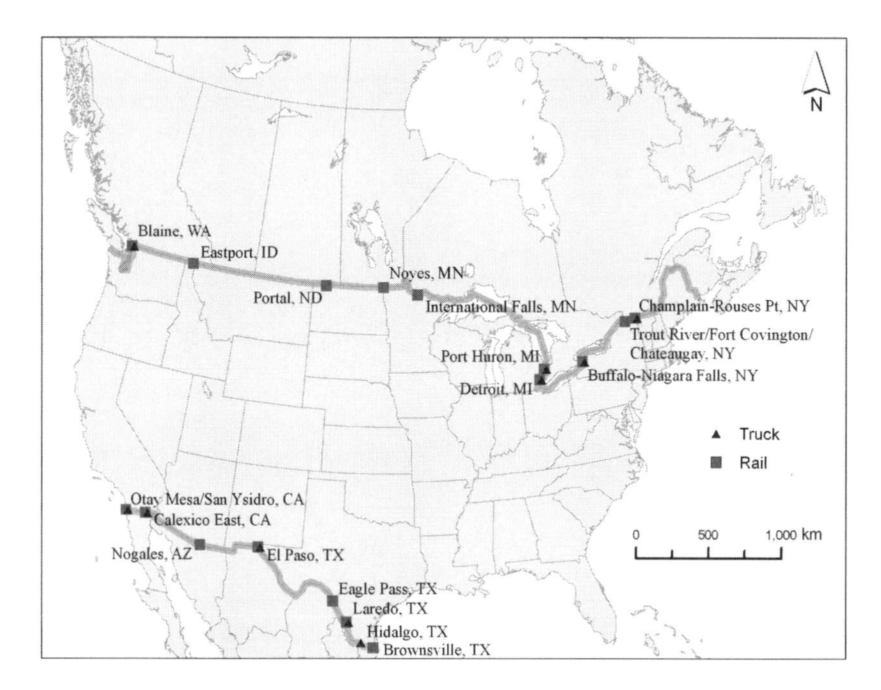

Note: Created for the author by Jennifer Milne of the Dalhousie University GIS Mapping Department to map the Top 10 crossings on the Northern Border and the Top 8 on the Southern Border based on 2005 crossing data presented in this chapter.

Source: US Bureau of Transportation Statistics and ESRI World Data

Figure 2.3 Top border crossings

of the revenue and about 70 per cent of the track miles (Association of American Railroads, 2006). The American network carries a volume in billions of ton-miles approximately ten times that of the Canadian system, the next largest (Table 2.6).

Over the past five years, rail traffic growth has been strongest between Canada and the US at the North Dakota border, with a growth of 81.3 per cent from 2001 to 2005 (Table 2.7). While North Dakota was the fourth largest market on the Northern Border in 2001, by 2005 its traffic had surpassed traffic via New York and Minnesota to take second place after the dominant Michigan access point. A large volume of international traffic accesses US Midwest markets via major rail corridors through the Windsor–Detroit area, with more than 50 per cent of Montreal's inbound container trade headed to the Midwest via this corridor.[6]

While earlier in this chapter it was noted that a few border crossing points

Table 2.6 A snapshot of North America's Class 1 rail industry

	2004		2005	
Number of US railroads*	7		7	
Miles of road operated	121 400		120 565	
Locomotives in service	22 015		22 779	
Number of employees	157 699		162 438	
Ton-miles (billions)	1 663		1 696	
Canadian railroads**	**CN**	**CP**	**CN**	**CP**
Miles of road operated	19 891	13 817	19 806	13 639
Locomotives in service	2 100	1 655	2 073	1 669
Number of employees	22 470	16 056	22 246	16 448
Ton-miles (billions)***	174	124	180	125
Mexican railroads****	**FM**	**KCSM**	**FM**	**KCSM**
Miles of road operated	5 375	3 043	5 034	3 046
Locomotives in service	501	467	492	384
Number of employees	6 185	3 399	6 105	3 393
Ton-miles (billions)***	22	20	24	19

Notes:
* The seven Class 1 are: BNSF Railway, CSX Transportation, Grand Trunk Corporation, Kansas City Southern Railway, Norfolk Southern Combined Railroad Subsidiaries, Soo Line Railroad, and Union Pacific Railroad.
** Two Canadian railroads meet US Class 1 Standards: CN (formerly the Canadian National Railway Company) and Canadian Pacific Railway. This data is derived from AAR's profiles.
*** The data for CN are in revenue ton-miles, not ton-miles, and the data for KCSM are net ton-miles. The CN data include the contribution of the Grand Trunk Corporation, which is also reported in the US data (Grand Trunk ton-miles were 54 835 in 2004). The CP data include the contribution of the Soo Line Railroad, which is also reported in the US data (Soo ton-miles were 24 522 in 2004).
**** Two Mexican railroads meet US Class 1 Standards: Ferrocarril Mexicano and Kansas City Southern de México. This data is derived from AAR's profiles.

Source: Association of American Railroads (2006). Carrier profiles from the same website were used for the data of Canadian and Mexican railroads. Used with permission.

accounted for a significant share of the transborder trucking activity, five ports of entry account for 68.3 per cent in the rail sector. Of these, traffic continues to grow at four of the top five ports of entry, including Portal, ND, and International Falls, MN; Blaine has successfully switched a substantial component of its truck traffic to rail over the past five years (Table 2.8). There is also good growth at some of the smaller access points. On the Southern Border, rail traffic at Laredo continues to dominate (with a share of 43.4 per cent of all rail container crossings) but there has been phenomenal growth (in excess of 200 per cent) at both Brownsville, TX and El Paso, TX, reducing

Table 2.7 Rail container crossings (loaded and empty) into the US from Canada and Mexico (2001–2005)

State	2001	2002	2003	2004	2005*	% change 01–05
Northern Border total	**1779345**	**1827384**	**1868245**	**1950909**	**1940666**	**9.1**
Michigan	794810	761795	757819	751600	730100	−8.1
Minnesota	274882	318460	325632	333657	251118	−8.6
New York	261565	256359	257598	276112	295236	12.9
North Dakota	168261	200013	219001	225284	304989	81.3
Southern Border total	**582361**	**601987**	**607370**	**675305**	**728559**	**25.1**
Texas	513367	539019	551088	613315	663415	29.2

Notes:
* 2005 data are preliminary. Border crossing data account for incoming vehicles only.
Rail containers also cross into the US from Canada via Alaska, Idaho, Maine, Montana, Vermont and Washington.
Rail containers also cross into the US from Mexico via Arizona, California and New Mexico.

Source: Selected data from US Department of Transportation, Research and Innovative Technology Administration (2006), Table A-3, p. 18.

Laredo's dominance. The top five southern rail gateways accounted for 97.5 per cent of all Mexican-originating container rail crossings into the US. This consolidation of activity at a few access points with infrastructure controlled by a small number of companies has enabled the rail industry to exceed security expectations applicable to the trucking industry in North America.

According to Phillips (2005), cross-border rail operations are different on the Northern and Southern Borders. On the Northern Border, a single rail carrier normally assembles and handles traffic for movement across the border, including foreign-originating container traffic. The crew will change at or near the crossing, but the equipment will not. On the Southern Border, trains often are completed and interchanged between the two carriers at the border crossing point.[7]

Rail issues in North America in the early 1990s centered primarily on investment in infrastructure, and on gaining the scale and scope needed to continue to make the business attractive to shareholders. The latter meant that there was significant interest in the rail sector on regulatory reform of the industry and on how *NAFTA* would address cross-border investment in transportation companies.

In conclusion, the *Canada–US Trade Agreement, 1988* addressed

Table 2.8 Top ports of entry for rail containers (loaded and empty) in number of crossings

Top 10 from Canada Northern Border port of entry	**2001**	**2003**	**2005***	**% change 01–05**
Port Huron, MI	449 299	458 551	457 275	1.8
International Falls, MN	205 430	252 699	251 118	22.2
Portal, ND	168 137	217 390	231 832	37.9
Detroit, MI	304 591	254 688	231 482	−24.0
Buffalo-Niagara Falls, NY	150 525	149 916	153 772	2.2
Blaine, WA	73 713	98 752	123 209	67.1
Champlain-Rouses Point, NY	78 799	68 762	90 716	15.1
Eastport, ID	59 323	74 499	88 821	49.7
Noyes, MN	69 452	72 933	71 666	3.2
Trout River/Fort Covington/ Chateauguay, NY	32 241	38 920	50 748	57.4
Top 5 from Mexico Southern Border port of entry	**2001**	**2003**	**2005***	**% change 01–05**
Laredo, TX	273 935	313 244	316 402	15.5
El Paso, TX	44 537	50 893	143 741	222.7
Brownsville, TX	101 787	98 622	105 175	303.0
Eagle Pass, TX	93 108	88 329	98 089	5.3
Nogales, AZ	58 667	45 685	46 831	−20.2
Calexico East, CA	5 460	6 924	12 358	126.3
Otay Mesa/San Ysidro, CA	3 453	3 441	5 862	69.8

Note: * 2005 data are preliminary.

Source: Selected data from US Department of Transportation, Research and Innovative Technology Administration (2006), Table A-4, p. 20.

conditions affecting Canada–US trucking and rail operations. While it was a mechanism to liberalize access to international transport markets, it retained cabotage[8] restrictions for domestic traffic. Most of the changes in transport operating conditions for Canadian and American companies were achieved through the implementation of *CUSTA*. Investment restrictions were lifted and Canadian and American trucking companies, for example, were able to consolidate operations in a much more competitive environment through an M&A strategy (Brooks and Ritchie, 2005). Trucking companies were able to exploit some of the benefits of deregulation in the two countries so that efficiency gains would be reflected in dramatically reduced unit costs for transport. They were also able to aggressively grow business,[9] although they were not able to fully exploit the asset utilization potential or network efficiencies that might have been possible had cabotage been removed or equipment standards fully harmonized. The addition of Mexico to a more liberalized international trucking and rail environment offered the promise of even greater benefits. The question the next section addresses is: what did *NAFTA* change?

WHAT *NAFTA* DID

In theory, *NAFTA* made substantial changes of importance to land transportation suppliers – it opened the market for international point-to-point traffic, and it extended many of the gains made for Canadian and US companies in *CUSTA* to Mexican firms, albeit through a phased-in approach. It proposed timelines and milestones for market liberalization.

> A US negotiator summarized the results: 'We gave the Mexicans generous phase-in schedules. We broke down the liberalization process into discrete processes: first the border states, then the entire country are liberalized. Only international cargo is included. Then, in seven years, they can come back and there will be further liberalization' (Cameron and Tomlin, 2000, p. 145).

However, *NAFTA* did not change the domestic cabotage restrictions; domestic traffic would still be required to use national carriers. It also did not address the uneven playing field in terms of subsidies to transport users, immigration, and access to capital, or critical differences like rules regarding exit from the market (bankruptcy, abandonment of right of way, or conveyance), corporate taxation or governance. It did make gains, however, in two key areas: (1) international cargo access, and (2) investment restrictions and screening.

International Cargo Access and Cabotage

A critical element of the negotiations was the agreement by the three countries not to use standards-related measures as unnecessary obstacles to trade. In the agreement, both national treatment and most-favoured-nation treatment were accorded to NAFTA partners. *NAFTA* provided a timetable for the removal of standards-related barriers to the provision of land transportation services between NAFTA countries, and established a mechanism for the further negotiation of access barriers – the Land Transportation Standards Subcommittee (LTSS) – under Article 913 and Annex 913A. The three countries also agreed to encourage cooperation between private standards organizations for mutual acceptance of test results and certification procedures.

Although the development of the LTSS was expected to go some way towards dealing with contentious issues like vehicle weights and dimensions, there were grounds for some scepticism, given the wide range of standards in use in the US, and the significant differences between these and Canadian regulations. Mexico had no vehicle weights and dimensions regulations and so had the opportunity to cooperate or become more protective.[10]

NAFTA did not alter the existing cabotage restrictions for domestic cargo, but did open access to international point-to-point traffic and phased out rules preventing the movement of international cargo from Canada through the US into Mexico by Canadian operators. Canada agreed to continue to permit American and Mexican truck operators to obtain operating authority in Canada. The critical breakthroughs in negotiation were for the Mexican carriers and for Canadian and American carriers in the Mexican market.[11] Prior to the negotiation, some American carriers had established interchange agreements or subsidiaries in Mexico to enhance their transit times to market, but there were no known interchange agreements between Canadian and Mexican carriers (External Affairs and International Trade Canada, 1991). Most Canadian carriers interlined with an American carrier rather than travel the full distance to the Mexican–US border.

As a result of the *NAFTA*, Canadians gained the right (phased-in) to pick up in the US and drop off in Mexico. Three years after signature of the agreement, Mexico was to allow US and Canadian operators to make cross-border deliveries to, and pick up cargo in, Mexican border states, and the United States was to allow Mexican truck operators to perform the same services in US border states. Prior to the signing of *NAFTA*, if a Canadian company wanted to interline with a Mexican company, that had to happen in the US, but if there was no backhaul cargo bound for Canada, the Canadian operator faced a long empty return as US cabotage rules prevented a domestic leg. As an interim measure, Canadian companies either had to acquire US trucking companies or sign interline agreements with US carriers in order to have a less-tilted playing field on which to offer a service to the US south. As the US decided to maintain its moratorium on operating authorities for truck carriage of domestic cargo, along with the requirement to use US drivers and equipment, this meant that carriers wishing to compete needed to gain access via equity-based investment or strategic alliances. Any trucking company seeking greater access needed to be creative about how they structured their operations.[12]

The rail environment was less restrictive. Article 305(5) enabled rail equipment and trucks to enter through and exit from different points, providing freedom of routing and greater flexibility in accessing cargo. However, *NAFTA* did not affect each country's immigration law requirements for crews to change at or near their borders, according to Article 1201(3)(a). The clarification of the immigration rules for operators of international transportation services (Article 1203[3]) provided carriers some certainty, but personnel restrictions have continued to this day to be problematic for transnational transport entities. Rail standards were to be addressed by the LTSS.

Investment Restrictions and Screening

In Canada, at the time of the *NAFTA*, investment restrictions were applicable to all modes, and Canada maintained all existing transportation investment restrictions through Annex 1 Schedule of Canada. Under the *National Transportation Act, 1987* (Chapter 34, Sections 252, 253), acquisitions of at least 10 per cent of the voting shares in a transportation business with assets or annual gross sales over C$10 million were to be reviewed by the National Transportation Agency. The *Investment Canada Act, 1985* (Chapter 28) dealt with acquisitions on a case-by-case basis but tended to assume control at one-third ownership, and maintenance of control in Canada was clearly important to the Government of Canada. Ownership restrictions would ease somewhat in subsequent years but not for reasons associated with *NAFTA*. In the United States, Canadians were free to establish companies for the carriage of domestic cargo point-to-point, although they were required to use US drivers and equipment; these restrictions, a non-controlling interest in US trucking firms under the same driver and equipment conditions, were also available to Mexicans.

The Mexican trucking market was closed in 1981, followed quite closely by an internal restructuring process, accelerated by the Salinas government. Although transportation in Mexico was liberalized on 24 January 1990, trucking remained closed to foreign carriers; ownership of a Mexican trucking company was required to be by nationals, and operations to be performed by a Mexican driver and truck. The Mexicans were quite firm on this position, but anticipated that ownership would be phased in on a schedule that reflected the phase-in of Mexican trucking access to US markets. Under the *NAFTA*, Mexico agreed to reduce investment restrictions on transportation with a staged timetable as follows (Annex 1 – Schedule of Mexico – Investment in Land Transportation):

1. Three years after the agreement was signed, Mexico would allow 49 per cent Canadian and US investment in bus companies and in truck companies providing international cargo services (including point-to-point distribution of such cargo within Mexico).

2. By 1 January, 2001, Mexico would allow 51 per cent Canadian and US investment in Mexican truck companies providing international cargo services.
3. By 1 January, 2004, this investment limit would increase to 100 per cent, but the advantage would still only be available to carriers of international cargo.

The Annex also clarified that foreign ownership of Mexican transport entities carrying domestic cargo would not be permitted.

According to Article 1102 of *NAFTA*, each country would accord NAFTA investors and their investments national treatment. Under the investment review provisions of Annex 1 – Schedule of Mexico, a sliding scale for calculating review thresholds over the 10 years after the agreement is in force would curtail Mexico's review of takeovers of existing enterprises. To keep its part of the bargain, after the agreement, the Mexican government passed the legislation necessary to open the industry to foreign investment, but did not implement it when the Mexican trucking dispute began in December 1995 (to be discussed later).

According to Brooks (1994, p. 111), these investment restrictions, the investment screening process and the timetable for phase-in all existed to protect the weaker partners from the stronger one. The differential timetable indicated 'the weaker parties, Canada and Mexico, retained some clout during the negotiation process'. The promise of a continental trading area was further assisted by the removal of Mexican import licensing requirements for goods as a way of growing the cargo business for international carriers.

AFTER THE *NAFTA* WAS SIGNED

At the time the *NAFTA* was signed, Chow et al. (1994) reported that the typical US trucking company was much larger than the average Canadian one, but less heavily leveraged, which they attributed to better access to equity capital in the US, although that equity investment was not performing well for shareholders in US trucking firms (Terry, 1991). After the agreement was signed, both Canadian and US trucking industries continued to have difficulties. The financial performance of US truckload and LTL carriers deteriorated, becoming inferior to that of their Canadian counterparts with respect to operating ratio and return on equity. Net profit margins, however, were another matter. US LTL carriers had higher profit margins than their Canadian counterparts; Canadian TL carriers had higher profit margins than US TL carriers. Moreover, Canadian carriers continued to have a greater reliance on debt financing than their American counterparts (Bowland and McKnight, 1996). Although there were a substantial number of mergers and acquisitions following *NAFTA*, trucking continued to be highly fragmented, with many small firms struggling to survive (Brooks and Ritchie, 2005).

As for the rail sector, it was historically privately owned (with the sole exception of the Canadian National Railway, which was privatized via Initial Public Offering in 1995). After deregulation, Canadian railways expanded their links in the US (American railroads appeared to have little interest in expanding north of the US–Canada border). After *CUSTA*, Canadian National Railway created CN North America with its US subsidiary, Grand Trunk Corporation, and signed marketing alliances in 1991 with Norfolk Southern and Burlington Northern to handle transborder shipments. Canadian Pacific acquired the remaining shares in the Soo Line in 1990, purchased the Delaware and Hudson Railway in 1991, and entered into bilateral traffic agreements with other US carriers (WESTAC, 1992). The US railroads acquired by the Canadian companies retained their US legal identities as railroads could not be foreign-owned. After the signing of *NAFTA*, the acquisition of Mexican railroads was still not available, as the Mexican government retained control over the operation and maintenance of rail infrastructure under Annex III Schedule of Mexico. This did not deter efforts, over a long period of time, by the Kansas City Southern to bring the Kansas City Southern de México into being, an event which finally occurred in 2004 (Machalaba and Millman, 2004); this enabled the smallest of the US Class 1 railroads in terms of 2005 ton-miles to become a true NAFTA player after years of growth through strategic alliances.

THE EMERGING REGULATORY ENVIRONMENT OF *NAFTA*

The creation of the Land Transportation Standards Subcommittee (LTSS) by the agreement provided an institution for resolving standards issues in order to facilitate trade. As technology was viewed to be a key element of the standards issue, the three countries signed the *Memorandum of Understanding (MOU) on Science and Technology Cooperation in the Field of Transportation* on 30 March 1995. According to the 1998 *NAFTA Plenary Report* (Transport Canada, 1998), by mid-1995, the LTSS had established five standards-focused working groups: Compliance and Driver and Vehicle Standards (Group 1), Vehicle Weights and Dimensions (Group 2), Traffic Control Devices for Highways (Group 3), Rail Standards (Group 4), and Hazardous Materials Standards (Group 5). Furthermore, five transportation consultative groups were also established to address outstanding areas where trilateral cooperation would be beneficial; these five were Cross-Border Operations and Facilitation (TCG 1), Rail Safety and Economic Issues (TCG 2), Automated Data Exchange (TCG 3), Science and Technology (TCG 4), and Maritime and Ports Policy (TCG 5). As the interests of Group 4 and TCG 2 were highly correlated, the rail sector quickly consolidated its efforts into one group to address both standards and policy.

The groups set a target to resolve the outstanding issues by 2000 and scheduled yearly plenary meetings to report on progress. By the plenary meeting of 2000, agreements were reported in the areas of driver legal age, driver logbooks (format and contents), reciprocity of medical standards, language of jurisdiction, and regulations governing hazardous materials transport. While all three countries agreed upon a minimum age for a motor carrier driver as 21, the insurance industry continues to require a minimum age of 23 for commercial operators. The US continues to struggle with the concept of mutual recognition for commercial driver's licenses, a matter of state jurisdiction, while Canadians and Mexicans granted each other mutual recognition for these in March 1994.

The agreement on driver logbooks for recording hours of service and other safety data resulted in logbooks with the same core fields, but driver hours of service continue to be different in each country. This has not prevented data-sharing across jurisdictions. For example, in Canada, the driver and vehicle data system run by Canadian Council of Motor Transport Administrators is gated to similar systems in the US; most Canadian and American jurisdictions electronically share data but the sharing is not fully exploited by most US states (Brooks and Kymlicka, 2007).

Progress was also reported at the plenary meetings in the area of hazardous materials (hazmat) transport. A *North American Emergency Response Guidebook* is available in all three NAFTA languages, published in 2000. The *NAFTA* gave each country six years to comply with UN regulations. Canada and the US were in compliance by 1994, while Mexico would have to work hard to bring its regulations in line. Most telling, however, is the progress on hazmat regulations; the UN regulations changed after 1994, and while both the US and Canada kept pace, they did not see this change as an opportunity to work together to seek regulatory convergence. Hazmat regulation implementations were also not identical. Mexico has still not succeeded in meeting the initially planned timetable. This seems to be another case of lost opportunity.

Other activities that have been undertaken include a baseline analysis of vehicle weights and dimensions (side-by-side analysis in the 65 NAFTA jurisdictions); analysis of traffic control devices; regulation of rail safety;

and data exchange, including port state control data for the regulation of vessel safety and vessel-source pollution (discussed further in Chapter 5). Clearly what is missing from this list is the harmonization of those 65 sets of rules regarding vehicle weights and dimensions, common regulation of truck safety, and a number of other irritants, which will be discussed in the next section.

While there has been some progress on resolving trilateral transportation issues, the lack of progress in market access and transportation ownership rules can be traced to the Mexican trucking dispute. The timeline for this dispute and the relevant key dates are detailed in Appendix 2.1. The primary conclusion that can be drawn is that it provides an excellent example of how to delay the timetable to implement negotiated obligations if that is the will of the administration. It also illustrates that while the US may have had the best intentions during the NAFTA negotiations, its political process is very much one where special interest groups can 'hijack' the process; the chattering classes can hardly be chastised for concluding that the US cannot be trusted to keep its promises. In spite of campaigning in 2000 on righting the wrongs, President Bush, too, did not deliver what he promised his most important trading partners of the day, although that may still happen before he leaves office.

The last meeting of the LTSS was held in May 2002. While there have been no trilateral meetings since then, each party has retained its portion of the LTSS as an implementation body. The establishment, at about this time, of two separate Transportation Border Working Groups (TBWGs), one for the Northern Border, and one for the Southern Border, signalled a shift from a trilateral relationship for land transportation issues to a bilateral one. Furthermore, the inability to resolve regulatory differences in land transportation standards across the three countries, coupled with the market access barriers found in the trucking dispute on the Southern Border, set the scene for the development of regionalism, not continentalism, in North American transport.

CRITICAL ISSUES IN NORTH AMERICAN TRANSPORTATION TODAY

Truck Vehicle Size and Weight

On US Interstate highways, Congress froze truck size and weight limits in 1991; trucks operating on most of the 46 000-mile Interstate highways can have a gross vehicle weight of no more than 80 000 pounds. This freeze occurred, in large part, because of concerns about the safety of longer and heavier trucks (as are currently allowed in Canada's western provinces and in Mexico). While American interstate commerce is regulated with a maximum set of truck size and weights standards, each state has its own variants for intrastate traffic. In Canada, vehicle weights and dimensions are also subject to provincial regulation, although there is some mutual recognition between provinces. In 1992, Mexico had no weight and size vehicle and equipment standards. As a result, Nix et al. (1998) noted that 'regional trucks' had developed as an industry compromise, as most Canada–US transborder traffic was of a more local nature.

Given the large number of variations within North America, it made sense for the negotiators to offload this complex issue to the LTSS, and for the countries to seek harmonization via consensus in Group 2 with a planned internal deadline of January 1997. (Differences in rail equipment regulation were seen as immaterial.) As noted above, while the *NAFTA Plenary Report for 2000* reported that a side-by-side analysis of regulations governing vehicle standards applicable within the NAFTA region had been completed, efforts in the early part of 2005 were fruitless in trying to find a copy of a single trilateral (or trilingual) publication. Brooks and Kymlicka (2007) reported that each country published its own manual for motor carriers operating across jurisdictions, noting that the Canadian *NAFTA Resource Manual* was 162 pages in length (Government of Canada, 2002) while the US version was 130 pages and the Mexican 71 pages. Problematically, neither the US nor the Mexican website links facilitated access to copies, in spite of repeated efforts to view the documents. It is difficult to understand the scope of regulatory convergence negotiations for 65 different jurisdictions when the content remains unavailable. It merely provides further evidence for a conclusion that trilateral efforts in this area are not a priority. The LTSS has only picked the low-growing fruit. The difficult issues have been left to fester.

Worse still is the fact that the issues appeared to have 'fallen off the table'. Since the on-line 'publication' of these three resource manuals, there does not appear to have been any effort to evolve the regulations to accommodate industry innovation. As noted by Brooks and Kymlicka (2007), a company wishing to use a long combination vehicle, for example, must apply to each jurisdiction for approval – not any way to run a business, improve efficiency or competitiveness. There is considerable work to be done by regulatory authorities to promote industry productivity gains that can result from reduced regulatory burden.

In conclusion, the creation of an institution, the LTSS, to deal with regulatory divergence was a valid approach to the diversity that existed at the time of negotiations. The failure of the LTSS to resolve the outstanding differences makes it difficult to revisit the issues today. One solution might be to develop trade corridor agreements or, in other words, sets of standards depending on needs to protect pavement life in cold climates where 'freeze thaw' cycles argue in favour of specific standards not relevant to authorities in the US south and Mexico or in climates where the ground stays frozen for most of the winter. It is clear that one standard will not fit all, but there are no agreed principles to address these differences and no justification for the multiplicity of regulations currently in play. While mutual recognition is one way of addressing the divergence in standards (although it is not one accepted under the existing agreement), the need to protect the system infrastructure can be argued to rank as a higher priority.

Safety

One of the foremost concerns of both Canada and the US, but particularly the US, was the continuing safety of the highways within North America.[13] Drennen (2004) noted that, in the early days after the signing of *NAFTA*, the Mexican fleet was old and vehicle out-of-service rates were very high. She argued that initial concern in the US about the entry of Mexican vehicles and drivers was related to the inability of US safety inspectors to verify Mexican carrier safety compliance. In fact, as can be seen by the 2000 statistics in Table 2.9, Mexican compliance reviews were still few and far between, but by 2004 they were moving in the right direction.

Drennen's assessment was that the initial Mexican trucking dispute was really a political battle that the Teamsters, anti-*NAFTA* and other special interest groups won against the advice of the American Trucking Association, among others. Had the trucking dispute not occurred, would highways be less safe today? Rothberg (2003, p. 120) noted that based on crash statistics in Texas, where more than 75 per cent of the Mexican trucks enter the United States, 'there are relatively few deaths and injuries from Mexican-registered commercial vehicles. Crash data from the other border states show similar statistics'. Table 2.9 shows that, by 2000, the Mexican authorities conducted far higher rates of driver and vehicle inspections than either Canada or the US conducted, relative to the size of their respective industries. Mexican driver and vehicle inspections exceeded 200 per cent in 2000 and 400 per cent in 2004. When compared with 39 per cent driver and 45 per cent vehicle inspection rates in the US in 2004, and 55 per cent and 40 per cent respectively in Canada in 2004, the Mexican effort to improve is obvious. While vehicle out-of-service rates in both Canada and the US have remained flat between 2000 and 2004, the Mexican vehicle out-of-service rate has declined to meet the US standard, implying that the inspections are working to improve Mexican truck safety standards. The biggest issue appears to be the compliance reviews.[14]

Table 2.9 Summary statistics for US DoT active motor carriers

2000 Motor carrier census	All domiciles	US	Mexico	Canada
Active carriers	583 429	555 763	9 856	17 810
Power units	3 605 024	3 470 806	22 760	111 458
Commercial drivers	3 524 239	3 395 394	15 408	113 437
Roadside inspections				
Inspections	1 911 808	1 791 596	52 926	67 286
Driver inspections	1 868 768	1 749 564	52 792	66 412
Driver out-of-service rate	8.0%	8.0%	6.9%	9.4%
Vehicle inspections	1 434 189	1 345 967	49 940	38 282
Vehicle out-of-service rate	21.7%	21.3%	36.1%	14.2%
Compliance reviews				
Compliance reviews	12 755	12 529	4	222
Satisfactory	6 722	6 635	0	87
Conditional	4 006	3 897	3	106
Unsatisfactory	1 760	1 730	1	29
Not rated	267	267	0	0
2004 Motor carrier census				
Active carriers	686 736	651 145	13 804	21 787
Power units	4 619 580	4 436 077	39 546	143 957
Commercial drivers	5 623 012	5 423 451	32 102	167 459
Roadside inspections				
Inspections	2 430 805	2 164 777	172 502	93 526
Driver inspections	2 389 061	2 124 190	172 179	92 692
Driver out-of-service rate	6.2%	6.6%	1.6%	6.4%
Vehicle inspections	1 773 857	1 557 963	158 216	57 678
Vehicle out-of-service rate	21.4%	21.6%	21.5%	14.0%
Compliance reviews				
Compliance reviews	10 475	10 104	236	135
Satisfactory	6 426	6 240	108	78
Conditional	2 941	2 801	92	48
Unsatisfactory	779	740	31	8
Not rated	329	323	5	1

Source: Federal Motor Carrier Safety Administration (2006).

If the Mexican trucking dispute were examined with fresh eyes today, it is clear that the Mexican industry and Mexican authorities have worked hard to address the safety concerns of its NAFTA partners; the Federal Motor Carrier Safety Administration (FMCSA) has documented this effort. From these statistics and, in particular, the nature of Canadian and US inspection rates, it appears that there is little room for criticism. However, Mead (2002) noted that the US continued to experience problems with unauthorized Mexican carriers operating in border states, and that states have not enacted legislation enabling authorities to put such violators out of service. If states were able to place vehicles out of service for operating without operating authority,[15] it might be possible to resolve the current impasse in the Mexican trucking dispute. Otherwise, the fear remains that Mexican drivers will operate beyond the limits of any authority they are granted.

Were the liberalization proposed under *NAFTA* to be in effect, the US International Trade Commission (2002, p. 135) concluded that Mexican trucks that would be found on the US highway system would be long-haul operators and significantly more likely to be in better condition from a safety compliance perspective than the short-haul dray trucks used in the border commercial areas.

It is quite clear that the American trucking industry is an elephant in size compared to the much smaller industry sectors of the other two (Table 2.9). This suggests that it is time to revisit liberalization of the trucking sector, perhaps considering using new technology and security-oriented certification processes to address the thorny issues in the regulatory climate. Even a partial opening would go some distance in improving the ability of North American transport operators to support North American competitiveness issues.

Hours of Service

Hours of Service (HoS) regulations for commercial vehicle drivers were, and are, quite different between Canada and the United States. In the US, HoS are regulated by the FMCSA. In Canada, HoS are regulated by Transport Canada, and reflect agreement with the provinces (via the Canadian Council of Motor Transport Administrators), Teamsters Canada and the Canadian Trucking Alliance.

The 1994 Canadian regulations permitted longer driving times in comparison with US regulations, and allowed for shorter off-duty (or rest) time between shifts. The resulting regulatory gap created confusion for trans-border drivers and caused concern in both Canada and the US over highway safety. 'Drivers using electronic logs are at even greater disadvantage in a border delay because of the traffic jams that ensue when the borders get busy. Electronic data recorders display these hours as "driving time"' (Park, 2003, p. 357).

The knock-on effect was confusion about applicable rules and known flouting of the rules by drivers (Park, 2003), making the relationship between drivers and the authorities even more confrontational than might otherwise have been the case. Furthermore, there was, and continues to be, some confusion about how to log stops at border crossings and inspection points, and thus rumours about these being disguised as 'off-duty' (rest) time persist. As long-haul drivers in the transborder market are usually paid by distance, there is also an incentive to avoid adding driving time if border crossings are 'known' as severely congested. According to Park (2003), hours of service and logbook violations account for more than 80 per cent of all driver out-of-service violations. Belzer et al. (2002) evaluated the relationship between driver safety and hours of service and concluded that there is a relationship between longer hours of service and highway accidents, and that there are strong incentives for drivers to under-report hours driving.

Both countries have revisited their regulations in the last few years, but have not coordinated the effort or ensured that the results are more aligned (Table 2.10). In the US, HoS regulations were revised in 2005, with effect 1 October 2005. In Canada, changes announced in October 2005 were enacted with effect 1 January 2007. The two sets of regulations are considerably different in tone and layout (Table 2.10). While the change in regulations reduced driving times in Canada by 19 per cent, Canadians are still allowed to have longer times on the road than are applicable in the US. In the US, truck drivers are permitted to drive only 11 hours compared to driving time of 13 hours within Canada. In Mexico, there are no HoS regulations. By establishing a common CUSTA region regulation, Canadian and US authorities might have been able to convince Mexican authorities to establish similar HoS regulations for commercial drivers; as it is, another opportunity for regulatory convergence was lost.

Border Infrastructure

When *NAFTA* was signed, there was considerable discussion about the growth in trade that would result. Nowhere in the implementation program was there any discussion about supplying additional border infrastructure to handle the growth in traffic volume. Drennen (2004) noted that a series of agreements – The *1995 US–Canada Shared Border Accord*, the *1997 Border Vision Initiative*, and the *1999 Canada–US Partnership* – are representative of a number of collaborative attempts by industry and various levels of government to draw attention to the lack of resources allocated to making the Northern Border efficient. The costs of doing business across the border continued to be a sore point with industry, but infrastructure investment did not seem to be a priority for either government.

The same has been said of the Southern Border. However, Edmonson (2003) noted that Laredo was infamous for its congestion and now is not

Table 2.10 Hours of service comparison

US HoS Rules 2005[1]	Canadian HoS Rules 2005[2]
May drive a maximum of 11 hours after ten consecutive hours off duty.	No driver shall drive more than 13 hours in a 24-hour period.
May not drive beyond the 14th hour after coming on duty, following 10 consecutive hours off duty.	No driver shall have more than 14 hours on-duty time in a 24-hour period.
May not drive after 60/70 hours on duty in 7/8 consecutive days. A driver may restart a 7/8 consecutive day period after taking 34 or more consecutive hours off duty.	A driver must have at least eight consecutive off-duty hours before driving again. Minimum off-duty time is ten hours in a 24-hour period. Other than the mandatory eight consecutive hours, off-duty time may be distributed in blocks of no less than 30 minutes each.
CMV drivers using the sleeper berth provision must take at least eight consecutive hours in the sleeper berth, plus two consecutive hours either in the sleeper berth, off duty, or any combination of the two.	Section 18 addresses single drivers in vehicles with a sleeper berth and how they may meet the requirements above. Section 19 does so for teams of drivers.
Passenger-carrying carriers/drivers are not subject to the new hours-of-service rules. These operations must continue to comply with the hours-of-service limitations specified in 49 CFR 395.5.	There are special provisions for drivers taking ferries where the crossing takes more than five hours (section 17).

Notes:
1. Applicable to property-carrying Commercial Motor Vehicle drivers; these rules are modified for short-haul drivers, operating within a 150 air-mile radius of their normal work reporting location.
2. The Canadian rules came into effect 1 January 2007.

Source: The complete US rules may be found at FMCSA (2005); the complete Canadian rules are available in Transport Canada (2005f).

as much of a problem; trucks no longer line up for miles. However, he concluded that the Laredo crossing is now so rigid in the way that it functions that shippers are not likely to see lower costs or more efficient border management. The problems of inspections on the Southern Border, the questions raised about the adequacy of the number of inspectors, and the way that the Mexican drayage system works are reported extensively in Rothberg (2003), Villa (2006) and Mead (2002). While Mead was much more positive that the Southern Border could handle the onslaught of inspection demands, Rothberg (2003, pp. 125, 131) was less positive:

> It is questionable whether there is sufficient number of inspectors to ensure an adequate level of compliance with the safety regulations at all of the border crossings. The inspection force is spread thinly. . . . FMCSA inspectors did not have dedicated telephone lines to access safety-related databases, such as those for validating a commercial driver's license, at some 20 crossings.

Most valuable in understanding the issues on the Southern Border is Villa's (2006) inventory of research completed to date. He concluded that while there has been substantial improvement in the management of the traffic flows on the Southern Border, there remain numerous problems and levels of bureaucracy to be addressed. In sum, issues remain with the commercial border crossing process itself, the information and data collection, interagency coordination, and the nature of bilateral cooperation. What is needed on both borders is an evaluation of truck transportation activities and adequate information for border planning purposes; this is already under way and was due to be completed for Texas ports of entry by the Texas Transportation Institute in late 2007.

In any event, it is clear that any growth in trade needs to be supported by infrastructure investment, and that issue will be explored further in Chapters 4, 6 and 7.

Taxation, Governance and Other Issues

Chow and McRae (1990) concluded, following the signing of *CUSTA*, that the tax advantages cited by others as accruing to the US had been overstated, but tax discrepancies nonetheless remained. Capital cost allowances, payroll taxes, municipal property taxes and corporate income taxes vary significantly between the jurisdictions, some of which favour American-based transportation companies and some of which provide an advantage to Canadian operators. The Canada Transportation Act Review Panel (PWGSC, 2001, p. 26) called for the Canadian government to bring Canadian rail taxation in line with other industries, and with that of the US, if the Canadian industry is to be able to compete, 'even if they [the policies] deviate from what would have been optimal in a perfectly competitive world'. KPMG (2001) found that the Canadian rail industry faced a substantially higher tax burden as a percentage of revenues (13.38 per cent) than US rail carriers (6.43 per cent), Canadian TL operators (10.38 per cent), airlines (5.07 per cent), marine carriers (5.43 per cent), manufacturers (7.07 per cent), and even Canadian financial services companies (10.74 per cent).[16] KPMG's findings varied little from those found by LaCroix et al. (1993), in an earlier study for the Transportation Association of Canada.

Cairns (2002) noted that there are specific concerns for the rail industry; in particular he noted taxation, economic regulation, the Canada–US exchange rate and productivity, ratification of the Kyoto Protocol, and uncertainty concerning enhanced running rights. The last of these, running rights, also appeared on Finn's (2004) list of NAFTA challenges. Of particular note, railways are subject to uneven application of municipal property taxes and a higher level of fuel taxes levied by provinces. In addition, they face the same income tax rates as other Canadian industries, and capital cost allowances for amortizing investments are more punitive in Canada; rail cars and equipment, for example, are depreciated more slowly in Canada than in the US. It remains to be seen in Chapter 4 if the industry believes that taxation is a critical issue for future regulatory convergence discussions.

Corporate governance in the US has been an issue for debate since the Enron scandal of 2001, and accounting irregularities surfaced at HealthSouth and Tyco. The resulting Sarbanes–Oxley regulations in the US are very restrictive and apply to Canadian companies operating transport subsidiaries in the US. In Canada, the corporate governance debate has been active since the Dey Report, *Where Were the Directors?*, was issued by the Toronto Stock Exchange (1994). Corporate governance is an issue that directly affects the global competitiveness of companies, and has been discussed at the OECD (OECD, 1999). It does not appear to have been examined in the context of North American transportation companies and the business climate they face.[17] It too remains to be seen (in Chapter 4) if the surface transport industry believes that corporate governance regulation is a critical issue for future regulatory convergence discussions.

After the signing of the *CUSTA*, Chow and McRae (1990) concluded that none of the non-tariff barriers they identified could be classified as overt violations of the principles of transparency (understandable), national treatment (equality of application), or the right of establishment (allowing participation). What they found was that non-tariff barriers violated the principle of 'commercial presence' (for example, ability of Canadian-domiciled carriers to sell their services in the US market). They concluded that the disadvantages faced by Canadian carriers were dependent on the type of carrier and the geographic area in which they chose to compete; those most severely affected were truckload carriers in the long-haul markets, principally as a result of immigration and equipment restrictions. *NAFTA* did not really address the second of these, and the first is still problematic.

Since the terrorist attacks of September 2001, immigration rules have become even more restrictive. Canada and the US have tightened passport security. Under the Western Hemisphere Travel Initiative, Canadians are now required to have a passport for travel to the US when only a birth certificate was previously required. (The land component of this legislation has been delayed in implementation.) Both countries have also tightened visa screening and admissibility standards, while retaining separate immigration policies.

One key outstanding issue for trucking companies (Brooks and Kymlicka, 2007) is insurance. The carriers operating in transborder markets are faced with a Band-Aid solution when it comes to the availability of insurance for transborder services. In 2001, the NAFTA Insurance Working Group (a subsidiary of the Financial Services Committee) was formed to find trilateral solutions. In the interim, an American trucker can buy private intermediary insurance for his truck from a Canadian company (for example, a Canadian company buys the American policy for the duration of the trip) and American insurers have similar layered plans available to Canadian truckers operating in the US. Condon and Sinha (2001) noted that there is no solution for Mexican truckers who, by Mexican law, are unable to reinsure the risk outside Mexico.

How important are these impediments? The survey of surface transport suppliers specifically addresses this question in Chapter 4.

CONCLUSIONS

Hufbauer and Schott (1993) concluded that the negotiators got far more than they expected, arguing that a North American network of transport services would evolve and that the agreement afforded the opportunity to deal with issues like vehicle weights and dimensions and cabotage restrictions in later talks. They saw infrastructure investment in roads and bridges as the challenge (but this assessment seemed focused on the Southern Border). In hindsight, it is very clear that their initial assessment of *NAFTA* was overly optimistic.

The Clinton Administration's lack of political will to deal with the Teamsters over the Mexican trucking dispute meant that the network of trucking services on the continent was never optimized to achieve international competitiveness for North American businesses. The necessary consolidation and restructuring of the trucking industry in particular, through phased foreign investment opportunities, was not realized. The result is a patchwork of regulations and a less efficient industry that today is faced with future driver shortages and no plan to deal with it. Although Brooks (1994) concluded that the Canadian trucking industry would gain greater freedom to carry cargo from Canada to the US and onward to Mexico, the retention of the exclusive right to haul domestic cargo by each of the countries ensured that market inefficiencies would remain. It was expected that US truckers would retain dominance of this market, particularly given the small volumes in Canada–Mexico trades. Canadian firms had no access to US domestic carriage unless they bought a US trucking firm and used US drivers and equipment. Within Canada and the US, M&As were often deployed by trucking firms to acquire licenses to operate in jurisdictions where the target did not previously have geographic activities (Brooks and Ritchie, 2005). However, market access was only one of the motives found to be at play, and the M&A option was unavailable for Mexico access.

For many American companies, the opportunities were a product of Mexican transport liberalization, and before that Canadian deregulation. The *NAFTA* just furthered a process of liberalization that had already begun, and provided new opportunities for US carriers with the financial and managerial capabilities to exploit them. The continuation of immigration restrictions, tariffs on operating equipment and the US moratoria on operating authorities probably perpetuated market inefficiencies that could have been corrected.

At the beginning of the NAFTA experience, Hufbauer and Schott (1993, p. 68) concluded that the most difficult issue within North America's transportation system would be the differing size and weight standards: 'Until these fundamental differences are resolved, a truly integrated continental transportation system will not be achieved.' Almost 15 years later, this issue has not been addressed and it is clear that, at this point in the book, the evidence is not all in to draw the same conclusion. Chapter 4 will explore the importance of this issue from a carrier perspective.

APPENDIX 2.1 THE TRANSPORTATION REGULATORY TIMELINE

Date	Key event or activity
1978	Deregulation in the US market takes hold with the *Airline Deregulation Act of 1978*.
1980	US Deregulation of other modes moves forward with the *Motor Carrier Act of 1980* (trucking) and the *Staggers Rail Act of 1980* (rail). The Motor Carrier Act eliminates regulatory barriers to entry to the US trucking market for foreign companies. In other words, it does not distinguish between Mexican, Canadian or US companies. Canada allows reciprocal access but Mexico does not.
1981	The Mexicans close their trucking market.
1982	The US passes the *Bus Regulatory Reform Act of 1982*, which contains a provision imposing a two-year moratorium on the granting of new trucking operating authorities. The US stops granting operating authorities for Mexican motor carriers to operate in the US. Five Mexican-based motor carriers are grandfathered permanent authority to operate in the entire US so long as they meet US regulations. The moratorium is lifted immediately for Canadian trucking companies, because the Canadian market remains open for US trucking companies and the US agrees that it is in the interests of both countries to retain the reciprocal agreement under the Brock–Gotlieb Understanding (NAFTA Secretariat, 2001, Para 39). The moratorium is repeatedly extended so as to be uninterrupted.
1984	De facto deregulation occurs in Canada's airline industry through changes to air regulations. The changes will be implemented via legislation in 1987.
1987	Canada passes the *National Transportation Act, 1987*, deregulating Canadian transport operations.
1987	The *Canada–US Trade Agreement* is signed.
1992	The *North American Free Trade Agreement* is signed with effect 1 January, 1994.
1 March, 1994	Canada and Mexico sign three Memoranda of Understanding (Condon and Sinha, 2001) that recognize each other's commercial driver's licences, Canadian training of Mexican drivers, and allows Canadian carriers to cross into Mexico to border facilities, instead of dropping their cargo on the US side for Mexican carriers to haul it across the border. This means that Canadian carriers may pick up backhaul cargo bound for US destinations without it being classified as cabotage cargo.

1995	US carriers gain the right to cross into Mexico instead of dropping their cargo on the US side for Mexican carriers to haul it across the border (Drennen, 2004, p. 265).
1995	The *Canada/United States of America Accord on Our Shared Border* is signed. The objectives of the Accord are to promote international trade, streamline processes for commercial goods and legitimate travellers, enhance protection against drug smuggling and illegal entry, and reduce the costs for both governments. (It is updated in 2000 and provides the foundation for interdepartmental cooperation between the two governments.)
17 December, 1995	This is the date Mexican trucking companies are supposed to gain access to US trucking markets in border states (California, Arizona, New Mexico and Texas). The moratorium continues entrenched in the *Interstate Commerce Commission Termination Act of 1995.*
18 December, 1995	The Clinton Administration denies access to Mexican truckers.
1996	Canada passes the *Canada Transportation Act 1996*, further reforming Canada's rail services in an effort to improve operating performance. The bill also provides further regulatory adjustment for other modes.
1 January, 1998	The first day in the history of Canada–US relations that not a single tariff is levied on two-way trade in Canadian and American goods (Hart, 2000, p. 132). Tariffs are still collected on goods that do not meet *NAFTA* Rules of Origin.
1998	Mexico brings its case against the US to the NAFTA arbitration process under Chapter 20 of the Agreement. A key feature of the case is that the US has breached its *NAFTA* obligations for both access to the market and investment in the US industry, although it affords Canadian carriers national treatment.
October 1999	*Canada–US Partnership* is launched to promote bilateral dialogue on border issues. (This is discussed further in Chapter 6.)
1 January, 2000	Mexican trucking is supposed to gain access to international point-to-point cargoes in all US states. As the earlier milestone (17 December, 1995) has not been implemented, this milestone is moot without the needed operating authority.
2000	Bush campaigns on Mexican access and wins the US Presidency. Vicente Fox is elected President of Mexico.
6 February, 2001	In early 2001, the NAFTA arbitration panel rules in favour of Mexico, concluding that the US is in violation of the *NAFTA*'s national treatment provisions. It is found that

Date	Key event or activity
	motor carriers operating in any NAFTA country are subject to all applicable domestic safety standards (NAFTA Secretariat, 2001).
11 September, 2001	Terrorist attacks in New York and Washington redirect the nature of the NAFTA relationship to focus on security rather than trade promotion and facilitation.
October 2001	Mexico announces it is preparing to exchange electronic data on driver and carrier safety records, as is Canada.
12 December, 2001	Canada and the US sign the *30-Point Smart Border Declaration and Action Plan* (Department of Foreign Affairs and International Trade, 2004). By 2007, the plan seems to have grown to 32 points on the Canadian Department of Foreign Affairs website.
May 2002	The US Congress establishes 22 new safety conditions applicable to motor carriers. (These are also the rules that will apply to Mexican trucks under the 6 February, 2001 arbitration panel ruling.)
27 November, 2002	President Bush lifts the ban on wider operation of Mexican trucks. There are 130 applications for operating authority by Mexican trucking companies by 29 November.
January 2003	The 9th Circuit Court of Appeals issues a ruling that again delays the opening of the southern US border to Mexico carriers. The case, based on environmental concerns, is brought by a coalition of labour and other special interest groups. The court indicates that the US Department of Transportation needs to conduct an environmental impact statement according to the *1970 National Environmental Policy Act* (NEPA) and the *1990 Clean Air Act standards*.
1 January, 2004	The milestone date for limits on cross-border investments in international carriers to be removed, but given earlier implementation failures, the day passes without change.
4 June, 2004	The US Supreme Court rules an Environmental Impact Assessment is not required to lift the ban on Mexican trucking.
November 2004	President Bush is re-elected.
8 December, 2004	Bush signs a bill preventing Mexican trucks from entering the US without a manufacturer's label certifying compliance with US vehicle safety standards.
23 March, 2005	The three leaders 'agree' on the *Security and Prosperity Partnership* (SPP) in Waco, TX. It is heralded as a new NAFTA relationship and a report on it is published in June (SPP, 2005). It is not an agreement or a treaty but a dialogue.

15 June, 2006	The North American Competitiveness Council (NACC), composed of 10 business leaders from each of the three countries, is launched to enable the business community to provide input into the SPP dialogue. The NACC is to meet with the leaders annually.
July 2006	Felipe Calderón is declared the winner in Mexico's presidential election, assuming office 1 December, 2006.
August 2006	A second report on progress under the SPP process is published. (This is discussed in Chapter 7.)
2007	In February, the US Department of Transportation and the US Federal Motor Carrier Safety Administration announce a year-long demonstration project for Mexican trucking (Peters and Hill, 2007). Details of the program requirements are published for comment in the *Federal Register* on 30 April.

Author's postscript: At the time the writing of this book was completed, Mexican trucks still did not have the access they were promised by *NAFTA* to have in 1995.

NOTES

1. In transportation, a firm practises triangulation when, because of cabotage rules or market demand characteristics, a carrier develops a triangular route network. For example, in North America, a common network pattern for Atlantic Canadian trucking firms is to carry Atlantic Canadian-originating goods to the Mid-Atlantic US states, pick up goods there destined for Quebec or Ontario, and then pick up a third load there destined for the starting destination. Such a network optimizes asset utilization in an environment where cabotage prevents the carrier from carrying domestic cargo between two US points.
2. In the end, they deemed the significant impacts would be equipment restrictions (both tractor and trailer) and immigration (for long-haul TL operators), US heavy vehicle duties in the short-haul TL market, and state economic regulations for short-haul LTL operations. The impact of the remainder would not be significant. See Table 5 of Chow and McRae (1990, p. 17) for details on all non-tariff barriers.
3. In Canada, for example, freight accounted for 89 per cent of all rail operating revenue in 2000 (Statistics Canada, 2002, Table 1).
4. There is always discussion in the rail sector about the ability of railroads to earn their cost of capital, given a long history in the 1990s of rail bankruptcy. Today, operating ratios in the rail industry indicate that some railroads are better able than others to offer sustainable transport services that are attractive to capital markets.
5. Class 1 railroads are the largest railroads. To be a Class 1 railroad in 2005, the railroad had to have revenue in excess of US $319.3 million. The Class 1 railroads as of 2005 are detailed in Table 2.6.
6. The data do not disaggregate international (non-Canadian) originating cargo from Canadian-originating rail cargo.
7. Prentice and Ojah (2002) noted that the Mexican rail network traditionally lost customers to truck because of service unreliability, a situation not easily repaired.
8. Cabotage is defined as the movement of goods or passengers between two origin–destination pairs within the same nation. Cabotage regulation often requires that domestic carriage use a nationally owned transport supplier. There is one small exception – incidental haulage. A US driver can, for example, drop off at Location 1, pick up a prearranged empty trailer near Location 2, conduct travel to Location 3 to drop off the empty trailer and pick up a load bound for the US. This incidental haulage may not be used to provide ongoing domestic service or to solicit return loads once inside Canada. The reverse situation applies to Canadian drivers in the US.
9. This had to be accomplished in a creative way as many tariff and non-tariff barriers remained.
10. There was some scepticism at the time (Brooks, 1994) that the LTSS would be able to resolve all as, according to Article 1210(2), NAFTA countries were not required to recognize licensing and certification, only in accordance with national treatment (Article 1203) and so this particular barrier to entry could continue to play a role and did.
11. As will be seen, these were negotiated but not implemented.
12. As will be seen in Chapter 4, how trucking companies chose to grow within the confines of these restrictions became a key strategic decision in the 1990s.
13. In fact, safety was of such concern that the US Department of Transportation established the Federal Motor Carrier Safety Administration in 2000 to address highway safety issues.
14. This may be moot as Delgado et al. (2003), in studying the Mexican trucking industry, noted that Mexican companies prefer the prospect of making alliances rather than entering the US market; they are more interested in protecting the *maquiladora* market from incursion by US trucking companies.
15. As of 2002, only two states, Arizona and California, had the ability to enforce operating authority compliance. Operating without operating authority is apparently not a safety violation elsewhere!
16. KPMG included income taxes, capital taxes, commodity taxes, payroll taxes and property taxes in their calculation of tax burden.
17. Even PWGSC (2001) was only interested in the governance of devolved infrastructure entities, and not concerned about Canadian and US differences in corporate governance rules.

3. Key issues for cargo interests

INTRODUCTION

In the last chapter, it was quite clear that both *NAFTA* and the *Canada–US Trade Agreement* brought about a changed regulatory environment for transport companies, as well as for the primary target of the trade agreements: manufacturing concerns. Before this chapter begins to discuss the impact of regulatory change and security on cargo interests, it begins with a brief comment on how manufacturing firms responded from a broader perspective to *NAFTA*, relying on two studies.

Based on a survey of US firms, Blank and Haar (1998) concluded that American firms have changed strategies since the implementation of *NAFTA*. They identified that the primary motivation driving corporate change by US firms was the opportunities that *NAFTA* presented to the companies; they also concluded that, for Mexican companies, the growth in the Mexican economy was primary, with the prospects *NAFTA* brought to firms running second. Globalization was also very important to both groups, while the *Canada–US Trade Agreement* was near the bottom of the list of motivating factors for change.

According to Blank and Haar (1998), six outcomes appear to have occurred in the 1988–97 period. First, there was a concerted effort by companies to integrate NAFTA markets into a continental corporate space. Second, companies undertook a rationalization of their work processes, focusing on economies of scale and shedding excess capacity. Third, there was a trend within North America to cross-border mergers and acquisitions, coupled with greater outsourcing of non-core activities; this happened in all sectors, not just transportation. Fourth, many companies standardized their product offerings. Fifth, companies developed new organizational structures and networks. Finally, there was a significant increase in intra-firm trade. In other words, North American companies integrated and moved further into an era of making things together.

Not unexpectedly, Blank and Haar (1998) found, for example, that the rationalization of work processes in Canada focused on the scale of production, new production opportunities and marketing changes. Canadian and Mexican subsidiaries of US corporations were hit with reductions in the scale of their production, though it is not clear whether the recession of

1991–93 or *NAFTA* was the cause. At the same time, a number of companies began to institute world product mandates and go so far as to develop an intra-firm bidding process for these mandates (Blank and Haar, 1998, pp. 56–61). Also, as rationalization of production and product mandates were instituted, the products themselves had to become more standardized. Technological advancements, however, allowed mass customization to take hold and automation allowed factories to produce a more flexible range of goods without losing much in the way of scale economics. The mixture of standardization and flexibility added a complexity to the question of what really happened in each sector. Blank and Haar also concluded that new organizational forms have accompanied closer integration of operations, but that many TNCs left local public affairs relationships, labour relations, training and other 'soft' functions in the hands of local subsidiaries (Blank and Haar, 1998).

According to McNiven (1999), the *Canada–US Trade Agreement* and *NAFTA* brought four types of potential corporate strategic responses as part of continental economic integration:

1. Larger multinationals could rationalize production on a transnational basis, either by closing inefficient plants on either side of the border or refocusing Canadian production, where manufacturing of diverse products solely for the Canadian market had meant a number of short (and inefficient) product runs.
2. Small companies that had grown up in a protectionist business climate would be threatened with extinction if they could not quickly acquire the scale economies of American competitors.
3. Product and service areas not previously available to Canadian firms were now opened, and firms could reposition their production and service capacities to meet the demands of a larger market.
4. American as well as other foreign corporations would see Canada as an increasingly attractive site for North American facilities expansion because of the removal of tariff and some non-tariff barriers between it and the larger American market.

These suggestions raise the question about how trade changed over the *NAFTA* period. Figures 3.1–3.5 examine Canada–US trade flows from 1998, the first year for which volume data is available (but the fifth full year of *NAFTA* and the tenth for *CUSTA*), to 2004 and how they changed. The figures were created using US Department of Transportation Bureau of Transportation Statistics databases and represent the weight transported by all surface modes, so that the impact of the trading relationship on the North American surface transportation network can be more readily understood.[1]

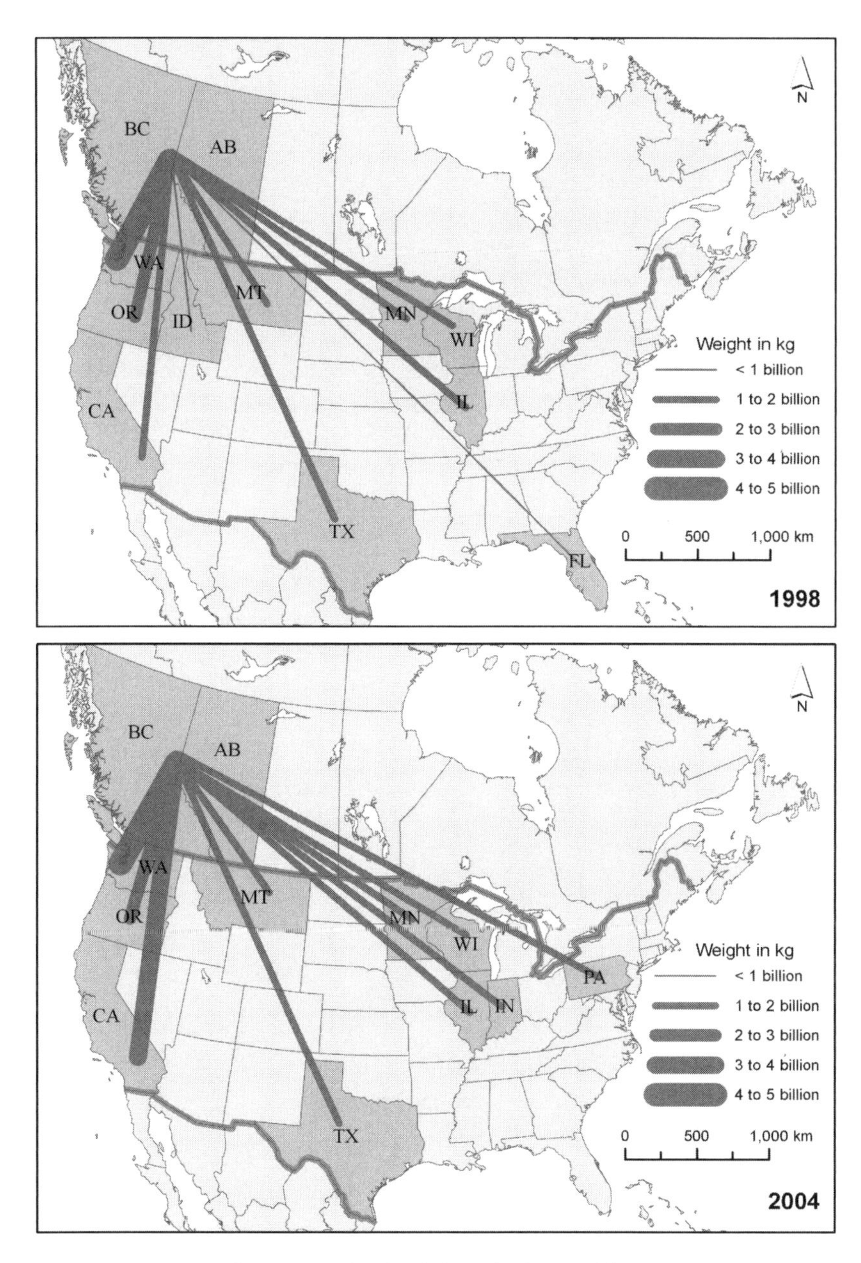

Source: US Bureau of Transportation Statistics and ESRI World Data

Figure 3.1 Canada–US trade from British Columbia and Alberta, 1998 and 2004 (in tonnes)

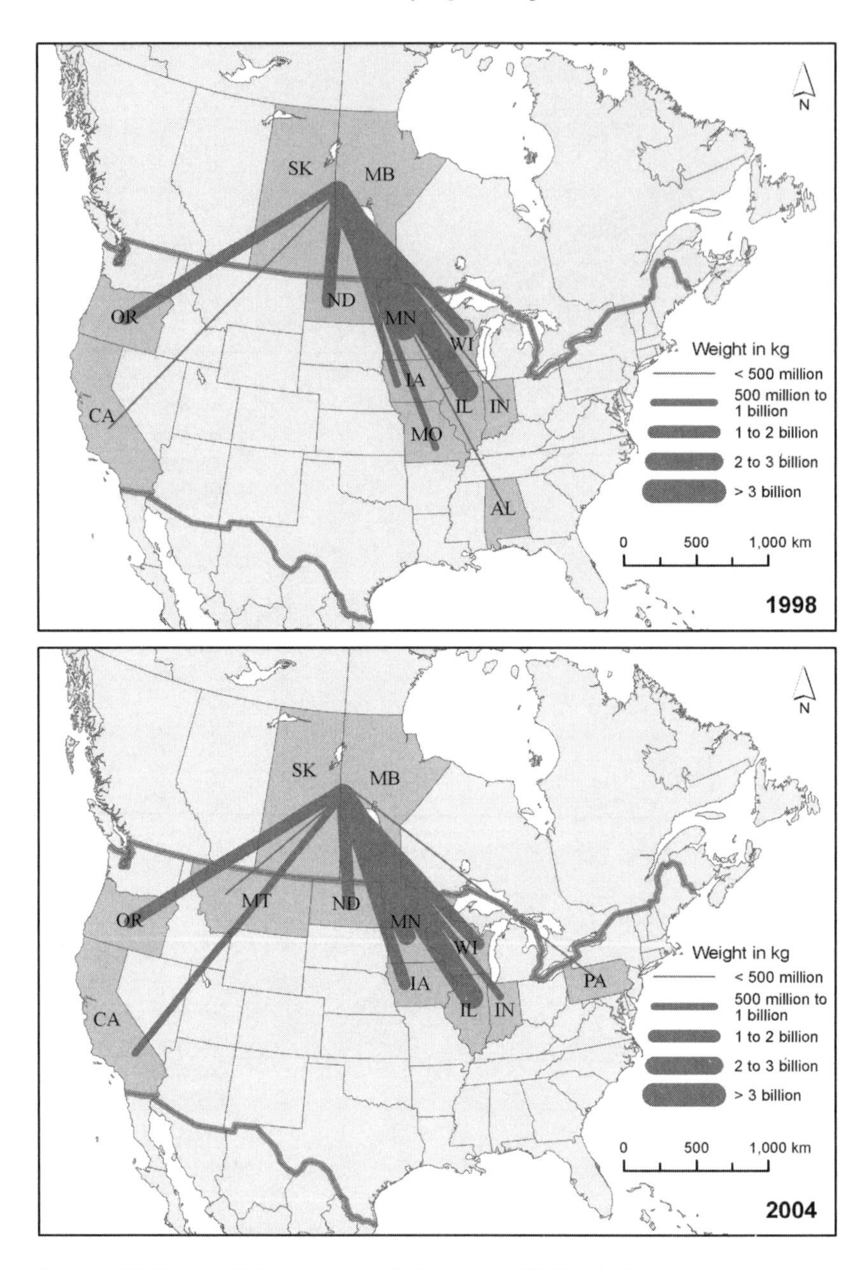

Source: US Bureau of Transportation Statistics and ESRI World Data

Figure 3.2 Canada–US trade from Saskatchewan and Manitoba, 1998 and 2004 (in tonnes)

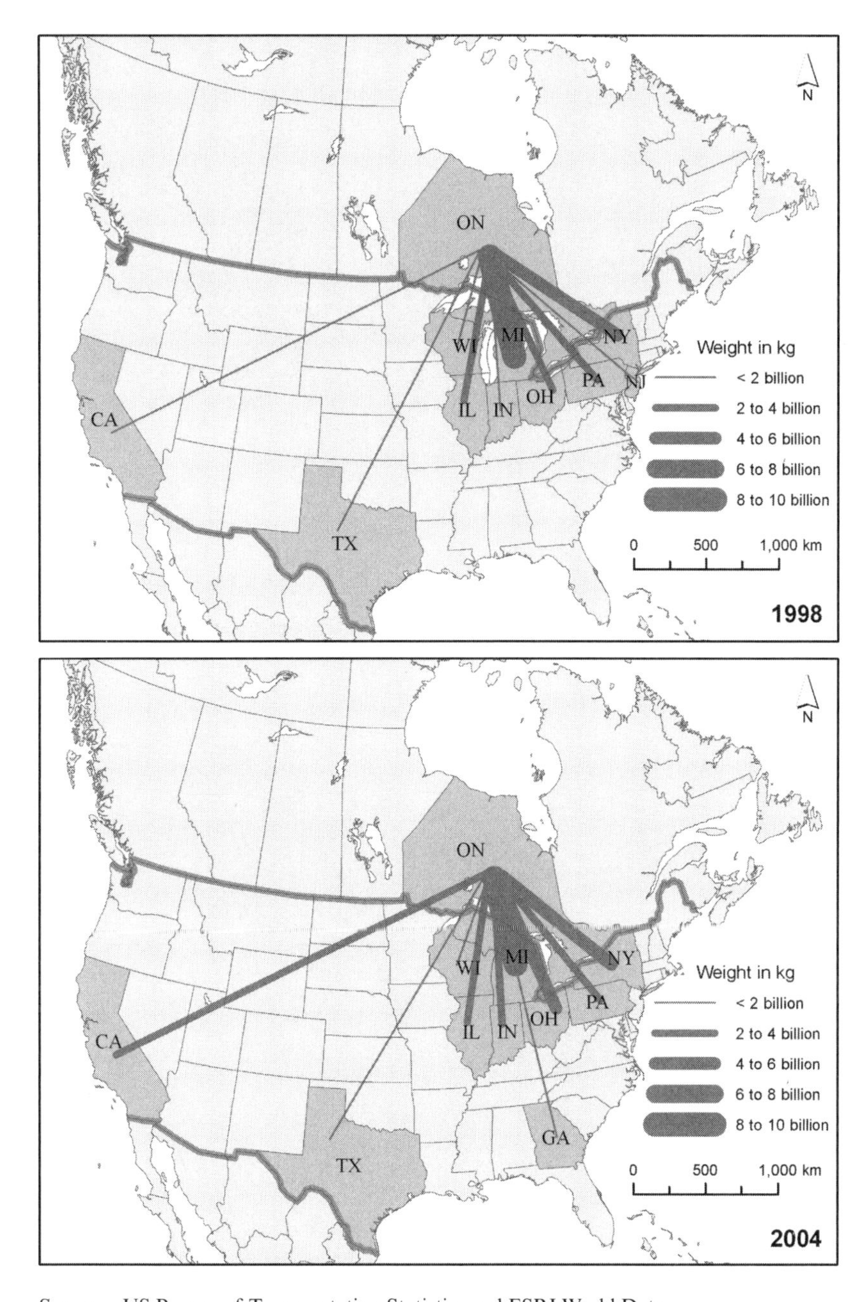

Source: US Bureau of Transportation Statistics and ESRI World Data

Figure 3.3 Canada–US trade from Ontario, 1998 and 2004 (in tonnes)

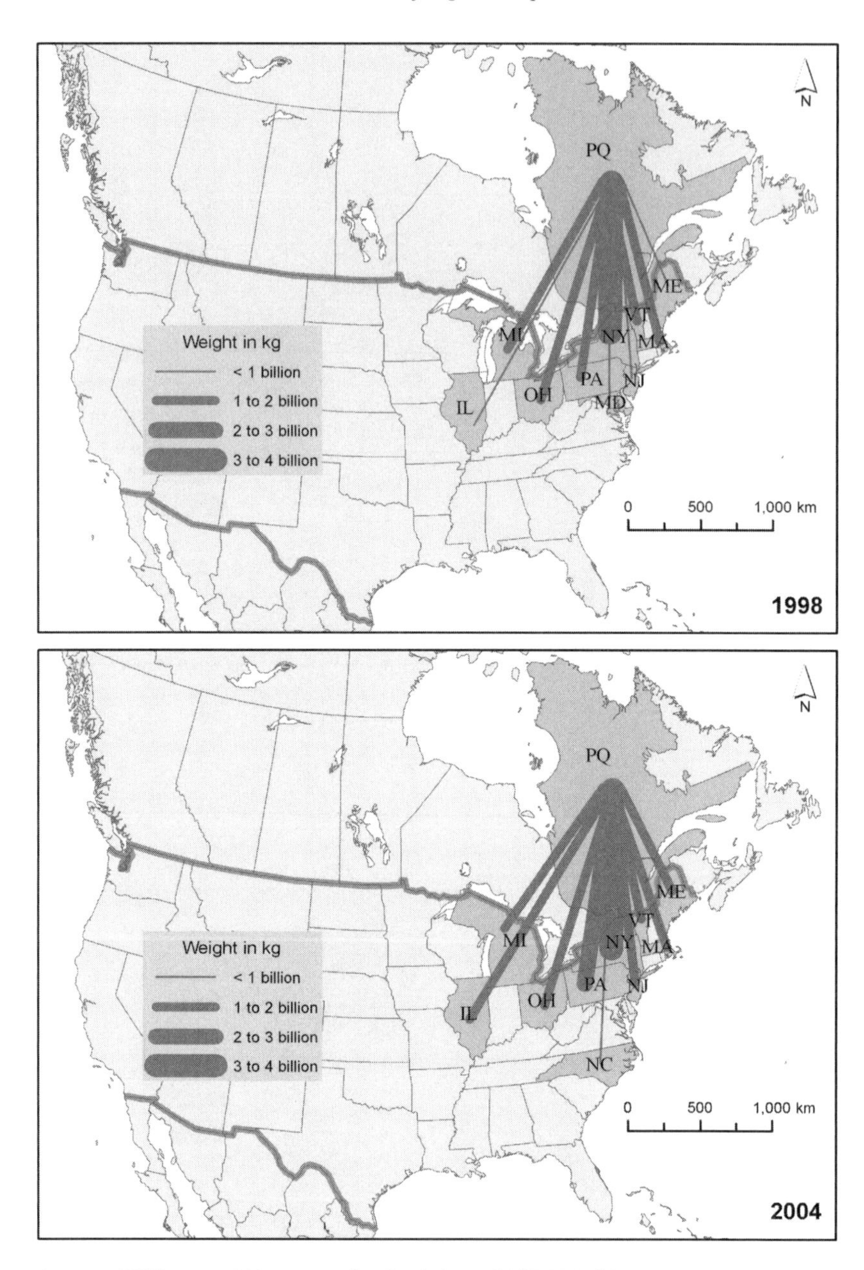

Source: US Bureau of Transportation Statistics and ESRI World Data

Figure 3.4 Canada–US trade from Province of Quebec, 1998 and 2004 (in tonnes)

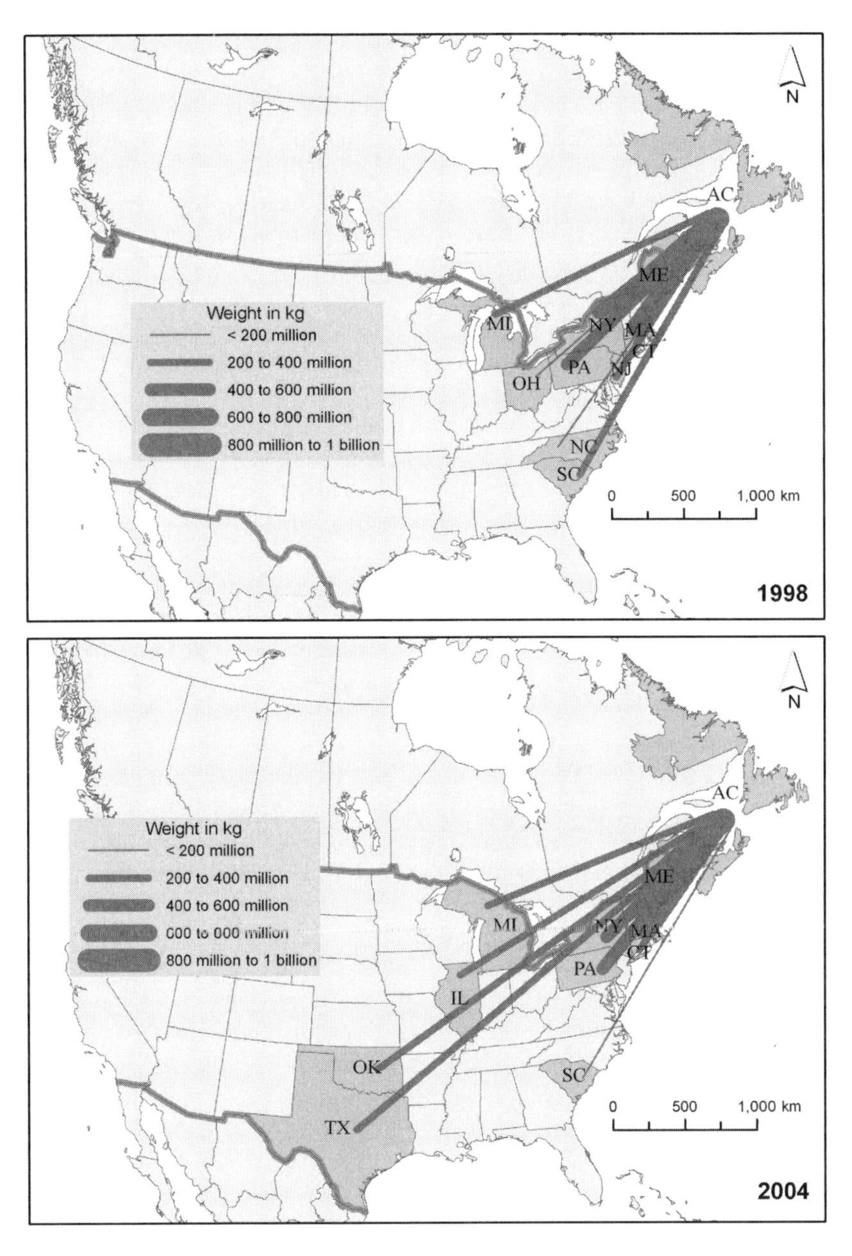

Source: US Bureau of Transportation Statistics and ESRI World Data

Figure 3.5 Canada–US trade from Atlantic Canada, 1998 and 2004 (in tonnes)

In 1998, the benefits accruing from the *CUSTA* and the earlier *Auto Pact* (for Figure 3.3) were well established and obvious. While Figures 3.1 to 3.5 are presented from west to east across the continent, it is quite clear that the largest trading relationship between the two countries (in both weight as illustrated and value) is between Ontario and the US Mid-West. The trade flows northbound are not illustrated as these data are not collected by either country in weight terms; for transport planners, it is difficult to use the data to evaluate impact on infrastructure needs.

In the period illustrated, Ontario's trading relationship with the US (Figure 3.3) changed only a little. The trade with its neighbours New York and Michigan were high volume and strong, but Ontario's dependence mainly on two states diversified somewhat over the period, as its trading relationship with the very populous state of California strengthened and Georgia moved into Ontario's top 10 markets.

The next largest trading relationship on the Northern Border was in the Pacific Northwest, with British Columbia and Alberta's trade with Cascadia (discussed in more detail in Chapter 6) strengthening as Florida dropped out of the top 10 states and Idaho joined (Figure 3.1). Third in size is the relationship between La Belle Province de Quebec and the US Northeast. Quebec companies shipped closer to home in 1998 and this pattern altered only slightly over the period studied. The volumes to Maine and Illinois grew but Quebec businesses did not expand their markets substantially through geographic diversification.

Smaller trading relationships existed for the last two groupings – the Prairie Provinces of Saskatchewan and Manitoba (Figure 3.2), and the four Atlantic Provinces of Nova Scotia, New Brunswick, Prince Edward Island, and Newfoundland and Labrador (Figure 3.5). For the Prairies, proximity of market presented a similar pattern between the years with strong north–south linkages and, like its West Coast neighbours, a growing relationship with California over the period. Atlantic Canada, on the other hand, saw a growing expansion of north–south trade with Oklahoma and Texas expanding relationships beyond the traditional New England markets and the post-*CUSTA* efforts to develop markets in the Mid-Atlantic states (for example, North and South Carolina). This is particularly interesting because the transport infrastructure is not supportive of these trade developments; surface transport links down the eastern seaboard are poor through northern New England (Maine and New Hampshire) and the I-95 interstate highway is congested through New York to Virginia. (This region is discussed in more detail in Chapter 6.)

This chapter focuses on the issues within North American transportation from the perspective of the key cargo interests, those of manufacturers and retailers. It examines very briefly what *NAFTA* meant for these traders. A number of quotes are provided by those interviewed, and as, in some cases, it is important to understand the perspective of the speaker, the quotes are attributed to a particular industry sector. 'Business equipment manufacturer' includes all types of products sold to businesses, 'automotive manufacturer' includes those in the parts industry as well as production and assembly, and so on. The classification should be taken in its broadest meaning.

The key focus of the chapter is whether *NAFTA* was seen as a market-growing opportunity, in the belief that understanding the strategic responses of buyers of transport services contributes to answering questions about what the next steps in the trade and transportation relationship need to be. The responses of retailers were initially expected to differ from those of manufacturers but only two retailers participated, many preferring to let the Retail Industry Leaders Association (RILA) speak on their behalf. RILA's perspective was that its members did not see *NAFTA* as a central concern, and that their focus was one of managing global supply chains in a security-dominated business climate. As will be seen, this means that the chapter has a strong security flavour to its content.

The remainder of the chapter discusses the methodology used to elicit a company's strategic responses to *NAFTA*, the transportation regulation changes it invoked, and then proceeds to assess the impact on the company of security requirements imposed in the aftermath of the events of 11 September, 2001.

THE RESEARCH METHODOLOGY

In order to understand the aspirations of the firms in the market and the strategic choices they make to respond to the regulatory environment determined by government, you need to first understand the environment and the opportunities and threats it presents as seen by the company, and identify the responses made by the companies. Second, you need to identify what they would want to see changed in future to make the regulatory issues less intrusive and more encouraging to market expansion or other growth strategies. Finally, the overlay of security concerns influences their perception of a changed environment and so their suggestions of what its impact is provides a useful starting point for discussing future issues of a continental or national or regional approach.

The perspective was a supply chain one. It was considered to be more important to connect with a variety of actors in the North American supply chain than to focus solely on the views on a part of the chain. This meant that each modal sector and cargo interest was approached with a tailored instrument specifically designed for them. The longest was the instrument for the trucking industry as they had seen the greatest change in their regulatory environment over the past 20 years. The shortest was the instrument for the maritime transport mode (as they were not part of either *CUSTA* or *NAFTA*).

The instrument itself incorporated both qualitative and quantitative questions, mostly the former. It was designed for use by personal interview, telephone interview, and mail or email solicitation. The data collection took place between January 2005 and May 2005 while the author was based at George Mason University in Fairfax, VA.

Research efforts were restricted so that firms could only respond to one of the questionnaires. This was done as many companies may operate both trucking and third party logistics services. Occasionally, companies opted to put together a team for a conference call so that diverse internal views could be rationalized through the interview.

Table 3.1 shows the response rate for this study; the next two chapters will discuss the responses of those offering transport services, while this one focuses on the demand side of the supply chain. By working through the industry associations as well as using 'Top 100' or 'Top 50' lists of companies, the approach can be considered a key informant approach; firms and individuals who are considered industry opinion leaders on these issues had the opportunity to contribute.

Many of the firms that responded did so only after the study had been vetted by their legal staff (due to current litigation or M&A activity in progress) or by public relations staff (for confidentiality reasons). Most of

Table 3.1 Response rate [1]

Type of company	Approached	Respondents	Response rate
Trucking companies	52	17	32.7%
Maritime transport companies	32	9	28.1%
Railroads	3	2	66.7%
Third party logistics firms	20	5	20.0%
Cargo interests (manufacturers and retailers)	36	10	27.8%
Carrier associations	6	6	100.0%
Cargo associations	3	3	100.0%
Total	152	52	34.2%

Note: 1. As this research is focused on looking at the response of those with regulatory risk, the table does not include the myriad of government agencies and departments in both Canada and the US contacted in the course of conducting the research.

the respondents also provided regulatory and security insights beyond those sought by the structured discussion document. This chapter is based on the findings of discussions with 10 companies and three industry associations. The diversity of these senior management respondents as well as their candour led to the conclusion that enough respondents had been contacted to gain a good representation of the insights and perceptions of senior executives, those with the ability to develop and execute strategic plans in response to regulatory change.

WHAT DID NAFTA MEAN FOR CARGO INTERESTS?

What the initial impact of *NAFTA* was on production and assembly location was a difficult question to answer. It was clear that, for many companies, too much time had passed since the agreement was signed and that most companies were much more preoccupied with the impact of China on their operations. There was considerable agreement that China is Mexico's biggest problem. That said, there was considerable agreement that production and assembly locations in the 1990s and the current decade are driven by total cost considerations and that the phase-out of import duties since implementation of the agreement changed cost considerations. To quote one manufacturer:

> Although NAFTA did not change our approach to the location of production or assembly plants, it along with other programs improved the cost environment making it more likely that plants will be located in the USA, Canada or Mexico.

Even more important was the strategic response to the changed transportation and distribution situation with the signing of *NAFTA*. The majority of manufacturers and retailers saw very little change. Some focused on taking costs out of the supply chain but others concluded that there were no *NAFTA*-related changes made to the way they did business. The few adjustments identified were:

> We formed an Expertise Center to focus on opportunities to reduce duty. *NAFTA* has not affected speed at the border, but it did significantly reduce the tariffs we face across the US–Canadian border. (chemical manufacturer)

> The reality is that Mexican truck carriers still may not travel in the USA. The next big change in this area will be if/when the obstacles to these carriers are removed. (automotive manufacturer)

> The *NAFTA* has not resulted in any reorganization of either the inbound materials or outbound (finished product) logistics due to the fact that these functions were already centralized . . . (another automotive manufacturer)

> The changes have not yet impacted our operation or organization, however we do plan to consolidate inventories when the security issues contributing to the transfer delays are resolved. (business equipment manufacturer)

In sum, the sentiment generally expressed was that the promise of the agreement was not delivered as expected and many cargo interests are waiting to see the promised changes to the transportation and distribution system realized. Otherwise, the primary benefits were reduced tariffs; a substantially improved distribution system was not the result of *NAFTA* but of other factors. It, however, encouraged some companies to think larger; it served as a catalyst for growth beyond the region for well-established US manufacturers. With the experience of *NAFTA*, they were ready for the outsourcing and off-shoring focus they would need in a global world economy.

THE SECURITY CONCERNS OF CARGO INTERESTS[2]

Generally speaking, it is fair comment that for manufacturers and retailers, the key focus before 2001 was the integrity of the supply chain in order to deal with issues of theft, both intrusive and trailer theft. Furthermore, maintaining cargo integrity was important, prior to 2001, in order to ensure that border crossings went smoothly and the potential for customs inspection delay was minimized, particularly for just-in-time cargo. No carrier or cargo owner wanted the headaches found from unknown drug trafficking taking place on their watch. For many of the manufacturers and retailers, cargo theft and customs concerns had already driven logistics processes in a direction that the new security requirements after 9/11 extended.

Border processing procedures were already well established as part of trade facilitation efforts in the 1990s. The Pre-arrival Processing System or PAPS enabled participating carriers to advance directly to the US primary inspection point without waiting in line behind those whose paperwork still needed to be completed; bar-coding speeded processing. It remains, however, not interchangeable with the Canadian border processing system, PARS. Prior to 2001, biometric pilot programs were in place to process drivers on the Peace Bridge route as a pilot project that has promise but has not yet been extended to all border crossings.

After 2001, two key US programs underpin the security applicable to NAFTA-originating cargo: (1) the Customs Trade and Partnership Against Terrorism (C-TPAT, called Partners in Protection or PIP in Canada) and (2) the Free and Secure Trade (FAST), and its Mexican counterpart, FAST-STEP (STEP standing for Secure Trade-Expedited Processing). These voluntary programs were imposed unilaterally and many shippers, importers, suppliers and manufacturers feel they have little option but to belong, at significant cost. Productivity gains with just-in-time manufacturing and delivery systems, and through faster, reliable and flexible transportation systems, are threatened by security delays throughout the supply chain.

Modal neutrality is not a feature of security regulations applied to the NAFTA region. In fact, the US did not make exceptions to its requirements if the cargo originated in NAFTA. As seen in Table 3.2, advance notification requirements imposed by the *Trade Act of 2002* are not applied equitably by the US on its imports.[3] There are two issues at stake: (1) the potential for modal choice sub-optimization, and (2) the likelihood of increased border delay for uneducated shippers. Of these, the first will be discussed further.

Given this background, it was not surprising to find that, when asked whether they had switched to outsourcing distribution/logistics or changed terms of sale, nine out of the 10 answered neither, and only one responded that a change in terms of sale occurred (Table 3.3). Some of those who had not changed terms of sale indicated that they had preferred to control the transport decisions prior to 2001 for risk, cost control, or other reasons, and so no change was necessary. To quote two of these:

> The supply chain is our lifeline and we almost never, and if so only reluctantly, yield control to anyone. (business equipment manufacturer)

Table 3.2 US advanced electronic notification requirements

Transport mode	Import rule	Export rule
Air/Courier	4 hours prior to arrival or 'wheels up' from nearby airports	2 hours prior to scheduled departure from US
Rail	4 hours prior to arrival at US port of entry	4 hours prior to attachment of the engine to go international
Vessel	24 hours prior to loading at foreign port	4 hours prior to departure of the vessel
Truck	For FAST carriers: 30 minutes prior to arrival at US border For non-FAST carriers: 1 hour prior to arrival at US border	1 hour prior to arrival at the border

Note: FAST carriers are those belonging to the Free and Secure Trade program.

Table 3.3 Strategic responses to changed security environment

Strategic response	n=	Frequency
Require C-TPAT of transport suppliers	10	7
Added requirements to transport contracts	10	6
Outsourced transportation and distribution	10	0
New terms of trade	10	1
Neither outsourced nor new terms of sale	10	9
Dropped markets	9	1

Source: Brooks and Button (2007), Table 1, p. 229.

> It has potential Customs compliance issues. Further, it limits your ability to leverage existing relationships for competitive rates that likely will be lower that those obtained by individual suppliers. Lastly, if you are not the importer, the ability to intervene to expedite hot shipments or work directly with Customs or other government agencies to solve an issue is greatly limited. (automotive manufacturer)

The one large retailer that changed its terms of sale did so 'to ensure that origin trucking is controlled by our company or a trusted 3PL (third party logistics supplier), as an increased security measure'. One large chemical company volunteered that they did re-examine their supply chain:

> Not all chemicals have the same risk profile. Our transportation safety and security measures are risk-based and, therefore, vary from one product or hazard category to another. Further, we enhanced our customer screening, qualification and selection processes to better ensure our products are used safely for their intended purpose.

Only one of the nine companies responding to the question about security responses indicated that the company had dropped a market because of security concerns.

Of particular interest is the issue of strategic changes in transport decisions as a result of September 2001 and the consequent new security requirements. Seven out of the 10 respondents indicated that they require their transport companies to be C-TPAT participants. One of the other three indicated that they encouraged it, a second felt they were too small a manufacturer to demand it, and the third believed it was more important to measure performance but that they 'have a role to educate our [transport] suppliers on security.'

Of those with the requirement for C-TPAT membership, one consumer goods manufacturer elevated this requirement to the highest level of corporate strategy:

> Membership in C-TPAT and validation of it protects our brand; we would not want a WMD [weapon of mass destruction] inside one of our containers. It's smart business. Theft is a critical issue given the value of the cargo. It is the right thing to do from a CSR [corporate social responsibility] perspective. It wasn't a big change for us given the value of the cargo and theft issues. We must make sure that our product remains highly desirable [to consumers]. C-TPAT was not that big of an effort.

On the issue of making changes to their transport contracts or their terms of sale, opinions were divided. Some felt that *all* suppliers must be C-TPAT compliant and that *all* Request for Quotations (RFQs) and purchase orders must include supply chain security clauses. Others felt that this formality was not necessary, that expectations could be conveyed to suppliers and that encouragement and coaching were appropriate roles for their companies. To quote one manufacturer:

> We work very closely with our transportation service providers to ensure the safe and secure transportation of our products. We have enhanced our transportation service provider assessment, qualification and selection process to evaluate security practices. We are very selective. In North America, for example, a dozen premier companies account for over 80 per cent of the volume we ship by bulk tank truck. We tell our transportation service providers what our performance requirements are, but we do not prescribe how they must do it.

As for terms of sale, only one company of the 10 made changes in their transport contracting to alter the allocation of responsibilities between buyer and seller.

Companies were very vocal on the issues of how they altered their transportation and distribution arrangements after September 2001. Many had already reduced the number of transport suppliers or contracted with carriers offering larger geographic scope in the 1990s, in an effort to gain greater control or to minimize supply chain costs. One manufacturer had reduced its transborder trucking suppliers to one. Particularly interesting was the comment by one company that the need to raise international security standards had also resulted in the implementation of the same program for domestic security, but that this was all in progress before 2001.

After September 2001, supplier reduction programs continued for many of the respondents. However, cargo interest concerns also turned to security compliance and transport network capacity constraints. These capacity constraints have some seeking to introduce supplier variety and routing options. One consumer goods manufacturer noted that it has instituted a port diversification plan to reduce the concentration of cargo through one particular port. To quote:

> This plan was initially driven by security (as opposed to congestion). We don't want to be too dependent on one place if there were an incident of terrorism in a port. We also needed to validate that we could manage in-bound flow through other ports.

Only five of the 10 companies were willing to discuss the cost of enhanced security, four claiming it to be less than 1 per cent and one claiming it to be 1 per cent. The others noted that it was hard to quantify but as requirements become standardized, it will be a cost for all companies. The cost of security, however, was not a key pressure point for many of the companies.

> [More than] 99 per cent of the items we sell are manufactured by our sister companies in Asia; therefore our security requirements were in-house in most circumstances, and quite stringent, before 9/11 but have been standardized since. We did not incur any significant added costs [as a result]. (business equipment manufacturer)

One company noted that the costs associated with C-TPAT were of concern:

> We are in the process of creating factory minimum-security standards and will utilize a third party to audit all factories. We will incur substantial costs to ensure that all factories are compliant with C-TPAT minimum standards. (large retailer)

When asked about their assessment of the security requirements with respect to production and distribution, and the impact of the requirements, companies were very vocal on the issue. While not all saw the benefits of streamlined logistics processes (yet), there were mixed reviews on whether the costs were outweighed by the benefits. Security was noted as slowing the supply chain down, although one company noted that this was being partially mitigated by the implementation of new technologies. The experiences of firms is best summarized by their thoughts:

> We are now focusing on our distribution center and are finding benefits from being 'forced' to document process and build requirements where none existed. This has not yet resulted in streamlining. (large retailer)

> Security measures have not been onerous. We consider our investment in security to be good business. Security measures have actually helped us reduce costs in some cases. For example, product tracking with RFID (radio frequency identification) and global positioning system (GPS) technologies have provided a win–win solution for us, enabling us to achieve a 50 per cent improvement in response time in identifying and resolving in-transit problems; a 20 per cent reduction in excess product/safety stock inventory; a 20 per cent reduction in the size of our container fleet; a 20–90 per cent improvement in delivery time

> reliability; elimination/early detection of product theft; elimination of historical 10–15 per cent human error rate associated with manual work processes to capture and enter data. In addition, we are looking at longer term ways to reduce hazardous material shipments. For example, we are seeking alternative sourcing options to reduce shipping distance, and pursuing opportunities for improved customer–supplier process integration and innovation to eliminate the need to ship certain materials. (chemical manufacturer).

When asked what would make transport security more cost effective, there were numerous suggestions, ranging from tax incentives for the adoption of new security technologies or for participation in pilot programs (expected), to calls for carriers to take a coordinated approach in standardizing tracking technology development and 'a standardization for multiple carrier/shipper tracking capabilities' (not expected). The cargo owners generally focused on the following issues known to the carrier industry:

1. Electronic manifest data, and in particular the need for a common platform and data elements across modes. It was recognized that implementation of the Automated Commercial Environment will help and that this could be of benefit to both carriers and cargo owners. One manufacturer said: 'The economic benefit is to the carriers in the form of asset control, and to the shippers in the form of data accuracy.' There is for cargo owners the positive benefit of better planning for inventory in transit.
2. The desirability of a US Customs and Border Protection (CBP)-rated country-risk index, so that companies would know where to place priorities.
3. Continued collaboration between government and industry and harmonization between governments (US and foreign). Particular mention was made of the hours of service discrepancies in the trucking sector.

Companies also called for US Customs and Border Protection to work with their counterparts in Mexico and Canada to employ FAST-type programs for all modes going between the three countries. It was believed that security costs will continue to go up with the implementation of smart containers, radio frequency identification tags, and the like, but that these costs may be balanced by the recovery of stolen items. One industry association made the following point on behalf of its members:

> One of our biggest issues is recovery post-incident. This is a critical issue for members. If an incident occurs, how much will be shut down so companies can develop contingency plans to minimize their consequential business losses (many of which are not insurable).

Furthermore, on this topic, the associations wanted to know that there would be a plan to waive regulations, like the Jones Act[4] for example, in cases of a port-closing incident. It appears that temporary changes to national policy have not been contemplated as part of incident-response, and this would allay some of the cargo owners' concerns about current government policy in the US. The belief that 'restoration is almost as important as prevention' was reported.

Finally, there was discussion about the level of communication between government and industry. Associations representing cargo interests felt that they have intelligence capability on the ground and can contribute; they have access to the companies with the most to lose from poorly implemented security programs. They also believe that government needs to share its concerns with industry. The cargo industry has been very supportive of US security initiatives, both within the US and in international forums, like the World Customs Organization.[5] It was noted by some of the associations that a two-way system of communication does not appear to exist.

There was one last issue discussed with the industry associations, and that was corridor standards and whether corridors need to step in to negotiate common standards if this is not happening at the supra-national level. One industry association believed that the current situation is untenable, and that while a tri-national agreement on trucking standards was preferable, at least uniform standards for major NAFTA trade corridors would provide a needed 'stepping stone' on the way to regulatory convergence.

Perhaps it would be best to sum up the security issues for the manufacturers and retailers interviewed as just another complexity for business. Costs are not seen as unbearable, and security programs are seen as having a benefit in the streamlining of logistics processes. However, there remains the question of equity, best summed up by a large manufacturer:

> Voluntary programs such as C-TPAT were an effective way to encourage companies to review and improve security. The program was designed to be one piece of an overall plan to secure the border and not disrupt business operations. We are concerned that this is evolving into a much more burdensome and costly program imposed on volunteers while at the same time little is being done to improve security for those not in the program. (automotive manufacturer)

LOOKING FORWARD: WHAT'S NEXT?

While not asked last, the question of importance to conclude this chapter was: if a second round of *NAFTA* negotiations were to be in the preparation stage today, what would you want to see on the table in terms of transportation or logistics elements?

This question opened the floodgates. It was interesting that most of those interviewed were well aware of the unresolved issues in the NAFTA implementation. They clearly were interested in the execution of the promises as a means to streamline their North American operations. In addition to the definite desire to streamline border processes and documentation as noted in Box 3.1, there was strong support for full and open access on the Southern Border, with free flow of goods and vehicles both ways and a fully integrated, no barriers (transportation and customs) system. In addition, the visions repeatedly expressed were of full cooperation on both security and efforts to resolve capacity issues; congestion was seen as a critical issue for these companies. In fact, their dream for the future went well beyond delivering on the existing agreement. Here are some of the ideas presented:

1. On Immigration and Labour

Freer immigration (for drivers): some of the empty backhaul can be removed; this also solves environmental problems (fuel). Immigrants would address the driver shortage. (industry association)

We would want to see the labor laws changed and allow Canadian carriers to be able to make an interstate movement before having to return to Canada or Mexico. (large US manufacturer)

2. On Regulation

Size and weight 80 000 pound [increase] LTLs and triples because cargo lightweight. (industry association)

Mexico is no different. Both countries have the same safety issues. (another industry association)

C-TPAT requirements for all companies involved in NAFTA [suppliers, carriers, . . .] (large retailer)

The specific compliance requirements also need to be coordinated and standardized, again to remove obstacles and to support the free flow of goods. (business equipment manufacturer)

3. On Information

In general, it would be more efficient for manufacturers as well as the respective government agencies if certification processes and requirements for the three NAFTA countries were made common and received reciprocal recognition. Then a company could become certified within their own country and receive the benefits from all three countries. Information exchange between the three countries would also create efficiencies by eliminating the need to file export data with one country and duplicate import data with another for shipments that incur no duty. (automotive manufacturer)

BOX 3.1 ONE CANADIAN COMPANY'S WISH

Any moves related to standardizing government requirements would be welcomed. This might include a very wide range of standards. Some examples might be common rules for what kind of wood packaging is acceptable to the three NAFTA countries, or country of origin marking rules, or standards for food products, etc.

An area that I work with as customs manager for [the company, a consumer goods manufacturer] is customs clearance, particularly into the US. Late last year [2004] it became mandatory to electronically report very detailed information to US Customs at least one hour prior to arrival at the border. This required a great deal of re-engineering of our customs process and made scheduling much more difficult. We previously arrived at the border with bar coded information and invoices and then had ten days after release to account for a shipment with a formal customs entry.

So, under the Pre Arrival Processing System (PAPS) it's required that electronic information is waiting in US Customs computers when the driver shows up with bar coded invoices. The code is read and all the shipment details come onto the inspector's screen. If no electronic information is in the system, the driver can be fined $5000. We are aware of this happening quite often.

The PAPS system is very difficult to work with and the US Customs computer is not user friendly. The system is also down frequently. While we do our own brokerage, many Canadian shipments are cleared by customs brokers. Shippers have to FAX documents to the brokers who input data, hopefully an hour before the truck arrives. Again, if the information is not with US Customs an hour before arrival, at best the truck is refused entry and goes to the broker to find out what happened and waits an hour after the broker enters information. At worst, the driver is refused entry *and* gets the $5000 fine. Any clerical typing errors negate the validity of the electronic information.

That's a long explanation to suggest a change to transport security that would save some money. US Customs should give interested parties involved with a shipment the possibility of enquiring whether shipment pre-notification has been properly received (by the US Customs computer). This would allow the carrier to confirm before taking a chance on showing up and getting the fine. Until such transparency is available, US Customs should not be issuing such heavy fines. In addition to the above-mentioned improvement to the PAPS system, the process of deleting or adjusting information should also be improved. Given that the US Customs computer is so difficult to work with, importers should be given some tolerance with time limits before penalties are issued.

14 July 2005

Source: An email received from the company (which was offered anonymity) in the course of data collection for this research.

4. On Congestion

> [Our] biggest issue is 'capacity.' [It is a] nightmare to schedule routes. (business equipment manufacturer)

> The US and Canada have much stronger transportation infrastructures than does Mexico, and it is essential to match the capabilities across the region to take full advantage of the agreement. (another business equipment manufacturer)

However, in spite of these ideas, cargo interests have focused much of their lobbying capital on addressing the future security environment. Such ideas noted above do not appear in the mainstream reports representing cargo interests. The Retail Industry Leaders Association (undated) has posed a list of questions of the US government to try and understand what it will do in the event of a terrorist attack to secure the speedy recovery of the trading system. The Retail Industry Leaders Association (2005) has also focused on the critical issues of business continuity and contingency planning as an overarching concern. Against security, there appears to be some concern about congestion arising from security measures but even less on the other issues that would facilitate trade.

In summary, the key conclusion that can be drawn about the views of cargo interests in the US interviewed for this chapter is that the North American transportation system still has plenty of room to improve if it is to be efficient in the global context, and that progress is possible on several fronts, such as regulatory convergence, changes to immigration requirements and labour practices, and so on. For cargo interests, they see security and the future of China as dominating the thinking of those in a position to make system improvements desired. With hindsight, it is interesting that the topic of environment was not raised by any of the companies interviewed, although it would be if the interviews were conducted in 2007.

NOTES

1. The BTS data southbound is a richer data source as it contains the weight for each commodity. (There are no northbound weight data in this data set.)
2. A synopsis of these findings was presented in Brooks and Button (2007).
3. US Customs and Border Protection (CBP) published the final *Trade Act of 2002* regulations in the Federal Register on 5 December 2003. The rules required advance transmission of electronic cargo information to CBP for both arriving and departing cargo and provided for various effective dates depending on the mode of transportation. This effectively meant all carriers, not just those using PAPS or working for large manufacturers with just-in-time cargo, now had to provide advanced notification of what they were carrying.
4. US maritime cabotage legislation requiring the use of a US flag vessel on domestic routes. This legislation is discussed further in Chapter 5.
5. 'The World Shipping Council, the International Mass Retail Association, and the National Industrial Transportation League, and their member companies have supported the *Maritime Transportation Security Act of 2002* and its '24 hour rule,' the Container Security Initiative, and the C-TPAT program as well as the development and implementation of analogous efforts at the international level through the World Customs Organization. . . . The industry strongly supports the governments of trading nations establishing predictable and transparent, and mutually consistent, security rules governing these issues' (WSC et al, 2003: 2).

4. Key issues for surface transport suppliers

INTRODUCTION

Since the implementation of *NAFTA*, the growth in trade has meant a concurrent growth in transport opportunities within the region. More recently, growth has also come from a burgeoning trade between China and North America through continental gateway ports. Over the 1990s, Canadian land transportation companies grew transborder business at a faster pace than their US counterparts, as receipts for transborder transport services grew faster than payments (Figure 4.1). There was also significant consolidation of the Canadian and US trucking industry (Brooks and Ritchie, 2005), and absorption of smaller railroads into the current seven Class 1 railroad systems. As noted in Chapters 1 and 2, land transportation services were the primary focus of *NAFTA*'s regulatory reform of international transportation.

This chapter will explore what *NAFTA* meant for those carriers supplying surface transport – road, rail and third party suppliers (3PL) – and the opinions of carrier associations for surface transport. Specifically, this chapter will identify what surface transportation companies concluded about the benefits of *NAFTA*, how they responded to its implementation in terms of strategies and new opportunities to be exploited, and what issues they believe still remain to be addressed. The chapter also examines these companies' views of European-style integration, and what changes they think are needed to make North America's transportation system more effective in the future. Finally, the chapter addresses the impact of security requirements. Because each mode has differing structural issues, each section in this chapter cuts across the modes but presents their points of view separately.

THE BENEFITS AND CHALLENGES OF *NAFTA*

If you listen closely to the economists and the political scientists, the *NAFTA* is all about benefits and positive outcomes. If you listen to the unions and labour leaders, there does not seem to be much positive to say.

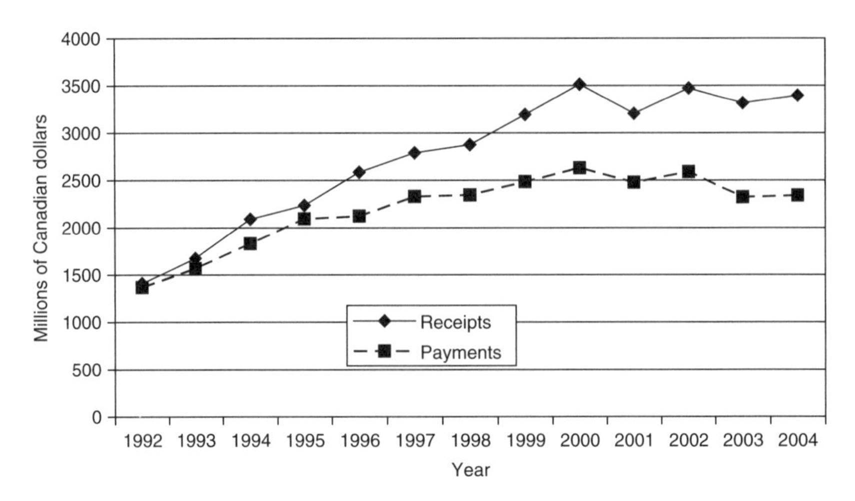

Note: This category includes all but air and marine payments and receipts, both passenger and freight.

Source: Adapted from data extracted from CANSIM Table 376-0032 ('International Transactions in Services, Transportation by Category, Annual Dollars', special tabulations) by Statistics Canada staff, 28 February, 2006.

Figure 4.1 Payments and receipts for Canada–US land (and other) transportation services

As the trucking sector was one of the primary beneficiaries in the transport industry of revision to the rules of engagement, one would expect to hear positive outcomes from freer international markets. The growth in international trade should benefit the companies by providing more cargo to move. Therefore, it seemed highly relevant to ask trucking companies and third party logistics suppliers of land transportation services, as well as the carrier associations, about the benefits they believed *NAFTA* generated.

Beginning with the *carrier association perspective*, all three associations interviewed had quite divergent views. One noted that their members had experienced growth, particularly in volumes to be carried, warehousing and logistics, but reported that security requirements discouraged small and medium-sized truckers and owner-operators. A second was very critical of Mexican access to the US market, while the third was very much against opening of the market at all. Furthermore, this last one was very concerned about driver privacy and vehicle tracking, seeing these as undesirable. One can only conclude that the different associations have different positions that may not be reflected in the needs of the largest operators that were interviewed for this book.

Table 4.1 Profile of trucking company respondents

	n=	Mean	Range
Fleet statistics			
Size of fleet (in trucks) (1)	18	4244	225–18141
% owner-operators (2)	8	36%	15%–85%
Business practices			
Vehicle replacement time (in years)	16	6.0	3–14
Years for depreciation of trucking assets	13	5.5	4–12
Location of current operations			
Canada	15		
Mexico	11		
United States	18		

Notes:
1. The total size of the fleet represented by these companies was in excess of 75000 trucks. As some heavily used owner-operators did not include these in their fleet size estimates, it is clear that the answers present the views of key informants in the industry.
2. Of the 16 companies responding to this question, four did not use owner-operators at all and four used more owner-operators than they had trucks in their fleet. The remaining eight provided the statistics reported on this line. Four of these used less than 20% owner-operators.

Initially, it had been planned to evaluate the responses to *NAFTA* by the type of *trucking* business, with particular focus on truckload (TL) and less-than-truckload (LTL) sub-groups. Of the 18 respondents, 17 had truckload services, six offered LTL services and seven offered intermodal services (Table 4.1). The companies' business models are no longer as discrete as they once used to be and, given this overlap, issues and strategies could not be disaggregated by business type, so the chapter reports the findings for all business models without separation by sub-group.

All 18 trucking companies provided their comments on the benefits. Of the 18 companies, 11 were already doing business in more than one North American country or planned to expand geographically at the time of the signing of the agreement. Although seven of the companies indicated that they had no plans to expand beyond the US, by 2005 all but two of the 18 had operations in Canada, Mexico or both. Times change and, in spite of original intentions, service expansion geographically was one definite outcome of the agreement.

Respondents reported the full spectrum of outcomes to the *NAFTA*. Five companies were quite blunt in noting that they had not seen any benefits at all. Two reported that they had lost business as their customers struggled with a more competitive marketplace after the agreement had been signed, and one complained that its international revenues had declined by 75 per cent. Another noted:

> NAFTA has not changed the way we have operated. We have an operation with a Mexican forwarder who has a yard in Laredo, TX. Our equipment is dropped in this yard and then picked up and delivered in Mexico by a Mexican carrier. The equipment is then returned to Laredo, TX. This is how we operated prior to NAFTA and it is how we continue to do business in Mexico.

Five companies indicated that positive outcomes had been variable, difficult to judge, or that the impact was neutral. One trucking company identified that the trade pattern had changed but the volume had not:

> We have gained some shipments south of the border, but in most cases these shipments originate from the very customers we lost here in the States when they moved the plant to Mexico.

The remaining eight trucking companies saw benefits, primarily in the form of more cross-border traffic and more transportation-related growth opportunities. Two of these attributed their improved circumstances to more than just the agreement, citing customs modernization and opportunities for growth through acquisition as the key factors in their improved state of affairs.

As for the negative impacts, these were quite diverse and well represented by the quotes below:

> Cohesiveness of rules in first four to five years [were frustrating]. [The] interpretation of rules differed by [border] crossing resulting in time delays.

> Requiring an 'over the road' truck driver to carry a birth certificate in order to cross the Canadian border has required us to reduce our US–Canada traffic.

> International freight is more time consuming than domestic freight. It increases our cost by requiring more employees to move each load. Now that all of the security programs are being put in place, the costs are rising. This does not even take into account the time spent by drivers waiting at the border.

Two more companies found that the shifting pattern of trade forced them to seek other, less compensatory freight while they waited for the three countries to resolve issues or for the market to stabilize. Some companies used the opportunity to vent their frustrations with politicians, bureaucrats or lobbyists. Only one company expressed the concern that 'cheap Mexican non-regulated trucking' might be allowed to compete in the US.

Table 4.2 The service offerings of 3PL respondents

Current services offered by 3PLs	**n=**	**Yes**	**No**
Transport	5	4	1
With owned assets	5	4	1
Using purchased services	5	5	0
Warehousing	5	4	1
Electronic documentation	5	5	0
Customs brokerage	5	2	3

Note: The respondents were asked to check all services they currently offer in the market.

As for *third party logistics providers*, five companies participated in the research. Four of the five owned transport and warehouse assets as well as providing transport services purchased from others (Table 4.2). All provided electronic documentation but only two also operated customs brokerage services.

The third party providers were more positive about what the *NAFTA* offered. One believed that the increased complexity of the expanded market created more need for third party logistics services and another found more business in the burgeoning transborder trade in auto parts. Perhaps most interesting were the views held by two companies:

> NAFTA was [the] catalyst for thinking larger.

> NAFTA caused us to look at the supply chain services we were offering our clients and put more emphasis into developing logistics solutions for their Mexican operations. This included developing new competencies and hiring more bilingual coordinators.

On the negative side, two were disappointed that the opportunities they envisaged did not materialize as hoped; one of these wished for cabotage to be eliminated and the market truly opened.

Only two *rail companies* chose to participate in the survey on their views of North American expansion, the impact of security and where they saw the future of rail within the region going. The ability of rail service providers, given the fixed nature of their networks of operation and geographic scope of business, to benefit from the agreement was expected to be a product of that built network, as adding rail capacity is extremely expensive and borne solely by the company. That said, one rail provider said that

> It is our view that liberalized trade is good for business.

The other noted:

> The NAFTA agreement allowed our customers to extend their marketing reach . . . This was and is important to them and to [us] as it allowed us to extract greater value from our . . . rail network.

It is not surprising that *NAFTA* was not the only factor seen as important to rail growth in North America. All railways in North America are looking at the impact of China on their operations, not just those that responded to this research inquiry.

> The rise of China as both an importer of North American raw materials and an exporter of finished goods back to North America has fueled transportation demand. In addition [our company's] long-range strategic plan envisioned the need for major productivity improvements. This need forced us to re-evaluate how we ran our railway and think about how we could better position ourselves to take advantage of a dynamic, competitive, market place. . . . capital spending . . . combined with an operational redesign has allowed us to capitalize on the recent growth in Asian demand which has helped fuel the North American economy of the past several years.

The remaining question concerned perceptions about the benefits of *NAFTA*. In short, were the achievements of the Land Transportation Standards Subcommittee already discussed in Chapter 2 passed down to the operating businesses? It is one thing to achieve consensus between governments through an institution established for the purpose of continuing negotiations, but quite another to find that the regulatory convergence has been used by those for whom it was negotiated. From the mean scores awarded by interviewed companies to the key issues listed in Table 4.3, it appears that the gains were less important to each company's growth strategies than was expected. What is clear is that access to international point-to-point cargoes figured strongly in the business planning for some companies and not at all for others (given its wide range on a scale of one to five).

STRATEGIES FOR EXPLOITING THE *NAFTA* OPPORTUNITY

From the survey it is easy to conclude that the companies, for the most part, saw the *NAFTA* as a path to growth (Table 4.4). Most of the companies used the opportunities the agreement provided to grow their businesses, and there was no one preferred path to growth. The trucking companies opted for a range of responses from growing geographically (to adjacent

Table 4.3 Importance of changes introduced in NAFTA *to the growth of business in the last 10 years*

Change negotiated by the *NAFTA* or LTSS	n=	N/A	Mean	Range
Access to international point-to-point cargoes				
Trucking	16	2	2.50	1–5
Rail	2	0	4.00	3–5
3PL	4	1	4.50	4–5
Carrier associations	2	0	3.00	1–5
Cooperation on Intelligent Transportation Systems development and other transportation technologies				
Trucking	15	3	2.47	1–5
Carrier associations	1	1	2.00	
Rail	2	0	2.50	2–3
3PL	4	1	3.50	3–4
Agreements on log book format and contents				
Trucking	16	2	2.38	1–5
3PL	3	2	1.67	1–3
Carrier associations	1	1	5.00	
Agreements on emergency response				
Trucking	14	4	2.43	1–5
Rail	2	0	2.50	2–3
3PL	3	2	2.33	1–3
Carrier associations	1	1	4.00	
Agreements on hazardous materials regulation				
Trucking	15	3	3.07	1–5
Rail	2	0	3.00	3–3
Carrier associations	1	1	5.00	
3PL	3	2	2.33	1–3

Note: N/A = not answered. Question asked: On a scale of 1–5 (5 being very important), how important were the changes introduced in *NAFTA* to the growth of your business in the last 10 years?

states) to acquiring other trucking companies or establishing new hub operations. Alliances were a favoured option, with nine of the 16 companies responding to this question choosing alliances with Mexican firms, three entering into marketing agreements, two buying a minority interest in a Mexican operation, and four looking to activate other approaches.[1] For the third party businesses, the pattern of addressing the Mexican opportunity was similar but sales agreements were favoured.

The inability of non-Mexican trucking companies to buy Mexican trucking companies, as a result of the stalling of the investment provisions

Table 4.4 How the companies grew their businesses after 1993

Growth by	Yes	No
Expanded into adjacent states		
Trucking (n=16) (1)	7	9
Third party logistics (n=5) (2)	3	2
Established a new hub		
Trucking	6	10
Third party logistics	2	3
Expanded operations internationally		
Trucking	7	9
Third party logistics	2	3
Acquired trucking company		
Trucking	7	9
Third party logistics	0	5
Identified new partner(s) in other jurisdiction		
Trucking	9	7
Third party logistics	3	2
Other means of growth		
Trucking (3)	5	11
Third party logistics (4)	5	0

Notes:

1. Of the 23 trucking and third party logistics companies, two trucking companies chose not to answer the question.
2. Of the five third party logistics suppliers, four reported they owned trucking assets.
3. For trucking companies, the other means of growth included organic means (hiring more drivers, buying more equipment, and so on), and setting up sales offices or offices at or near the border.
4. For third party logistics suppliers, this included acquiring freight forwarders, customs brokerage operations and transport management operations or identifying new agents in the market. One company said it shrunk, rather than grew, closing operations.

implementation timeline (Appendix 2.1), did not appear to dampen American interest in Mexican opportunities. Of the 18 trucking companies interviewed, 11 had Mexican operations and 15 had Canadian ones at the time of the interviews. (As all respondents were listed in the top 100 US trucking or third party logistics firms, all had a presence in the US market.) One company with Canadian and US operations rightly noted that the benefits they had accrued resulted from the *Canada–US Trade Agreement* and not from the *NAFTA*.

Whether these approaches to new market opportunities were optimal is debatable. Some companies were satisfied with the way they approached the opportunities, while others would have preferred differing entry methods – ones not available because of the continuation of some regulations. One logistics supplier praised the necessity of using a Mexican partner because 'Mexican owned companies bring a lot of value to the relationship in terms of local knowledge of the customer base and transportation regulations.' Another would rather have bought its operations in Mexico but was thwarted by the ownership restrictions. A third was so disappointed with the outcome it experienced that it left the market.

Of the nine trucking companies using strategic alliances (or similar partnership arrangements) to enter new markets, seven were satisfied with the approach. For the most part, strategic alliances worked. One company noted:

> Utilizing strategic alliances to provide intra-Mexico carriage was the best alternative. Mexico's foreign investment restrictions and the seesaw political environment that accompanies any third world emerging economy require prudence when considering capital expenditures.

One company noted that alliances taught them how to deal with the Mexican market and provided a good first step from a learning perspective. Even some of those satisfied with their use of strategic alliances noted that, in the long run, alliances can be less than satisfactory:

> Initially strategic alliances and marketing agreements have allowed us access to additional markets and customers that we did not previously have. Going forward, Canada, the US and Mexico are becoming one trading bloc much like the European Union. As such, LTL transportation providers must be able to offer a consistent customer experience regardless of origin or destination NAFTA country. This will result in the need to own a service provider with capabilities in all three countries.

> [We] would prefer company operations in Mexico because alliances do not provide adequate service to customers.

While alliances offered local expertise, a few indicated that their satisfaction with alliances was a result of their concerns about risking equity in the Mexican market.

During the course of these interviews, there was considerable discussion about the relative importance of the agreement as a driver of change. Many trucking companies and third party logistics suppliers saw the 1990s shift of production to *maquiladoras* and the more recent relocation of production to China as more important factors than *NAFTA* in influencing their corporate growth strategy decisions. One company indicated that they believed currency fluctuations drove the shifting trade patterns more so than the *NAFTA*. Other factors driving change were driver shortages and capacity issues; several companies raised these issues.[2] As infrastructure issues will be explored further in Chapter 7, they will not be discussed here.

THINKING ABOUT EUROPEAN-STYLE INTEGRATION

In the European Union (a political union), the maintenance of cabotage has been Europe-wide rather than country-specific, and there is freer movement of labour and equipment. Europe has a considerably more liberalized road transport market than North America. As a catalyst for discussion about the future, the issue of the European-style liberalization was raised.[3] It sparked a lot of comments from the trucking companies but less interest from the third party logistics suppliers and the industry associations. One of the third party suppliers, however, noted that:

> Anyone who thinks protectionism will work is only looking short-term. Freight is like water; it takes the path of least resistance.

One association thought that customs procedures, hours of service, and immigration (and security standards) should be harmonized, but with the caveat that the Mexican industry is not at all similar to those of Canada and the US. In fact, one of the associations was quite blunt about how the Mexican safety culture just did not meet their standards. To quote:

> [We] are concerned about US trucking companies not having access [to Mexico]; [we] don't want Mexican trucks in the US. . . . [We] do not advise [our] members to enter Mexico. [We] are concerned about the Mexican safety culture plus the economics for members will be undermined by lower wage rates and safety costs would be less. Driver records [in Mexico] are suspect because of traffic police corruption plus the cop just confiscates the license.

The trucking company responses ran almost the full spectrum. At one end of the range was enthusiastic and emphatic endorsement of total harmonization; at the other end was concern about what regulations would be implemented, and a strong belief on the part of two companies that Mexican drivers should not have access. One of these companies said:

> At this point in time I'd be concerned with allowing access to the US by Mexican firms. US firms have too much to lose. Margins are too low now and the industry is extremely supply and demand sensitive. In the event trucking supply increases dramatically, the US truck market could fail.

The negative end of the continuum focused on regulations that would put companies at a disadvantage. Not on the continuum but expressed nevertheless was the sentiment that less regulation in total would be appreciated. The weight of opinion was clearly at the pro-liberalization end of the spectrum. As is usually the case, however, the situation was not seen as straightforward but as one where the 'devil is in the details' – it was the qualifiers to the positions taken that yielded the most insights into the mindset of the industry players consulted.

The reasons for supporting further liberalization centered on beliefs that such a path would reduce the time required for border crossings and address the current concerns about bottlenecks and inefficiencies at the border. The following two comments illustrate:

> Any reforms that would reduce the entry times into Canada (several hours) or into Mexico (several days) would be beneficial.

> Definitely yes. Much time is spent by [company division] and myself dealing with immigration and Customs issues. Trying to comply with US Customs is like trying to hit a moving target. What is OK today could get you a fine tomorrow. Even worse is there is no continuity . . . You can clear a load today at Windsor and everything is fine. Tomorrow you take the same load, driver and paperwork to Niagara Falls and you receive a fine for some obscure reason. Customs enforces its own rules differently at different border locations.

Companies often cited issues in their qualifying comments. The ones most frequently mentioned were concerns about equipment restrictions (vehicle size and weights), licensing, environmental compliance, and not just Hours of Service issues but other labour regulatory differences. Security concerns were also raised. To quote one company in favour of greater liberalization:

> Yes, provided border security was not compromised, and foreign vehicles entering the US complied with all US safety and emission standards. All drivers (US and foreign) should meet stringent background checks.

It was also not just about regulatory divergence; six of the companies provided quite extensive comments regarding their concerns about current differences in interpretation and enforcement of the existing regulations, and inconsistency in these throughout the supply chain. It was quite evident that regulatory divergence within each of the three countries added some measure to the level of interest in greater regulatory convergence between the countries.

Finally, some of the companies felt that dealing with the immigration rules needs to be part of any reform discussion, and noted that immigration could be a path to easing the driver shortage.

> Regulatory reform would be beneficial in transportation. Today, we have an uneven playing field with regard to compliance issues, licensing, environmental compliance, insurance limits and the like. Freight is moving across the border in the present system, legally and illegally. With respect to labor, I think it is unlikely that such reforms would have an immediate impact in our business. Our drivers do not want to drive into Mexico, and Mexican drivers do not want to drive into the US. There are language and cultural barriers, harmonization of Commercial Driver's License and Hazmat issues, etc.

THE KEY REGULATORY ISSUES OF IMPORTANCE

Hours of Service Requirements (Trucking)

Trucking companies were asked specifically about the Hours of Service discrepancy (between Canada and the US as noted in Chapter 2), as it was a highly charged topic of discussion during the time of the research and so was singled out for direct questioning.[4] The comments made by 16 of the companies indicate a spectrum of concerns. Either companies have adapted their operations, viewed the impact as a market-restricting non-tariff barrier, or have not found it to be a problem at all. This last group included those companies managing cross-border operations via strategic alliance, LTL operators or those in the oversize/overweight commodity business.

Hours of Service regulations were noted to be a particular challenge for companies when a driver encounters congestion or border delay or routes with excessive wait times. One company declared it to be more of an issue for Canadian drivers heading into the US than for US drivers heading north. Three of the comments indicate the range of beliefs about the issue:

> Mexican hours of service compliance training is not acceptable.

> It is not a major problem, but a driver working for us should have the same log book regulations in Canada as in the US. It just creates confusion and will someday lead to an accidental violation.

> If the driver was in line, it didn't count and now it does. This means the truck gets left at the side of the road. It could be a serious problem.

One company's view of the issue was pointed:

> There is a 'disgraceful' gap between the countries [Canada and the US]; we see the balkanization of Canada.

The carrier associations also saw Hours of Service as a critical issue. One noted the particular difficulty it faced in getting agreement on Hours of

Service from its membership. As the Hours of Service issue was in the throes of discussion during the time of the survey and the final regulations were not yet in place, to discuss the issue further here is not particularly useful.

Equipment Standards

There has been considerable discussion over the years about the number of jurisdictions in North America that impose divergent truck vehicle size and weight regulations. Under *NAFTA*, the Land Transportation Standards Subcommittee was supposed to develop a common set of North America-wide regulations. While each state in the US has differing regulations, there is a common standard for interstate trucking. In Canada, some provinces have agreed to regional standards. As a result, there are numerous options for firms to adopt depending on their market reach. As this is the primary area of regulatory divergence in road transport, several questions focused on trucking companies' views on the issues, what it meant for their companies, and how they opted to address the divergence. Similarly, the divergence affects the third party providers as well and so they were also asked about its impact. Finally, the carrier associations were tapped for their views.

Beginning with the carrier associations, there was consensus that this is a critical issue for their members. Key issues were tractor wheel base limitations, trailer length and axle spreads, and the associations noted that the variance by state, on particular routes like domestic west coast to Alaska and for some operators to Canada, was especially difficult. One association believed that American truckers have less trouble going north than Canadian truckers have heading south. As for how their members deal with differences, the answers can be summarized as follows: as best they can, often opting for the lowest common denominator or choosing to purchase equipment from only one supplier (manufacturer) and opting to turn the assets over on a shorter replacement schedule to gain the advantage of any new technologies. One association noted that some states are more flexible than others in their requirements; to quote:

> Uniform rules on size and weight are a good thing, except [we] do not want to see bigger and heavier. Harmonization should begin and end with the standards of the biggest – the US industry.

Of the 18 trucking companies, 16 chose to answer the questions on weights and dimensions. Of these, six did not know how many differing sets of regulations applied to their business operations. Of the remaining ten, five indicated that they only had to meet one set of regulations. The remaining five had to meet two (two companies), five (one company), between three and ten (one company) and more than 50 (one company). It is instructive to assess strategies for operating in multiple jurisdictions, and so these companies were queried further on their approaches with a set of three questions focused on identifying problems with the regulatory divergence within the multiplicity of jurisdictions, and how the company deals with the issue.[5]

The variety of answers to what causes the most problems was almost equal to the number of companies responding. Only two companies indicated that they had no problems. The remainder provided illustrations that reflected the variety of business activities and specific restrictions that make daily operations incredibly complex for these companies. They also reported the substantial documentary burden this places on them, and the question sparked a few complaints about protectionist attitudes. In summary, the pain can be best described by the company that indicated somewhere between three and ten jurisdictions:

> We actually have over 40 different trailer types in operation, if we consider each brand, capacity, and axle configuration as a choice. Varying regulations, whether it be 13-feet six-inch trailers for the Eastern US states, 14 feet for the West, or 13 feet seven inches for Canada, or three-axle for the Pacific Northwest to haul 88 000 pounds or two-axle trailers to haul 80 000 in California, etc., have all created significant operating costs in our fleet.

As for strategies to deal with the multiplicity of regulations, seven of 14 companies indicating problems with multiple jurisdictions indicated that they standardize their fleet to the lowest common denominator or to a single standard (one tractor specification and one trailer specification); this could be seen as company-imposed convergence. Two companies opted to work to the highest specification in each market to maximize payload and accept the accompanying inefficiencies in fleet management. The strategy of one of these companies was to compete through customer service:

> We look to the highest common denominator. How can we provide the most value for any given customer? Over the years, we have custom built trailers to match the exact upper limits of the region's legal specifications, allowing maximum carrying capacity.

The remainder of the companies opted for geographically differentiated strategies. One of these concluded that it was possible to focus on productivity gains for the fleet within specific geographic markets. One company indicated that it makes routing decisions that avoid states with regulations that are too restrictive or too slow in issuing special hauling permits. From this discussion, it would seem clear that there are significant savings to be had from regulatory convergence within each country and even more if the market between countries was liberalized.

Companies were also asked about how they might change their strategies if there were fewer jurisdictions. About half of the companies assumed that the standards they had already adopted would become the new standards or that they would have to selectively adapt depending on where their largest markets were. Many did not see themselves making changes because they had already decided on a 'single standard' strategy and they believed this approach to doing business would continue. Several companies indicated that fewer jurisdictions would enable them to expand their use of owner-operators (this was expressed positively), and that they would appreciate the opportunity to acquire greater flexibility in operations expecting that better fleet utilization would result. One company noted that it would mean they could do their existing business with a smaller fleet. One company did not want fewer jurisdictions as they saw the complexity as a barrier to entry. As a final comment on this issue, it was clear that some firms were worried about their existing fleet investment, and that if weights were raised, existing fleet value would diminish; a phase-in of any regulatory change was clearly front of mind for most.

As a first step towards assessing the promise of regulatory convergence, the proposition of trade corridor-specific or geographic-zone standards was raised.[6] Here the responses were split, almost equally. For those in favour of geographic or corridor standards, the potential for productivity gains or efficiencies were front of mind:

> The biggest benefit again would be in streamlining our trailer purchases. If a standard was set that would allow us to use the same axle configuration and obtain the same axle weights through the zone, we could operate more efficiently and at a lower overall cost. We would also see a savings in obtaining oversize/overweight permits as this operation could also be streamlined.

> Trade corridor-specific standards could be helpful. Something similar to 'B' trains in Canada, or 'Rocky Mountain Doubles' with the ability to run from Canada, the US, and Mexico would enhance commercial movements while limiting the number of heavy trucks on the road.

> It would be better than no ability to improve efficiencies, but it complicates issues as well.

The reasons why such an approach was not favoured are also quite valid:

> It will be more difficult to change [later].

> More balkanization [will result]. It would be better to resolve the overall problem rather than [engage in] bilateral deals.

> The critical infrastructure of our nation is not keeping pace with our nation's economic growth. We are not properly maintaining our current highway and bridge infrastructure. Our nation is throwing away billions of dollars annually through highway congestion and damages sustained by personal and business equipment. Further, our nation's highway safety is negatively impacted by this same root cause. If private-funded trade corridors are developed, we will have to determine if utility would be beneficial beyond the roads we travel currently. We are adamant that no effort should be made to create trade corridors and then mandate their use by commercial vehicles. The trucking industry fully understands that we fund highway construction and maintenance through fuel use tax and equipment excise tax. We will fight efforts to 'toll' existing roads, or any efforts to require carriers to utilize solely trade corridors.

One of the carrier associations indicated that corridor-focused regulatory convergence could create problems for off-corridor cargo interests, raising the question that governments in both Canada and the US have been trying to grapple with: how do you define a corridor and what does it mean if you do so? (The corridor or regional approach is dealt with in Chapter 6.)

Finally, there is the question about savings possible from fewer jurisdictions (if regional standards evolve). Most companies felt quite uncomfortable with this question and some sought extra time to contemplate it further. Only nine companies were prepared to commit to an estimate. No one thought that cost savings would exceed 15 per cent of equipment operating costs and, on the other hand, no one thought it would add costs. The nine were evenly split between no savings, less than 5 per cent, and 5–15 per cent. One company expressed the issue of estimating financial impact differently:

> This is difficult to estimate and would depend on what the single applicable vehicle size and weight regulation turned out to be. For example, if triples were allowed everywhere, we would use higher horsepower tractors across the country, which would increase costs but we would also experience significant productivity gains.

The third party logistics companies were also asked about financial savings possible from a single set of equipment standards, but as none were able to say how many different standards regulations they faced for their asset-owning operations, they were unable to find consensus on the savings possible.

In the rail industry, there has been a push to standardize regulation in the industry and to implement common equipment specifications. This has also encouraged railroads to establish equipment pools to improve asset productivity within the total rail system.

> Equipment specifications are governed under the auspices of the American Association of Railroads. As such, the Canadian and US railroads use similar if not identical types of equipment that are easily interchangeable between rail company and rail customer.

It is worth thinking that reduced variation in equipment standards might allow more companies to focus on improving asset productivity, and hence network competitiveness as a whole.

AREAS FOR FUTURE NEGOTIATIONS

While it is of interest to know the perceptions of the current state of play when planning for the future, it is of greater importance to know what industry needs to be competitive. Therefore, it was seen as absolutely necessary to explore those areas where companies believe government can be useful in dealing with regulatory divergence. For this reason, the companies were asked what should be on the table for future negotiations between Canada and the US; this was only asked of companies with operations in both Canada and the US, as these are the companies already indicating an interest in broader market operations. The companies were asked to evaluate what areas of their business regulatory environment would provide the greatest benefits of change, and their evaluations appear in Table 4.5.[7]

Changes to border crossing infrastructure and streamlined documentation are seen as areas offering the greatest benefits to the *trucking industry*. The development of cross-trained customs officials implementing US rules in Canadian facilities and Canadian customs officers in US facilities as possible under the Container Security Initiative also holds some promise for improvement in the land border congestion and delay situation between the two countries. If the question had been worded to contemplate an external security perimeter, it would be interesting to speculate what perspectives might have been found. The issue of common data collection is certainly also seen as a simplifying and beneficial prospect to the companies.

When discussing their opinions on these issues, one trucking company said:

> A lack of capacity at northern border crossing points creates delays and increases cost. If in fact Canada and the US truly want to improve security and efficiencies at the northern border, they must invest in creating additional physical capacities to properly and effectively process cross-border commerce.

Table 4.5 Identification of Canada–US issues for bilateral action

Issue	n	Mean	Range	n Ranking in top 3
Harmonization of corporate governance regulation	10	3.70	3–5	2
Trucking only	8	3.63	3–5	2
Similar tax treatment of parents and subsidiaries	11	3.45	1–5	2
Trucking only	8	3.25	1–5	2
Common competition policies on anti-competitive practices	13	3.77	2–5	3
Trucking only	10	3.90	2–5	3
Common rules opposing state subsidization	13	3.31	1–5	0
Trucking only	10	3.20	1–5	0
Common rules on preferential access to capital	13	3.15	1–5	0
Trucking only	10	2.90	1–5	0
Freedom of drivers/crew to work in both countries	14	4.64	2–5	9
Trucking only	11	4.55	2–5	6
Removal of cabotage provisions	13	4.15	3–5	3
Trucking only	11	4.18	3–5	3
Common data collection and documentation procedures	14	4.36	2–5	5
Trucking only	11	4.18	2–5	3
Common bi-national border zones and clearance areas	12	4.50	3–5	5
Trucking only	9	4.44	3–5	3
A bi-national investment partnership for border infrastructure investment	14	3.86	1–5	3
Trucking only	11	3.73	1–5	2

Note: This table only includes those surface transportation suppliers with business activities in both Canada and the US. The response rate varied by sub-question and so the number (n=) responding is reported.

On the other hand, the absence of common rules opposing state subsidization and common rules on preferential access to capital on any of the companies' 'highest priorities' list, and their low mean score, indicates that the harmonization of this type (as seen in Europe) is of little interest. The research by Heads (1992), Chow and MacRae (1990), and Cairns (2002) all indicated that this is an issue in Canada, where taxation hits companies harder than their US competitors. It is not surprising that US companies operating in Canada do not see the need for this uneven playing field to be addressed! The interest in this issue came from the Canadian owners of leading US operations (as only top US companies were approached).

Although there were divergent views associated with the evaluation of important issues, the key areas for targeted bi-national attention concentrate on border infrastructure and market access. While one company stated that freedom of drivers to work in both countries was the same as removal of cabotage, other respondents did not share this point of view. Technically, they are similar; however, cabotage might be maintained but immigration requirements or incidental move regulations relaxed.

Did *3PLs* have the same opinions as trucking companies? Only two 3PLs of the five interviewed were eligible to answer this question and so this assessment cannot be made. What can be said is that both responding 3PLs placed 'common bi-national border zones and clearance areas' and 'common data collection and documentation procedures' as 'five' on the scale of one to five and ranked them in their top three priorities. The other one of importance was addressing the 'freedom of drivers to work in both countries'. As four of the five 3PLs operate trucking assets, it is not surprising to see this desire for further liberalization.

What is particularly interesting is *rail companies*' perception of the issues of importance in future. There is a strong interest in seeing the issue of labour integration addressed. In Table 4.5, the strongest area for improvement between Canada and the US is the ability to use crews and train drivers, wherever in the network they are needed.

> Unlike the trucking industry, train operating personnel are generally changed at the border. This is to say, Canadian crews will pull their train just over the border into the US handing over responsibility for the balance of the US journey to their American counterparts. The same holds true going north with Canadian crews taking control at the border.

One company indicated that, while such flexibility might be appreciated by management, it would not necessarily be seen as desirable by labour. One difference noted was that drug testing in the US is random while, in Canada, probable cause is required for testing. Furthermore, the requirement for passports under the Western Hemisphere Travel Initiative was raised as a concern.

When asked to look to the future and provide their comments on possible areas for harmonization, one company noted that corporate governance regulation applicable in Canada has already risen to meet the higher US standards. On the other hand, it was clear that no one wished to see the tax treatment of parents and subsidiaries align with the Canadian standards, the higher tax environment. As for a bi-national infrastructure investment partnership to invest in border infrastructure, it was seen as 'not likely'. Harmonization of procedures had strong support as an area where economic benefits could be the greatest.

In summary, there was very little evidence (from this survey of the larger trucking companies) of protectionist sentiment; the higher priorities of the companies centered on improving the functioning of the border and eliminating the uncertainty associated with it. The fact that such improvements might be accompanied by market opening did not seem to raise too much concern, although one company thought greater access would grant Canadian companies the opportunity to drive prices down (without any counterbalancing recognition that tax advantages currently accrue to American companies). With the appreciation of the Canadian dollar over the 18 months prior to the survey, any currency advantage had probably already evaporated. There was sufficient concern about Hours of Service, vehicle weights and dimensions and the coming driver shortage, that these areas warrant further focus on the part of regulators and industry.

THE IMPACT OF SECURITY

What has changed since 9/11? In response to the changed security environment,[8] many *trucking companies* noted that the new security requirements are layered onto security of cargo requirements in place before 11 September, 2001. Customers have asked many more questions, required greater scrutiny of identification documents presented by drivers, and generally have been much more focused on security issues. Most companies noted that their efforts (prior to the September 2001 terrorist attacks) were on the safety of hazardous materials and the theft of desirable products. The additional layering from a customer concern point of view has caused trucking companies to accept an educational role, as reflected in the following comments:

> We had stringent security regulations in place prior to 9/11; however, we have had to provide education and proof of those security regulations, procedures and processes to our customers since 9/11.

> [Our company] has always taken necessary precautions to provide security for all aspects of our chain-of-custody responsibilities handling our customer's shipments. Security is reviewed regularly, and appropriate action taken when risk assessments dictate. We are more than concerned about well-intended, under-informed Government officials that legislate laws, rules or regulations

> without fully understanding implications or looking downstream far enough to avoid unintended consequences. Legislating emotionally always results in unintended consequences, and often times does not even meet the goals that dictated actions in the first place. Typically, we have customers who do not fully understand cost implications associated with less-than-fully vetted mandates and once enlightened rescind their requests.

The impacts of security requirements have been felt in various ways. While few trucking companies or 3PL companies reported losing customers or a change in customer mix due to security regulations (Table 4.6), the commentary on the mix of customers, and how it changed, is quite instructive. Altered markets and customer mix were attributed to new hazardous materials regulations, the *Bioterrorism Act* or the US *Patriot Act*. It seems that the changing customer mix is only partly explained by new security requirements. Seven trucking companies attributed it to changing economic conditions or knock-on effects of security on freight rates. One company believed that future changes to pre-notification rules would cause further changes in the customer mix for that company.

Not all impacts have been adverse. One trucking company reported growth in business as a result of their security decisions. To quote:

Table 4.6 Impact of security regulations

Impact	**n=**	**Yes**	**Don't know**
Loss of customers			
Trucking	18	2	0
Rail	2	1	0
Change of customer mix			
Trucking	17	3	0
Rail	2	0	0
Additions to transport or forwarding contracts required			
Trucking	18	10	5
Rail	2	0	1
Third party logistics supplier			
Acquisition of new customers			
Trucking	18	1	5
Rail	2	0	1
Dropped markets			
Trucking	17	2	0
Rail	1	0	0
Third party logistics supplier	5	0	0

> We have experienced NAFTA customer growth from a broad array of customers as a result of our knowledge and experience handling business between the NAFTA countries. Customers are concerned about the liability and risk they may take on as a result of not doing business with LTL carriers that have experience or security procedures on international transportation for NAFTA countries. Customers also want the confidence that their LTL transportation providers will have the resources to keep up with anticipated additional government security requirements that are coming as a result of NAFTA countries tightening access in an effort to protect their residents.

The implementation of additional clauses or requirements in transport and forwarder contracts was the most common response to the changed security environment. Some trucking companies resisted changes sought by customers, such as more stringent seal requirements or the requirement for C-TPAT certification. To quote two on the changed security requirements:

> When you have 1000-plus loads at any given time, sealed with a five-cent seal that any driver or passerby can snap open, it's perhaps unfair to expect the carrier to purchase the load. We've pushed back on contracts with language that is bilateral.

> More shippers are 'forcing' carriers to grant waivers of subrogation, grant indemnity for any and all acts of negligence, and are requiring higher levels of excess insurance over DOT mandated amounts.

Membership in C-TPAT was not always seen as a good thing. Of the trucking companies interviewed, 16 were prepared to talk about security and its impacts. Of these, 12 belonged to C-TPAT and nine of them saw it as a necessity of doing business (Table 4.7). One 3PL pointed out the conundrum of C-TPAT: it is a necessity for doing business but 3PLs are not allowed to belong!

Perhaps most important to companies and their strategic responses to the changing environment are the impacts security requirements have had

Table 4.7 C-TPAT and competitiveness

Impact	n=	Yes	Don't know
Belong to C-TPAT			
Trucking	16	12	1
Rail	2	2	0
Third party logistics supplier	5	1	0
C-TPAT as a necessity?			
Trucking	16	9	1
Rail	2	2	0
Third party logistics supplier	4	3	0

on their business operations. In the research undertaken by Thibault et al. (2006), many container shipping lines, when faced with the new security requirements and the 24-hour advanced notification rules, found that companies benefited from the rules because it streamlined their documentary processes and forced them to address shippers' less-than-complete documentation on the contents of a container. Was the same factor at play in transborder surface operations where the advance notification rules are significantly less stringent or were the costs of security uncompensated even partially by such benefits?[9]

Certainly it was expected that there would be costs incurred in implementing security regulations. One company very bluntly advised that they had calculated the cost to be US$20 per border crossing and, given the number of crossings per day, this put total costs for them into the millions of dollars. Several others indicated that they had not been able to quantify costs fully because it was not possible to calculate the investment in time accurately.

> The largest expense by far is the increased time at the border into Canada. Time is money in trucking. If a driver is sitting, he is working for free which drives up turnover, which creates an empty truck.

One company noted they had not been able to calculate the cost of their FAST certification as it was leading to a significant rise in the cost of driver retention and acquisition. Another company said the full cost was not yet known (as implementation was not complete):

> We have added security cameras, fencing, automatic gates, and the like to facilities. The cost impact of the Patriot Act will be extreme. We estimate that as many as 20 per cent of current Hazmat, 'X' endorsed drivers will not pass the background check, or will refuse to subject themselves to the background check The cost to our industry will be enormous.

One large LTL trucking company noted that it had always, for cargo security reasons, managed its cargo responsibilities tightly. Its view was clear on why they had not followed government guidelines:

> [Our company] has always taken necessary precautions to provide security for all aspects of our chain-of-custody responsibilities handling our customer's shipments. If we were to put in place all the security recommendations made by the CBP and DHS at all locations (which are not necessary based upon our risk assessments), we would have to spend over $30 million and we would not materially improve security.

Last but not least, the documentary costs imposed by changes to data entry requirements and hazardous materials endorsements received a substantial number of supplementary comments. In particular, it was noted that these requirements impose significant costs on those who had already developed proprietary systems for internal use and now must accommodate the information technology and Electronic Data Interchange requirements of US Customs and Border Protection; these requirements were declared to be 'in some cases not industry standards and [they] require special programming'. The security checks for hazmat drivers were noted to be costly. There were even complaints about the costs of background checks for Commercial Driver's Licenses; one company wanted to know why existing drivers with three or more years of service could not have grandfathered arrangements. Furthermore, it was noted that the current security environment penalizes the less-than-truckload sector disproportionately:

> Only because customers believe they receive benefit from the CBP (US Customs and Border Protection) with this accreditation. In fact, C-TPAT works fine for customers or trucking companies dealing with a single bill trailer or a single bill commodity. When confronted with multi-bill trailers and commodities, there is absolutely zero benefit from expedited customs clearance, including those multi-bill carriers who have even become FAST accredited. . . . FAST ain't fast as the border facilities lack the necessary capacity to process the amount of commerce crossing the border, and they lack 'standards' associated with staffing and due process.

It is fair comment to say that there was no shortage of opinions on the cost of security to operations in the trucking and 3PL sectors. From the perspective of rail service providers, one company summarized the impacts:

> Both customer and carrier security requirements have been driven by the US and Canadian customs agencies. The impact on [our company] is as follows: 1. Increased capital investment to support US Customs and Border Protection Vehicle and Cargo Inspection System (VACIS) at points where [the company] crosses into the USA. 2. Tripling of the physical inspection of shipments by CBP resulting in train delays and increased operating costs to [the company].

The other rail company indicated that while customers did not impose requirements, the company determined that it should move quickly to take advantage of any program. The company's view was also that any program that would eliminate or reduce delay in trains crossing the border 'would provide the biggest benefit to the company'. In fact, both rail companies indicated that moving the security perimeter out to the ports would be their number one priority in a second round of *NAFTA* negotiations because of those border-crossing benefits. As one noted, on inbound boxes for North America, the Container Security Initiative assesses the box at the foreign port, and again at the North American port, and the company therefore questioned whether a third inspection is really needed when the box crosses the border if the carrier is C-TPAT compliant. Both rail companies indicated that the increase in inspections has not led to any benefits, has not assisted them in streamlining operations, and generally concluded that the benefits seen in other modes have not been applicable to them. In conclusion, the rail industry respondents have reported a different impact than the others. Perhaps it is because the rail network, as a private one, was already better controlled and less complex before September 2001 and, therefore, the 'benefits' accruing from security improvements are perceived as generally less or negative.

Two of the three *industry associations* complained about the implementation of the FAST program and the problems it posed for members, one noting it was costly and that the government needed to make infrastructure investments to support it or its usefulness would not be realized. There was also concern expressed by one of the associations that the next fear would be that voluntary programs would become mandatory, excluding even more of its members from the market.

What would make security more cost effective? One solution proposed was quite interesting: 'Increasing size and weight allowances would put fewer shipments on the road, possibly allowing tighter security focus on a smaller number of shipments.' Another company suggested applying differentiated hazmat regulations so that 'dangerous' hazmat commodities would be treated differently than 'common hazmat products like commercial soap'. One industry association proposed that a consolidation of all the background checks into one multilateral standard would make the complex situation simple; the current four processes (Transport Workers' Identification Credential, FAST, Hazmat endorsement, and US Visit) could be streamlined and there would only be one credential.

Most of the responses focused on the issue of border crossings. Several companies suggested single border clearance zones, common administrative procedures, and single bi-national security and quick clearance programs (one noted that C-TPAT and PIP are not enforced similarly). There was a strong theme of greater intergovernmental cooperation at the border and many repeated that the time to cross the border is far too long.

Differences in enforcement were raised on a number of occasions. One trucking company was particularly vocal and makes a point that was echoed throughout the discussions with the carriers:

> One thing you did not address and I would like discussed is a US Customs agent's absolute authority at the border. Over the years we have had situations arise at the point of a driver at the border trying to cross. An agent makes an arbitrary decision to deny entry to either the driver or the cargo. At that point

> in time, the agent is the law. I have had agents tell me that verbatim. The agent can be wrong but at that point in time the carrier has no recourse. It is very costly to have loads/drivers turned back at the border.
>
> I want to assure you I have pursued some of these erroneous decisions and proven the agent wrong. By the time you get the correct decision (it could be the next business day or the next week), the driver has already taken the load back to the shipper. The damage is done. I realize the need for our country's security, but some of these agents see themselves as a deity.
>
> There is a real difference between the way US Customs and Canadian Customs operate. US Customs offers no help or hands-on guidance. Canadian Customs has given me a liaison contact person for any questions I might have. The difference seems to be US Customs has an adversarial attitude and Canadian Customs has more of a partnership attitude.

The only conclusion that can be drawn from this forceful opinion is that a streamlined approach to border management (or possibly a change in attitude about what consistutes a border) could go a long way to stemming the underlying frustration.

CONCLUSIONS

Looking forward, companies with operations in both Canada and the US expressed throughout the interview process a continuing concern about the future driver shortage in the trucking industry in North America. The source of future drivers, the potential for undocumented drivers to participate in the industry, and the impact of a number of regulations on the ability to recruit drivers were reoccurring themes. The requirement for passports was repeatedly raised and very well expressed by one trucking operation:

> One of the challenges coming up that will be difficult is the requirement for all entrants into the US to have passports. This may make it even more difficult to get drivers to go into Canada. If we have 1000 drivers, it is a $100 000 expense to refund all drivers for Canada legal (passports). If we do not offer to assist drivers with the passport, we risk having no drivers available for Canada.

Second, there was strong endorsement in the industry for a future agreement to be more open with mutually agreed means of managing the border crossings and standardization of rules, both security and otherwise.[10] A common Hours of Service regime, harmonization of vehicle size and weight standards, common insurance requirements, and generally a 'level playing field' were repeatedly proposed. The issue of border delay resonated throughout and the solutions seen by many focused on improvements to the documentary and regulatory processes. Consistent enforcement would also be appreciated.

These views were echoed by the 3PLs surveyed. The need for true North American standards (for equipment, driver qualifications and documentation), a more open border, and streamlined border crossing procedures were underlined. One 3PL wanted a European-style arrangement within North America, a common perimeter.

When asked where priorities needed to be placed, views were divergent on the single most important issue but three consistently appeared near the top – common Hours of Service, a focus on improved border processing, and harmonization of equipment requirements. The fourth priority is greater market access.[11] While the first three did not appear to be as onerous in the discussion in this chapter, they are clearly the prime irritants the industry would like to see resolved. It is particularly interesting to note that two of these three – Hours of Service and equipment standards – do not need a second round of *NAFTA* negotiations; the mandate given the Land Transportation Standards Subcommittee already exists. The third, improved border processes, could easily be added to existing trilateral institutions. The fact that the *Security and Prosperity Partnership* does not address any of these three in particular is discouraging.

Finally, the industry associations reflected similar opinions. They are concerned that procedures be harmonized, that infrastructure investment is needed and that there be standardization of security checks, program consolidation and simplification. The current situation is not cost effective for their members. One association felt it was time to get a North American Trucking Agreement in place with 'clarity' on the cabotage issue; it believed generally that discrepancies between agencies are frustrating and need to be eliminated.

NOTES

1. These four companies noted that other options included setting up more sales offices in Mexico, adding equipment and drivers, and restructuring border operations.
2. Interestingly, one company indicated that the capacity issues allowed them to raise rates and become more profitable, and so it was a positive rather than negative factor for them.
3. The question asked: Europe has increasingly eliminated the rules governing access to trucking markets within Europe, reduced restrictions on European trucking businesses, and harmonized the business environment (standards, taxation, labour and immigration, and so on) applying to transportation services within Europe. Would you want to see more of this type of regulatory reform within North America? Why? Why not?
4. The question was: does the continuing discrepancy on Hours of Service pose a problem for your cross-border operations? Please explain why or why not.
5. The three questions were: 1. What are the differences in equipment regulation that cause you the most problems? 2. If there were fewer jurisdictions, how would you operate differently? Would you have a different fleet structure with fewer vehicle models? Use more or fewer owner-operators? 3. What is the company's strategy for dealing with

variety in vehicle weight and dimension regulation? Do you just work to the lowest common denominator?
6. The question was: do you see any benefit to developing trade corridor-specific standards? Geographic-zone standards? Please provide your thoughts on this.
7. The question was: if you currently have operations in both Canada and the US, for each of the elements (or factors) below, identify the importance of further harmonization to the future growth of your company. Next, select the top three and rank them in your order of priority, with 1 being the single most important area for bilateral government attention (i.e., which of these would have the greatest positive impact on your company?).
8. The question was: what has changed since September 2001 in terms of your customers' security requirements that have affected how you do business?
9. The questions were: what is your assessment of the security requirements you have had to meet? Have they assisted you in streamlining business operations? Have they been costly? The cost of enhanced security requirements has been about_____ per cent of operations. Have security requirements led you to drop markets?
10. The final question was: if a second round of NAFTA were to be in the negotiation preparation stage today, what would you want to see on the table in terms of transportation or logistics elements? (Please develop a list of your top priorities and explain why.)
11. There is a clear sub-group that is frustrated with access to the Mexican market and with cabotage rules in general, and believes that this needs to be a direct focus for the future.

5. Forgotten modes

INTRODUCTION

This chapter will explore what the *NAFTA* meant, or rather did not mean, for transportation services and the transport network supplied by the marine and air modes. They were left out of the *NAFTA* and present a very different picture from the land modes discussed in Chapter 4. This chapter examines each of these 'forgotten' modes separately. In the case of both, however, regulation is a key driver of industry structure today, and the corporate strategies employed have long developed based on that regulatory climate and so are not especially flexible, particularly in the case of shipping, to any changes that might arise from market liberalization.

The chapter begins by painting a picture of the marine industry, before examining the history of the regulation of the mode as a way of explaining the challenges the mode faces today within the NAFTA region. The points of view of marine suppliers are examined as was done in the two preceding chapters, in an effort to understand the network and its suppliers today, as well as their views of the security requirements. The marine section concludes with a brief discussion as to whether short sea shipping between NAFTA countries will be a potential future growth direction. The chapter then moves to the air mode, presenting a history of Canada–US air liberalization efforts beginning in 1966 and leading to the *Open Skies Agreement of 2005*. The state of the market throughout this period is examined, laying the foundation for a discussion of the current international air market between the two countries today. The air industry is one of bilateral agreements and so this section only includes Mexico where major events are relevant, or where the *Security and Prosperity Partnership of North America*, signed by the three governments, is discussed. While this chapter follows a somewhat different format from the last two chapters,[1] it rounds out the transport supply picture within North America.

MARINE TRANSPORTATION WITHIN NORTH AMERICA

Chapter 1 has already indicated that the North American transport network is dominated by land transportation services (specifically Table 1.4), and that this was the primary focus of the negotiations for both trade agreements. Also noticeable in Chapter 1 is the sheer volume of US domestic shipping, both brown water (inland) and blue water (coastal), with coastal shipping at 10 times the size of Canadian and Mexican shipping combined, and inland at 20 times that of Canada's inland shipping (Table 1.4). Maritime transport is a complex and critical component of the North American transportation network.

North America has an extensive coastline and inland river systems. The Gulf of Mexico region boasts that it is home to 59 million in population and seven of the 12 busiest US ports (Springer, 2005). North America also has the largest freshwater lake system in the world. The North American market in shipping is composed of four, quite distinct segments:

1. *US domestic marine transportation*. This market is quite large, totalling a little more than 1 billion short tons in 2000, in a total US foreign and domestic market of approximately 2.5 billion short tons (USDOT Bureau of Transportation Statistics, 2002). The size of the market is a product of an extensive inland waterway system (in particular the Mississippi River Basin) and a number of overseas territories. The separation of Hawaii and Alaska from the continental US adds considerably to the size of the domestic market. Carriers in the market are heavily regulated, but subsidized by numerous Maritime Administration programs and protected by the cabotage rules[2] to be discussed later. Despite the protection of the market, US operations are sufficiently costly that the market is depressed and much of what could travel by vessel moves on rail or road, where the cargo interests are not captive by virtue of product characteristics or network structure to marine options. The age of the US-flag fleet is testimony to the problems of earning sufficient capital for fleet renewal, given the US-build requirements. Of all of the vessels flagged in the three countries, those sailing under the US flag comprise 91.5 per cent of the total deadweight tonnage (UNCTAD, 2006, Annex IIIB).
2. *Canadian domestic marine transportation*. Compared with the US, the Canadian domestic market is considerably smaller, with an estimated 69.5 million tonnes handled of a 395 million tonnes of total domestic and international cargo (Public Works and Government Services Canada, 2006). Like the US, it too is a protected one supplied by aging

vessels. Existing services in Atlantic Canada are quite extensive and often built on geographical necessity, such as the services to Newfoundland, outport resupply, and energy shipments. On the west coast, the log trade is substantial and captive. The other two significant markets comprise of largely bulk trades on the Great Lakes and northern resupply in the summer months. In Canada, the primary deterrent to domestic fleet renewal is not a 'build in Canada' requirement but rather a punitive tariff on imported ships (25 per cent), and the Canadian Coast Guard's vessel regulatory regime that requires an operator to convert the vessel to meet unique Canadian regulations.[3] Of all of the vessels flagged in the three countries, those sailing under the Canadian flag comprise 5.9 per cent of the total deadweight tonnage (UNCTAD, 2006, Annex IIIB).

3. *Mexican domestic marine transportation*. Here, too, the market is closed and it has been very difficult to find information on the industry and its characteristics. Off-the-record discussions with industry watchers indicate that the Mexican industry is also not healthy. Of all of the vessels flagged in the three countries, those sailing under the US flag comprise 2.6 per cent of the total deadweight tonnage (UNCTAD, 2006, Annex IIIB). As little more is known about Mexican shipping activities, this region is sadly not included in most of the discussion in this chapter.
4. *Foreign flag international shipping*. Foreign flag carriers have the ability to operate within NAFTA, as long as they meet the restrictions imposed by the cabotage regulations of each country. This means that a non-national flag vessel cannot carry cargoes between two domestic ports, but all moves must be international. This usually results in a one call per country network. Excellent examples of the resulting route decisions of shipping companies include the transborder ferry operations between Victoria, BC, and Port Angeles, WA; Yarmouth, NS and Bar Harbor, ME, and the truck ferry that operates between Detroit, MI, and Windsor, ON. If more than one port is called, ballast legs[4] become a feature of the service and result in lower asset utilization and diminished profitability. The inability to triangulate operations has been blamed for the failure of businesses forced into shuttle operations.

The state of the existing maritime market can be seen in its small transport share accruing to each of the NAFTA countries, compared with their position in global trading circles (Table 5.1). The region is a key global trading area, yet the size of each country's participation in maritime transport is not commensurate with its role as a global trading nation. It could be argued that this is a result of the large land mass that comprises North America.

Table 5.1 The relative state of North American shipping

Country	Rank in goods exports	Rank in goods imports	DWT owned[1]	Share of world fleet	% Domestic flag
US	2	1	46.3 M	5.5%	22.2%
Canada	9	10	5.9 M	0.7%	42.4%
Mexico	13	14	NA	NA	NA

Note: 1. Total cargo carrying capacity (DWT) of the number of vessels over 1000 gross registered tons owned. 1.3 million DWT are registered under the Mexican flag; how much is owned is not known. Mexico's circumstances as beneficial owners of shipping are not available as UNCTAD tracks only the top 35 *owning* nations.

Source: Calculated from data provided by World Trade Organization (2006), Table 1.5, and UNCTAD (2006), Table 16.

However, short sea shipping is the second most common mode of transport in that large land mass called the European Union; in North America, with its extensive coastline, maritime transport is a less visible option.

As already seen in Tables 1.4 and 2.1, marine transport is not as large a player in North American transport as might be expected, given this continental geography. Problematically, most of the international trade between the three countries is carried in foreign flag vessels. The participation of Canadian and US owners is predominantly through foreign flag tonnage (Table 5.1). Canadian owners in international shipping activities prefer to choose a foreign flag, with 57.6 per cent of the Canadian-owned fleet registered under foreign flag; the US percentage is even higher at 77.8 per cent (UNCTAD, 2006, Table 16). That said, the US flag fleet is significant, with 5.3 per cent of the world fleet measured in deadweight tonnes, while as already noted, the Canadian and Mexican registered fleets are a small fraction of the size of the US-registered fleet. Given the magnitude of shipping owned by US interests, and the industry expertise held by Americans, the US stance on protecting their maritime transport market from 'challenge' by Canadian and Mexican shipping interests is, to state the obvious, surprising.

Prior to the *North American Free Trade Agreement*, Canada's sales of water transportation services to the US were substantially less than its purchases from the US, but in the years since the agreement was signed, the two have moved within a narrow band of activity. It was only in 2003 and 2004, when Canada's currency began its sharp appreciation against the US dollar that the relationship between sales and purchases of water transportation services seemed to move out of sync with each other (Figure 5.1).

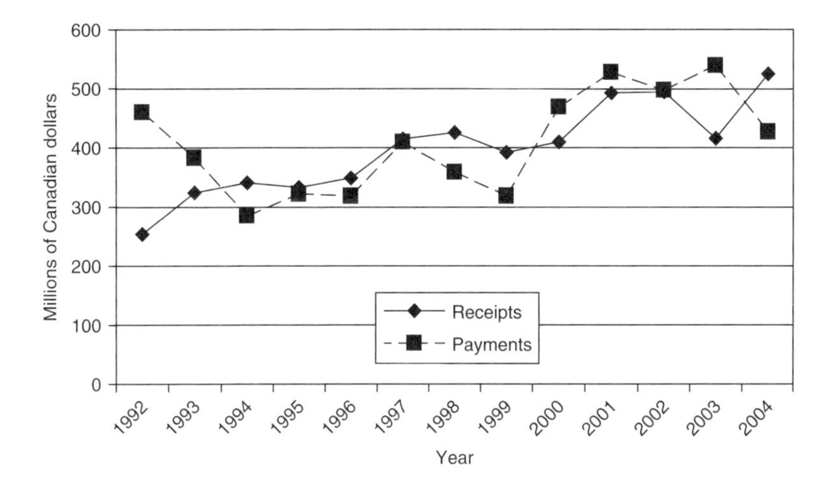

Source: Adapted from data extracted from CANSIM Table 376-0032 ('International transactions in services, transportation by category, annual dollars', special tabulations) by Statistics Canada staff, 28 February, 2006.

Figure 5.1 Payments and receipts for Canada–US water transportation services

Table 5.2 identifies the NAFTA international marine cargo activity between the US and its two NAFTA partners. The importance of Great Lakes and Gulf traffic is clearly evident, but most noticeable is the distinctive cargo imbalance between imports and exports for particular origin or destination states. This further underscores the inefficiencies in protecting maritime trade for a particular flag; it is quite clear that triangulation is needed to ensure optimum asset utilization.

Canada's domestic marine traffic volumes are considerably smaller than its transborder waterborne trade with the US. While the domestic traffic, subject to cabotage regulation, has had very low growth levels since the *Canada–US Trade Agreement*, transborder growth has been healthy (Figure 5.2). Transborder waterborne cargo was relatively well balanced prior to the *NAFTA* (Figure 5.3) but ex-Canada volumes have grown much more rapidly since *NAFTA* than ex-US volumes. The traffic has become more imbalanced over the past decade, with US export volume to Canada stagnating in the period after 2001.

Most of Canada's cabotage trade uses Canadian flag vessels; in the last few years, the share held by foreign flag vessels operating under waiver has grown to an average of 4 per cent (Transport Canada, 2006, Table A8-14). A waiver system does not exist in US cabotage operations and interpretation of the *Jones Act* has resulted in a totally closed market. The less

Table 5.2 Maritime cargo activity in the NAFTA region, 2005

Weight of exports by vessel (short tons)			
From US state	**To Canada**	**To Mexico**	**US–NAFTA**
All US states	**39 190 569**	**25 120 293**	**64 310 863**
Texas	1 695 576	13 475 618	15 171 194
Louisiana	540 451	7 517 188	8 057 639
Missouri	6 101 266	4 555	6 105 821
Michigan	5 620 094	10 151	5 630 245
Minnesota	4 747 915	30 273	4 778 188
Weight of imports by vessel (short tons)			
To US state	**From Canada**	**From Mexico**	**US–NAFTA**
All US states	**79 149 518**	**112 413 751**	**191 563 269**
Texas	3 751 136	62 727 840	66 478 976
Louisiana	756 814	16 512 097	17 268 911
Mississippi	23	11 933 995	11 934 018
California	4 360 430	6 998 145	11 358 575
Ohio	8 874 523	56 893	8 931 416

Source: Selected data from US Department of Transportation, Research and Innovative Technology Administration (2006), Table A-8: 24.

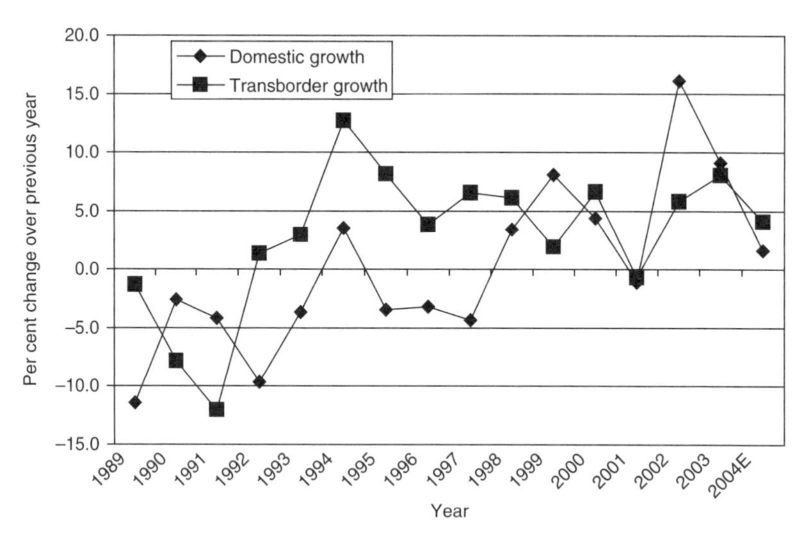

Source: Adapted from data from Statistics Canada as reported by Transport Canada (2006), Table A8-13: 'Canada's marine traffic statistics by sector, 1986–2004', *Shipping in Canada* (Catalogue 54-205), Ottawa: Statistics Canada.

Figure 5.2 Growth in Canada's maritime traffic (1989–2004)

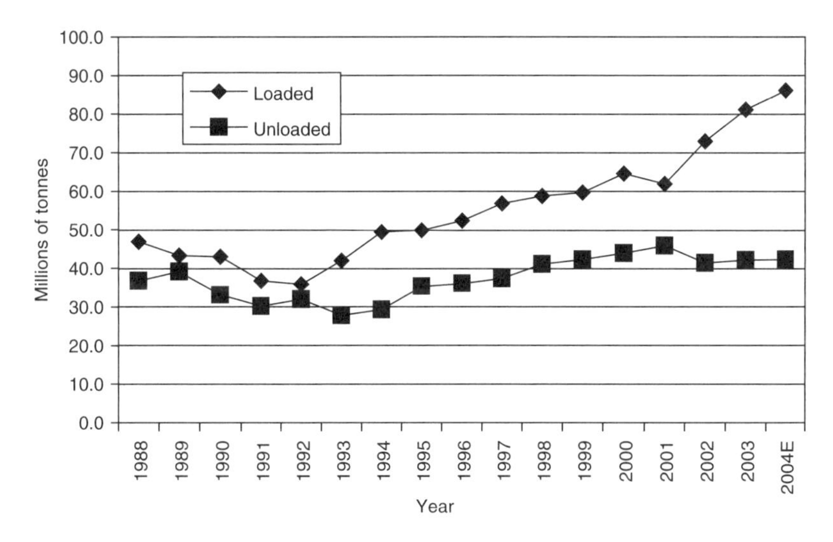

Source: Adapted from Transport Canada (2006), Table A8-16: 'Canada's marine traffic statistics by sector, 1986–2004', *Shipping in Canada* (Catalogue 54-205), Ottawa: Statistics Canada.

Figure 5.3 Canada–US waterborne cargo loaded and unloaded in Canada

protected transborder market has the appearance of being a slightly healthier one.

The regulation of domestic shipping in all three countries reflects long-held protectionist philosophies. In the US, Chapters 24 and 27 of the US *Merchant Marine Act of 1920* (also known as the *Jones Act*) state that cargo may not be transported between two US ports unless it is transported by vessels owned by citizens of the US, built and registered in the US, and manned by a crew of US nationals. While the *Jones Act* looks to be a philosophy of the last century, it actually reflects anti-British sentiment dating back to the American Revolutionary War. The second act to be passed by the new Congress in 1789 promulgated cabotage as a response to the pre-war requirement to use British-flagged ships in colonial traffic (Brooks, 2006). The cost of cabotage protection to the US taxpayer has been well documented by the US International Trade Commission (2002).

Canada and Mexico also practise protectionist policies. With the passage of the *Coasting Trade Act* in 1992, Canada closed domestic shipping to all but Canadian ships, albeit with a waiver provision, reconfirming 'the same protectionist philosophy that has existed ever since Canada inherited its coasting trade regime from Britain' (Hodgson and Brooks, 2004, p. 51). Mexico too wishes to protect its small and aging domestic fleet.

While the protection of coasting trade is contrary to the overall liberalized trade intentions of both the *NAFTA* and the *CUSTA*, as already noted in Chapter 1, the US was not prepared in either negotiation to open the market by providing access in shipping. While many countries do impose restrictions on domestic shipping, 'the scope of US restrictions is almost certainly unparalleled' (Hodgson and Brooks, 2004, p. 62). This means that North American cabotage policies are significantly at odds with trends in other shipping markets. For example, in Europe, an EU-flagged ship is eligible to participate in the cabotage trades on any other EU state. Furthermore, tonnage tax, or an equivalent, is formally endorsed as EU-wide policy and available in the large majority of European States, effectively reducing corporate tax to very low levels[5] and eliminating the difference in the cost of conducting operations between the domestic and the international sectors of the industry. The result is that maritime transport companies can allocate vessels to either domestic or international sectors of the industry as circumstances dictate, and each part of the business is able to support the other through an adverse business cycle. Such is not the case in either Canada[6] or the US.

The pro-cabotage (or protectionist) political lobby in the US is currently very strong; this has meant that the maritime transport sector has received less attention within NAFTA than the land transport modes in the network. It has also meant that trade irritants in the sector have not had a forum like the Land Transportation Standards Subcommittee for discussion and resolution.

In Canada, the desire to continue coasting trade protection is less fervent than in the US. In 2001, as part of the government's mandated transportation regulatory review, the Canada Transportation Act Review Panel recommended that Canada make its preference for eliminating the restrictions on entry to domestic shipping in the *Coasting Trade Act* clear to the US and offer to negotiate equivalent bilateral elimination (Public Works and Government Services Canada, 2001, p. 146). It does not appear that this recommendation has been accepted.

Both Canada and the US face a situation where the capital cost of a new vessel makes many service possibilities uncompetitive, there is a looming crew shortage, and the regulatory climate erects a firewall between domestic and international shipping (the rest of the world does not have such a firewall). In the maritime transport sector, it is reasonable to say that the interests of each country are not well understood by the others. As a result, operators, with only a few exceptions, focus on retaining protectionism and subsidies. It is also likely that the situation in Mexico mirrors that in Canada and the US.

Among developed countries, there is currently nowhere in the maritime transport world more dysfunctional than North America.[7] However, all is not doom and gloom. Both Canada and the US have cooperated in their efforts to reduce substandard shipping, and they have cooperated on studying short sea opportunities within the region.

As for the former, both Canada and the US participate in vessel inspection programs to keep continental waters safer and to prevent pollution from substandard shipping, and cooperate on the exchange of data supporting these efforts. While Canada belongs to both the 1982 Paris *Memorandum of Understanding on Port State Control* and later joined the Tokyo MOU, the US has adopted the principles of port state control, but not membership in these organizations. The US preference for its own program (and observer status at international meetings on port state control) has not prevented the two countries from exchanging data and working with the US Coast Guard to coordinate efforts.

As for the second area of cooperation, Canada and the United States signed a *Memorandum of Cooperation on Sharing Short Sea Shipping Information and Experience* (*MOC*) in July 2003, and the agreement was renamed and extended to Mexico on 6 November 2003.[8] Its objective was to collaborate on examining the future potential of this transport option to all-land transportation, and it provides a vehicle for the three countries to share research findings and advance knowledge in areas like new technologies. The promise of change in North American maritime transport in future is discussed further in the section on short sea shipping, later in this chapter.

MARINE COMPANIES' VIEWS OF *NAFTA*

Because maritime companies did not gain a more liberalized environment, the questions posed to maritime companies clearly needed to be different from the questions posed to those who had seen changes to the rules of engagement. The questions were asked of US shipping companies, and nine interviews were undertaken with those engaged in domestic trades, of which five had some form of international operations as well.

When asked about European-style regulatory reform,[9] eight companies had opinions they were prepared to share. Several were interested in seeing liberalization in other modes but not in the marine mode! One company was hopeful that the federal government might be interested in working with state governments to standardize regulations domestically. There was a clear indication of being comfortable in a protected market, and little interest on the part of those serving solely domestic markets to exploit any opportunities to grow their business through freer access to North American maritime markets. Two specifically mentioned that they would like to see US-build provisions relaxed, and one company was actually intrigued by the concept of an EU-style cabotage arrangement; this company thought that access to cheaper crew from elsewhere in the NAFTA region, plus relaxation of the build provisions might make them very competitive against their primary competition, the railroads. One company summed up liberalization within the NAFTA region using that great metaphor: 'It's got a snowball's chance in hell.' Two companies saw great opportunities in Mexico, while a third thought that the Canadian and Mexican markets were so small and therefore 'not worthwhile'.

Further probing about the concept of an expanded NAFTA cabotage region elicited three responses. One repeated the 'snowball's chance' comment, a second indicated that such a region would result in unfair and unwelcome competition, and the third was extremely positive towards the concept, seeking a 'NAFTA-endorsement' that would enable development of Gulf and Great Lakes short sea business.

Finally, the question on priorities for future negotiations[10] elicited seven responses. These focused primarily on improvements for other modes, but one was focused on the maritime sector:

> [We need a] review of the Seaway Commission and its fees. [The] Great Lakes needs to be made more competitive. It would make sense to explore a coastwise endorsement that was NAFTA-wide. Efforts on short sea are too hypothetical. Tomorrow's 1-95 is worrisome.

Brooks et al. (2006) would agree with this sentiment. They concluded that if short sea were to develop further on the East Coast of the US in any significant way, it would be forced by automobile owners desiring to remove trucks from this congested corridor.

MARINE COMPANIES' ASSESSMENT OF THE IMPACT OF SECURITY

In the US, following 9/11 and the subsequent reorganization of security agencies, the US Coast Guard was maintained as a separate entity within the Department of Homeland Security (DHS) to deal with maritime security issues, and not part of DHS' border and transportation security directorate. As the lead federal agency for the maritime component of homeland security, the Coast Guard is responsible for maritime border and transportation security in the US (Congressional Research Services, 2004, p. 3).

When companies were asked about maritime security from their point of view, the interest in the topic was palpable. The group was vocal and the messages consistent; there has been a change in focus by the company, an increase in paperwork (regulatory burden), the necessity of adding security-focused personnel, and one company indicated it felt forced to add a 'security surcharge' of 5 per cent to its freight rates.

To quote two marine carriers:

> There is much more focus on the requirements for security and on Health Safety and Environmental (HSE) plans. We now have an HSE director (new position) who is in charge of developing, administering and documenting HSE and Terminal Security plans.

> Container security is now of much greater importance, [both] site access and vessel security. Business tends to be more administratively burdensome as we comply with the requirements for security and record keeping. We have also experienced delays in port operations due to USCG security procedures, but in general we have adapted.

While customer mix did not change in any significant way for maritime companies (and they indicated they did not lose customers although some customer gain was noted), the views of maritime companies were divergent in their assessments of the impact of new security regulations. One felt forced into C-TPAT because customers demanded it; therefore, it was not a voluntary program. Some were quite vocal that the mandatory rules were costly to implement with little benefit to be gained, while others found that the costs were not too excessive, or that there were offsetting benefits such as efficiency gains and the ability to extract additional revenue. These opposing positions are reflected in the selected quotes from three different companies below:

> The security requirements that we've been forced to implement have been costly and have put up more barriers to conducting normal business. There is no way that any security requirements have aided us in streamlining business – quite the opposite.

> There have been efficiency gains from the 24-hour rule; we no longer have to chase people for documents; documentation is better. Difficulties complying with the ISPS Code and 24-hour rule are offset in benefits. Radiation monitoring and naturally occurring radiation were initially a problem.

> They [security requirements] have become part of the cost of doing business. In some ways, the additional security requirements have led to better accountability of our freight and have reduced loss.

When asked what changes would make security more cost-effective, the responses were quite diverse and given in a spirit of cooperation. There was some commonality of concern about the way in which grants have been awarded (those getting grants of course having a different view from those not), and the 'one size fits all' approach that not all felt was appropriate. Again, the quotes from five different companies are quite instructive:

> Implementing a tiered level of security requirements for port facilities depending on location, size, etc. would be helpful. It's not practical to require small port facilities to have the same level of security as the Port of Long Beach, for instance.

> We need to raise awareness and force our partners in the supply chain to adopt security measures. High security bolt seals should be used on containers; the manifest should list what is on the ship not necessarily its origin.

> Maybe a lot more electronic tracking instead of having our ships stopped for searches before they enter US ports.

> Regulations more tailored to the level of potential threat in a particular evolution or vessel type would be helpful. There are also regulations that add little to actual security and are administratively costly which could also be modified. Lastly there are some regulations that may actually impair security, AIS being an example.

> I believe the US Government must take responsibility for things that carriers cannot deal with, such as security on the offshore side of vessels.

Most surprising of all was the response of one company approached but who declined to participate in the research. The reasoning was that *NAFTA* is not only irrelevant but maritime security was not its problem; the security rules were only applicable to foreign companies! It was also clear that this one company believed that security was solely a problem for those who charter, not for those who own vessels. The concept of hijacking a vessel in US waters obviously did not occur to this company.

THE PROMISE OF NORTH AMERICAN SHORT SEA SHIPPING

While North America's coastline and river system is quite similar to Europe's marine network, the pattern of modal choice in the transport sector differs substantially from that seen in Europe; in Europe, road accounts for 44 per cent of the European Union's goods transport market, with short sea shipping accounting for the next largest share at 41 per cent (European Commission, 2001, pp. 12, 24). These facts indicate that short sea shipping could be a stronger player in the continental transportation network.

Since 2003 and the signing of the *MOC*, Canada and the United States have begun to examine the potential of short sea shipping, primarily because it affords a means to remove trucks from congested highways and is seen as an environmentally-friendly option to road transport. Both Transport Canada and the US Maritime Administration have provided financial support to workshops and studies to examine these issues. They also, along with the Mexican government, supported a three-country conference, the *North American Marine Conference: Towards a North American Short Sea Shipping Strategy*, in Vancouver, BC in the spring of 2006, to discuss publicly the issues needed to make short sea more institutionally likely to happen.

Shortly after signing the *MOC*, the Canadian government embarked on an assessment of short sea shipping through a series of workshops and studies. The US has explored short sea domestically through SCOOP (the Maritime Administration's Short Sea Shipping Cooperative Program), through the US Department of Transportation support for other initiatives, such as those of the Whatcom Council of Governments (discussed later), and regionally through the Gulf of Mexico States Accord. These are, of course, in addition to state-funded initiatives such as that undertaken by the Connecticut Department of Transportation (2001). Each of these larger studies is discussed below.

As a result of the cross-Canada workshops run by Transport Canada, Brooks and Frost (2004) identified a number of impediments to the development of short sea shipping between Canada and the US in addition to the severe cabotage restrictions. These included the Harbor Maintenance Tax (HMT)[11] on shallow draft vessels, advance notification rules that were designed for transoceanic moves applicable to short sea operations, and Canadian Customs charges at new operations. These will be discussed in more detail later in this section.

On the East Coast, funding for a North American study was provided under the Strategic Highway Infrastructure Partnership program and the study was completed in March 2006 (Brooks et al., 2006). It drew a number of conclusions about the commercial feasibility of the trade, and about shipper requirements; more importantly here, it drew a number of conclusions about the changes needed in the regulatory and institutional environment. The issues raised differed little from those found by the earlier workshops, confirming that policy changes are needed before the market will commit to what is perceived to be a risky venture.

On the West Coast, the International Mobility and Trade Corridor Project undertook two studies of short sea shipping with funding from the US Department of Transportation and Transport Canada, and managed by the Whatcom Council of Governments. The purpose of the study was to determine the potential of short sea shipping in West Coast cross-border freight traffic, describe the most feasible service type(s), and suggest supporting actions that governments could take. Phase 1 examining existing services is complete and identified a number of problems similar to those found by Brooks et al. (2006) on the east coast, including problems with the advanced notification rules and the need to engage trucking as a partner. Phase 2 (Cambridge Systematics Inc., 2007) examined shipper requirements, commodity flows, locations of potential marine hubs, vessel options, intermodal infrastructure and technology, and found that high labour costs and customs clearance rules, delays and fees were significant impediments to the further development of commercially viable, cross-border short sea operations. Cambridge Systematics Inc (2007, p. 6) reported 'border delays (up to 2–4 hours per crossing), border surcharges (roughly $75 per movement), and the lack of delivery time reliability are the main problems with respect to cross-border trucking services. This is what is generating interest in short sea shipping.' While interest in short sea may be latent, as evidenced by many of these studies, the regulation of short sea remains an impediment to the attraction of cargoes from the road mode.

In the Great Lakes, there appeared to be interest in short sea services involving the Port of Hamilton, ON, both cross-lakes and between Hamilton and east coast Canadian ports. As most Ontario origin/destination cargo currently moves by rail and given prevailing rail rates between Halifax, NS, and Toronto, ON, a study was funded by the Transport Development Centre of Transport Canada to examine the potential of a Halifax–Hamilton service. MariNova Consulting Limited (2005) concluded that domestic short sea shipping is not viable where a short sea service would run parallel to an existing rail service that is competitively priced (that is, Halifax–Hamilton), and that it is useful in those areas experiencing road or border congestion.[12] While a domestic study, it underlined significant problems in the Canadian regulatory environment (including the high tariff on imported ships) that make short sea less likely to succeed commercially.

In the US, the US Department of Transportation hired Global Insight for a study due in the fall of 2005, but its focus was also for domestic short sea services only. Furthermore, the consultation process required that the consultant must include shipbuilding stakeholders, which ultimately indicated that the build provisions in the US would remain protected. Global Insight (2006) concluded that the principal obstacles to the development of short sea shipping are the high cost of domestically-built cargo vessels, high stevedoring and crew costs, and the HMT assessed on domestic shipments. When taken in combination with MariNova Consulting Limited (2005), it is clear that problems will exist in any effort to harmonize the regulation of shipping between Canada and the US.

The Gulf of Mexico States Accord is trying to get Gulf of Mexico routes on the radar screen in Washington and elsewhere but faces an uphill battle. The regional grouping clearly have a point: 89 per cent of total US–Mexico trade goes through the land border ports, and Gulf shipping would alleviate environmental problems, trade congestion, and disperse NAFTA trade while growing the total trade volume. The same can be said of Canada–US trade; bottlenecks at the border and on major land arterial corridors carrying Canada–US freight are becoming severely congested. Yet, while the US Government Accountability Office (2005) recognized the serious congestion problem the US faces in handling future freight requirements, it did not look beyond its borders and think continentally. The GAO report defines short sea as a domestic mode. Likewise, Cambridge Systematics Inc. (2005), in its study of East Coast ports and the potential for short sea shipping as an alternative to trucking in the I-95 corridor, included the Canadian port of Saint John, NB, in the list of coalition ports, but there was nothing in the conclusions and recommendations that indicated international short sea shipping was otherwise considered in the scope of the report. These two alone provide further evidence that continental perspectives are not first and foremost in the political mindset of the very country that dominates North American free trade.

To illustrate the challenge cabotage rules impose, a Canadian- or US-owned foreign-flag vessel could carry cargo from Halifax to Portland, ME, and Boston, MA (without the ability to pick up cargo in Portland for Boston), and pick up cargo in either of those two ports bound for Bermuda or Canada; given the imbalance of trading patterns resulting in unused capacity, coupled with the inability to fill the space between Portland and Boston, the vessel struggles to make a profit on the total route. Needless to say, the cargo is more likely to travel over the road (for all but Bermuda legs) or not at all. Currently, most cargo bound for Bermuda travels over the road to New York, and then on by sea or by air freight. A second example would be a vessel operating between Tampa, FL, and southern Mexico on the Gulf Coast; more than one coastal stop in the US (for example, New Orleans, LA) might provide enough cargo to make a Mexican service viable with an international flag vessel, but the imbalance of cargo northbound means that other destinations are needed, and yet a ballast leg is required to return to the starting point of the cycle; the resulting asset utilization means the traffic is handled by road.

Consistently, research has concluded that a number of policy challenges need to be addressed if short sea is to work. These are outlined below.

The US Harbor Maintenance Tax applies to marine cargo arriving from NAFTA partners as well as those from overseas. The HMT does not apply to passenger vessels so the vessel operator cannot really mix passenger and freight (if this were desired). The tax is not related to the type of vessel and therefore it applies to shallow draft vessels as well as deep-draft ones (clearly an ironic situation). As the tax is paid by the cargo owner on the value of the cargo ($125 per $100 000 of cargo), it discourages auto parts manufacturers from using the Detroit–Windsor Truck Ferry, even though the Ambassador Bridge between those cities is highly congested and LTL truckers returning from Canada would need to contact every shipper for permission to use the marine option (Ward, 2005). Furthermore, the HMT penalizes cargo owners who choose short sea shipping over truck, even though truck may be less environmentally friendly; Brooks et al. (2006, p. 71) note that:

> [The tax] may be viewed as working, at least theoretically, in Canada's favour since, by unloading US-bound cargo in Canadian ports and moving it overland, the tax is avoided, thus making Canadian ports attractive in relation to their US counterparts. . . . However, it serves to stimulate rather than discourage a shift to the use of land modes, and therefore works at variance with the thrust of the arguments for encouraging short sea shipping.

The primary purpose of the tax is to fund dredging activities, but most short sea services use shallower draft vessels in ports not requiring dredging. Furthermore, the US government collects far more tax under the *Water Resources Development Act* than is currently expended by the US Army Corps of Engineers in dredging. It is clear that a reconsideration of the tax is required in the context of not just US domestic shipping, as is currently happening with discussion of H.R.1701.[13]

Seasonality and weather pose challenges to year-round service. MariNova Consulting Limited (2005), a study of Canadian domestic short sea services between Halifax and Hamilton, concluded that the major hurdle to implementation of profitable short sea shipping in the St. Lawrence Seaway is the requirement by shippers for uninterrupted service in winter on a route where the Seaway is closed in winter. Furthermore, the study also noted that existence of the 25 per cent duty on foreign-built ships used in Canada was 'a serious impediment'.

Barriers to new route development also exist. For example, Canada charges a $3100 flat fee for ice-breaking in the Lakes, whether the vessel goes 10 miles or across the Lakes. Customs cost recovery in Canada applies to any new routing option but not to existing ones, which also discourages development of any new network options that might otherwise be viable.

Under the *Maritime Transportation Security Act of 2002*, advanced notification rules for marine cargoes are the most stringent when compared with those for truck, rail and air. While they may be relatively acceptable for overseas cargo, they raise an important impediment to the use of short sea. Brooks et al. (2006, p. 80) noted:

> Efforts must be undertaken to convince the Department of Homeland Security to reduce the advance notification requirements on NAFTA-originating ship-

> ments to terms more suitable to their geographic proximity. This has happened for US-to-Canada shipments, but not in the other direction. Without this, marine-based transportation will never succeed in securing cargo from the road mode.

This point of view is reinforced by the Phase 1 findings of the I-5 short sea corridor study (Whatcom Council of Governments, 2004).

Finally, it appears throughout all the research that social costs have not been addressed. There has been little focus on examining the issue of who should bear the costs of road congestion and air pollution and their mitigation. The prevailing dilemma in North America is one of no one wanting to deal forcefully with this growing global concern.

Brooks et al. (2006) concluded, as a result of their detailed examination of the current policy environment in Canada and the US, that the Canadian government should give some consideration to fixing the situation through regulatory convergence. Of particular interest, Brooks et al. (2006, p. 63) found that

> under current national shipping policy regime, the commercial benefits flowing from the provision of short sea service, beyond those accruing to the shippers and ports, would only likely be of modest benefit to Canada. At the same time, the shift of cargo off the land routes would presumably negatively impact land-based Canadian transportation service providers, be they truckers or rail services. Thus, unless there is some change in Canadian shipping policy, a successful transition to a short sea shipping service, for a given level of cargo transportation demand, is likely to result in a net loss of business to Canadian transportation service providers.

Yet, the likelihood of a move to regulatory convergence in this mode is minute. Neither the Canadian government nor the American government has maritime transportation high on the list of funding priorities. There was no SEA-21 money in the latest budget authorization process in the US, and the marine mode in Canada receives less financial support than either road or rail activities (Transport Canada, 2005a, Table 3-3). In 2005, the three governments signed the *Security and Prosperity Partnership of North America*, which sets out a plan of actions, committed to by the three government leaders, to push for further developments within the NAFTA free trade area. There is little action planned in the area of maritime transport, except as it relates to maritime security. More than continental security is at stake. It is time to begin to discuss the forgotten marine mode, and how change may be made to improve both the North American transportation network and marine access to and from the world. Future maritime competitiveness is a key component of North America's global competitiveness.

THE AIR MODE FROM OPEN SKIES 1995 TO OPEN SKIES 2005

The only mention of air services in Chapter 12 of the *NAFTA* is with respect to repair and maintenance services and specialty air services. Both Mexico and Canada have entered into bilateral air transport agreements with the US. Technically, however, it is not correct to consider air a forgotten mode. This mode has its own institutions and the International Civil Aviation Organization (ICAO) for debating and addressing the international regulation of the industry, although Oum (1998, p. 129) believed that liberalization of aviation would stand a better chance of succeeding if it was addressed in a multilateral framework like the General Agreement on Trade in Services. While it all began in 1919 with the *Paris Convention*, which established that each country controls the airspace over its territory, the primary multilateral treaty governing air transport today was signed during World War II. The *Chicago Convention of International Civil Aviation of 1944* sets the terms and conditions that apply to international aviation, both cargo and passenger. It not only continues the notion of airspace sovereignty, but it also establishes that all flights between any two countries are subject to the bilateral agreement signed between the countries; these are known as air service agreements (ASAs). The common language embodied in the convention lists nine 'freedoms' applicable to the specified routes, and unless both countries agree to higher order freedoms, the de facto default in most ASAs is a state of cabotage protection.[14]

Until 1966, Canada's air transport relationship with the United States was one of limited access and tight control; this changes in 1966 with a new ASA between the two countries permitting a significant increase in the number of transborder point-to-point flights. According to a timeline of Canada–US air relations reported by WESTAC (1991), more routes were added in 1974 and this marked the year preclearance was introduced to major Canada-US routes.[15] From 1979 to 1982, seven more rounds of negotiations took place and, in 1984, agreement was reached on new rules for commuter services for city-pairs not included in the 1974 amendment. It was during this period that the first offer from the US to 'open the border' was made.

On the US side, January 1977 marked the beginning of US interest in liberalization. The Carter Administration, according to Doganis (2002), was interested in harnessing the advantages of liberalization for US consumers and the US industry. This was articulated in a policy statement indicating that US air transport negotiations would aim 'to provide greater possible benefit to travelers and shippers' in a competitive environment and a fair market. While the US embarked, in the period 1978–1991, on a path of liberalization, beginning with a revised US–Netherlands ASA, the features of this liberalization approach focused on removing frequency and capacity restrictions, and on acquiring international open access (in the foreign markets), but did not incorporate cabotage. As such, the promise of open access did not materialize; domestic operations would remain protected.

By 1984, the Canada–US ASA consisted of five separate agreements: (1) the 1966 *Air Transport Agreement* (amended in 1974); (2) *All-Cargo Notes*, signed in 1966; (3) *Non-Scheduled Services Agreement* (1974); (4) *Preclearance Agreement* (1974); and (5) the *Regional, Local and Commuter Services Agreement* (1984).

Concurrently, deregulation of the air transport industry was taking place on both sides of the border, with Canada lagging behind the US. Canadian air transport deregulation took place in 1984, although the legislation that would put it into effect, the *National Transportation Act, 1987*, was not passed until three years later.[16] Carriers operating in domestic service must be safety certified by Transport Canada and licensed by the Canadian Transportation Agency. Otherwise, carriers are, for the most part, free to decide routes, aircraft type to be deployed on the routes, fares, and so on. Current legislation only permits Canadian-owned and operated domestic air services.

In 1985, Canada offered to open both domestic and transborder markets, but the US was only interested in liberalizing the transborder access. It also rejected the Canadian offer to operate domestically as an extension of a transborder service. When the Canada–US Trade Agreement negotiations began in 1986, air bilateral discussions were lost in the disagreement over marine issues. The air-specific negotiations restarted in April 1991. What is particularly interesting about the 1985 discussions is that Canada offered a more liberal environment than it has been prepared to accept in the period since, while the US established its baseline attitude towards 'open skies' agreements in general. The fact that this did not result in Canada gaining as many liberal access provisions as many other countries have achieved since raises questions about the benefits that may have been lost as a result.

According to Burney (2000, p. 6), the *Canada–US Trade Agreement* 'did pave the way for an open skies agreement, which is paying real dividends to the airlines and to the passengers'. The data available are clear; service has improved dramatically. In 1989, US airlines carried 62 per cent of the transborder traffic, yet it was much more important to Canadian airlines than to US carriers; 17 per cent of the traffic carried by Canadian carriers was transborder, while less than 2 per cent of US traffic was (WESTAC, 1991). Growth in transborder traffic after the agreement was quite dramatic, growing from 13.6 million passengers in 1994 (the last calendar year before the agreement) to 18.7 million passengers in 1998 (Transport Canada, 2000, p. 162). Annual growth was averaging 3.6 per cent in both 1992 and 1994, with growth after the agreement being 8.8 per cent in 1995, 15.6 per cent in 1996, 4.6 per cent in 1997 and 4.4 per cent in 1998. Both Canadian and US airlines participated in the growth; Canadian carriers grew market share from 43.3 per cent in 1994 to 50.6 per cent in 1998 (Transport Canada, 2000, p. 162).

By 2004, Canada had more than 70 air service agreements with other countries (Transport Canada, 2004), and in November 2005 signed an amendment to its Open Skies agreement with the US (to be discussed later). On the other hand, the US had, as of February 2006, signed Open Skies Agreements with 75 partner countries and Cargo-Only Open Skies Agreements with Argentina and Australia (US State Department, 2006).

Canada's approach to air transport regulation may be summed up as one that has gradually relied more on market forces but with gradual liberalization (Transport Canada, 2005d). As a result of this stance, Canada has not sought open skies agreements with non-US countries and now has a much less liberal international air cargo market position from which to grow than does the US.

Table 5.3 illustrates that transborder air passenger services followed the same pattern seen previously with cargo in other modes; there appears to be a reversal of fortune in the business, with a peak in 2000 and the possible beginning of a recovery in 2004. Part of this recovery may be traced to the establishment of new air services between Canada and the US; according to Transport Canada (2005a), in 2004, there were 34 new transborder services and seven discontinued services, for a net change in transborder air services of 27.

The pattern of a peak in 2000 and a subsequent decline is quite apparent on the goods side as well (Table 5.4). The intra-North America cargo

Table 5.3 Canada's air passenger traffic, 2000–2004 (000 passengers)

Air passengers	Domestic	Transborder	International	Total
2000	26 001	20 824	13 177	60 002
2001	24 994	18 568	13 196	56 757
2002	23 862	17 575	12 930	54 367
2003	24 434	16 809	12 661	53 903
2004	26 462	18 574	14 952	59 988

Note: Earlier years not available in this format.

Source: Transport Canada (2005a), Table 9-1: 'Air Passenger Traffic, 2000–2004', Statistics Canada, *Transportation in Canada 2004 Annual Report*, Ottawa: Public Works and Government Services Canada. Reproduced with the permission of the Minister of Public Works and Government Services Canada, 2007.

Table 5.4 Value of international goods shipped by air, 1998–2005 (in millions of Canadian dollars)

Year Canada/US	Air exports	Air imports	Air total	All modes	Air share (per cent)
1998	13 980	18 656	32 636	473 487	6.9
1999	17 521	20 182	37 703	523 649	7.2
2000	23 845	23 643	47 488	588 947	8.1
2001	21 875	21 114	42 989	570 040	7.5
2002	18 905	17 412	36 318	563 806	6.4
2003	17 290	15 418	32 708	530 397	6.2
2004	15 770	16 247	32 017	556 486	5.8
2005P	16 727	15 741	32 467	579 806	5.6

Source: Transport Canada (2006), Table A9-13: 'Value of international goods shipped by air, 1995–2005', adapted from Statistics Canada, special tabulations; *Transportation in Canada 2005 Annual Report Addendum*, Ottawa: Public Works and Government Services Canada. Reproduced with the permission of the Minister of Public Works and Government Services Canada, 2007.

market has strong truck–air competition. Crockatt (2005, p. 8) noted that 'In the United States domestic air cargo sector, the three largest express carriers (FedEx, UPS and DHL) carry nearly three times as much freight and mail as the remaining 11 passenger/combination carriers.'

He went on to examine the competition from transborder truck in the time-definite market.

> [T]he proliferation of time-deferred services into North American supply chains has had an impact on air cargo growth. . . . Their success spawned imitators among combination air carriers, logistics firms and LTL (less-than-truckload) service providers, all now trying to win some of the business carved out by FedEx and UPS. Compounding this, in the days immediately following 9/11, firms in North America were forced to manage their supply chains essentially with no air cargo service. Many companies quickly discovered they could survive quite well without air freight. Time-definite trucking services proved themselves to be reliable and could offer much lower rates than any company shipping by air. . . . [E]ven traditional air cargo carriers have realized they can provide excellent service at a lower cost and maintain profitability by using trucks instead of airplanes. (Crockatt, 2005, p. 9)

While Table 5.4 appears to indicate a peak in traffic in 2000 with a subsequent decline in value terms, it is somewhat deceptive. In tonnage terms, as noted in Figure 5.4, traffic inbound to Canada is somewhat more vibrant with outbound in distant second. Air is much less common in either Canadian or US trade with Mexico, being limited to highly perishable commodities.

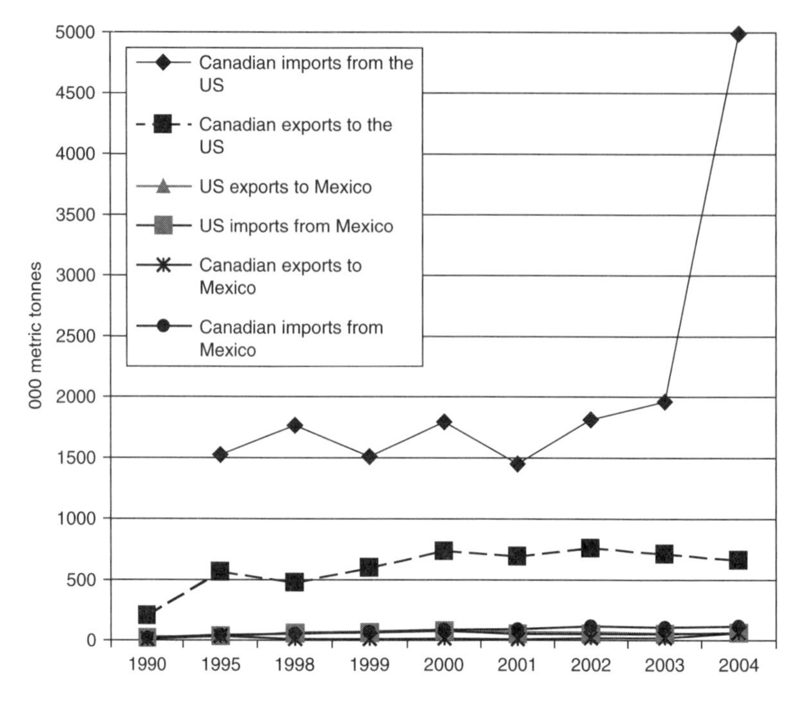

Note: Because each country defines and collects merchandise trade data differently, these numbers should be treated as approximate only. Detailed use should rely on the original data available at the NATS website. This figure is based on data in Tables 6-2c and 6-1c of the NATS.

Source: Selected from North American Transportation Statistics (NATS) database, January 2006.

Figure 5.4 North American air transport in tonnage terms

On 24 February 1995, an Open Skies ASA was signed between Canada and the US. (The key provisions are found in Box 5.1.) This agreement provided Canadian and US carriers with access to transborder routes and liberalized the frequency of service and fares that airlines could charge. It did not cover preclearance, which is negotiated separately, and a separate transition regime was applied to all-cargo services. Entry by US airlines was phased in at Canada's three largest airports – Montreal, QC, Vancouver and Toronto. All-cargo courier services were not permitted to practise co-terminalization;[17] the sole exception to be granted was a UPS northbound service from Louisville, KY to Hamilton and Toronto that was grandfathered as a permanent co-terminalization right for scheduled and charter services (Janda et al., 2005, p. 77).

BOX 5.1 MAIN ELEMENTS OF THE 1995 AGREEMENT

1. Airlines may serve any route between Canada and the US.
2. New US airline service at Montreal, Toronto and Vancouver to be phased in over three years.
3. Access to Washington National Airport (until now restricted to US domestic flights from Canadian airports) with customs pre-clearance facilities.
4. Fourteen free takeoff and landing slots for Canadian carriers at LaGuardia Airport (New York) and 10 at O'Hare Airport (Chicago).
5. Additional slots at congested US airports to be acquired under domestic 'buy-sell' rules.
6. Open code-sharing (i.e., ticketing passengers under their own code but carrying them on other airlines) among Canadian and US airlines.
7. Liberalization of the process for approval of Canada–US fares.
8. New dispute resolution process sets up an international panel to resolve violations of agreement.

Source: Transport Canada (1997), *Transportation in Canada 1996 Annual Report (TP13012)*, Ottawa: Public Works and Government Services Canada, p. 25. Reproduced with the permission of the Minister of Public Works and Government Services Canada, 2007.

Canada's Foreign Affairs Minister of the day, Lloyd Axworthy, said (Transport Canada, 1996, np): 'The new air agreement with the US has created the world's most competitive aviation market in support of the world's largest trade and travel relationship.' During the period between 1995 and 2000, air traffic grew by an average of 7.3 per cent per year and over 100 new routes were added by the airlines in that market (Transport Canada, 2005b, p. 1). The number of services grew quickly in the months after the signing of the agreements, as seen in Table 5.5, and continued to grow throughout the remainder of the 1990s. In 2001, the Canada–US Air Travel Agreement was reached with the objective of expanding pre-clearance services at Canadian and US airports, as well as in transit pre-clearance for third-country passengers travelling to the US and passing through a Canadian airport.

Table 5.5 Comparison of services before and after 1995 agreement

Services operated airport	February 1995			February 1997			As of December 1999		
	Canada	US	Total	Canada	US	Total	Canada	US	Total
Toronto/ Pearson	14	23	37	30	27	57	45	24	69
Vancouver	6	10	16	11	15	26	9	22	31
Montreal/ Dorval	7	10	17	9	14	23	12	13	25
Calgary	4	5	9	4	9	13	8	8	16
Ottawa	1	6	7	3	5	8	7	6	13
Edmonton	–	3	3	–	3	3	2	2	4
Halifax	2	–	2	3	–	3	3	2	5
Winnipeg	1	1	2	1	1	2	2	1	3
Others[1]	4	9	13	2	9	11	0	12	12
Total	39	67	106	63	83	146	88	90	178

Note: 1. Includes charter conversions for 1999 figures but not for 1995 and 1997.

Source: Extracted from Transport Canada (1997, p. 30, Table 4-3: *Transportation in Canada 1996 Annual Report*) updated by Transport Canada (2000, p. 166, Appendix 13-1: *Transportation in Canada 1999 Annual Report*), Ottawa: Transport Canada. Reproduced with the permission of the Minister of Public Works and Government Services Canada, 2007.

While the Canada Transportation Act Review Panel recommended a North American Common Aviation Area (Public Works and Government Services Canada, 2001, p. 123, Recommendation 7.1), it also believed that the US adherence to its entrenched position of no change to existing cabotage meant that Canadian carriers would lose out; because of 'scope clauses' in existing pilot contracts at Federal Express, UPS and other US companies, agreeing to modified sixth freedom rights would reduce demand for the Canadian air cargo industry. As a result, Recommendation 7.1 included a caveat:

> As a backup option if negotiations do not succeed, the Panel recommends that the government negotiate with other countries for the reciprocal granting of modified sixth freedom rights and of rights of establishment for foreign-owned domestic carriers. (Public Works and Government Services Canada, 2001, p. 124)[18]

Three years later, the Air Currents conference was held in January 2004 seeking Canadian industry opinion on Canada's international air policy. Reporting on that conference, Janda et al. (2005) identified four international air policy issues for Canada relevant to the Canada–US relationship: (1) the concept of a NAFTA common aviation area; (2) Canada's policy approach to US–EU liberalization talks; (3) foreign ownership and the right of establishment; and (4) air cargo liberalization.

Janda et al. (2005, p. 78) also reported that in 2004, the US Ambassador to Canada of the day, Paul Cellucci, called for a reopening of the bilateral ASA and that, on 29 October 2004, the then-Minister of Transport, Jean Lapierre, indicated Canada's willingness to review, in particular, issues of 'co-terminalization and cabotage and even the possibility of integrating the two markets under a single set of rules'. Based on polling of the audience at the conference, Janda et al. (2005) concluded that there was support for a North American Common Aviation Area in the medium term and that, in the shorter term, Canada should pursue a bilateral with the US that focused on cargo, fifth freedom rights and modified sixth freedom liberalization. 'It would be appropriately ambitious for Canada to seek a fully integrated transport regime with the United States analogous to the Common Aviation Area in the EU' (Janda et al., 2005, p. 79).

On a broader front, Janda et al. (2005) also noted the European Union efforts to seek a Transatlantic Common Aviation Area through the negotiation of an EU–US ASA, and believed that Canada's absence from this discussion would be detrimental to Canada's interests. If the current system of bilateral agreements evolves in the way that Europe seeks – to a set of regional common aviation areas – then Canada needs to convince the players to convert the US–EU discussions to a trilateral agreement. Such a position has a clear window of opportunity that might now be closing. This view was also held by the Review Panel (Public Works and Government Services Canada, 2001). As a fallback position, Janda et al. (2005, p. 81) proposed that Canada negotiate a separate open ASA with Europe.

The third plank in a liberalization program identified by Janda et al. (2005) had to do with ownership restrictions. The OECD (1997) concluded that foreign ownership restrictions should be relaxed as these can be used to protect national carriers and impede the long-term restructuring of air transport towards greater efficiency. Button (1998) concluded that the equity limits distort incentives and constrain participation, citing as examples the British Airways 1993 support of USAir and KLM's bailout of Northwest in 1989.[19] In Europe, caps are set at 49 per cent, while in the US and Canada, 25 per cent is the limit. Since the beginning of the decade, there has been considerable discussion in Canada (for example, Public Works and Government Services Canada, 2001; Lazar (2003); Transport Canada, 2005c) about allowing the limits to rise to the European threshold[20] but no action has taken place.

> Canada's foreign ownership rules are obsolete: they reduce access to equity capital, do not support the generation of jobs in Canada, constrain the return to Canadian investors, act as an entry barrier, and are an impediment to the needed consolidation and rationalization in the full segment sector of the industry. (Dr. Michael Tretheway, Vice President and Chief Economist, InterVISTAS Consulting, as reported by Janda et al., 2005, p. 83).

Janda et al. (2005) concluded that relaxing or eliminating foreign ownership limits on Canadian carriers would not necessarily be to the detriment of Canadian service levels; it might encourage carriers to look for opportunities to serve marginal routes. They proposed a three-pronged approach to ownership: (1) allow foreign-owned domestic carriers (as is the current practice in Australia); (2) raise the foreign ownership cap to 49 per cent; and (3) proactively seek to alter the current multilateral restrictions on right of establishment.

Finally, there was the question of liberalizing the air cargo regime. It was on this issue that there was a bifurcation within Canada as to the appropriate policy position to be taken. As illustration, Peter Wallis, President and CEO of Van Horne Institute 'indicated there was strong support for unilateral open skies for all cargo services from US carriers and from Canadian airports' (Janda et al., 2005, p. 85), while Barry LaPointe, President of Kelowna Flight Services (a Canadian cargo service provider), 'characterized co-terminalization as the 'kiss of death for Canadian air freight' (Janda et al., 2005, p. 85). It was expected that co-terminalization would be a critical battleground for the Canadian negotiators. To resolve this issue, Janda et al. (2005, p. 85) concluded that many consumers and Canadian companies rely on all-cargo express services for international trade worldwide, and that the restrictions on all-cargo co-terminalization add costs to businesses and consumers in order to protect the prices in the domestic market; on these grounds, they suggested that cargo flight co-terminalization should be allowed.

While Janda et al. (2005) provided an excellent evaluation of what the industry thought Canada's negotiating position with the US should be, the official stance of the Canadian government is not so easily discerned and appears to have been a bit of a moving target as there were four Ministers in the portfolio in the short period from the Chrétien to the Harper Administration. The Minister of Transport, LaPierre (Liberal) initiated a review of Canada's international air policy in November 2004 (Transport Canada, 2004), including its policy with respect to both the US–EU negotiations and the transborder open skies position. Noting at the time (based on 2003 statistics) that the four top airlines in terms of scheduled passenger kilometers flown were American and that Air Canada was thirteenth in the world, the mandate identified a series of issues for further consideration in revising Canada's international air policy, including relaxing the regulatory restriction on Canadian ownership for Canadian air carriers, removing the statutory obligation of Canadian control for Canadian air carriers, and allowing foreign air carriers to operate air services in Canada's domestic market (for example, altering Canada's current cabotage environment). The intent of the document was to begin the process of establishing a Canadian policy, not just with respect to transborder services, but also in the context of Canada's global trading interest.

Prior to the Open Skies Agreement of 1995, Canada's sales of air transportation services to the US were usually higher than its purchases from the US (with the exception of 1999); in recent years the gap has closed, and in 2004 the balance of payments in air transport services is, well, balanced (Figure 5.5).

During 2005, the Government issued several documents (for example, Transport Canada, 2005c, 2005d, 2005e) as part of the consultation process with industry and the Canadian public, and this process helped it to define its position with the US and in the run-up to the meetings in Waco, TX in March 2005. The consultation process (Transport Canada, 2005c, p. 9) identified several restrictions that the 1995 Agreement and the US 'Open Skies' model do not address (Table 5.6), including fifth freedom

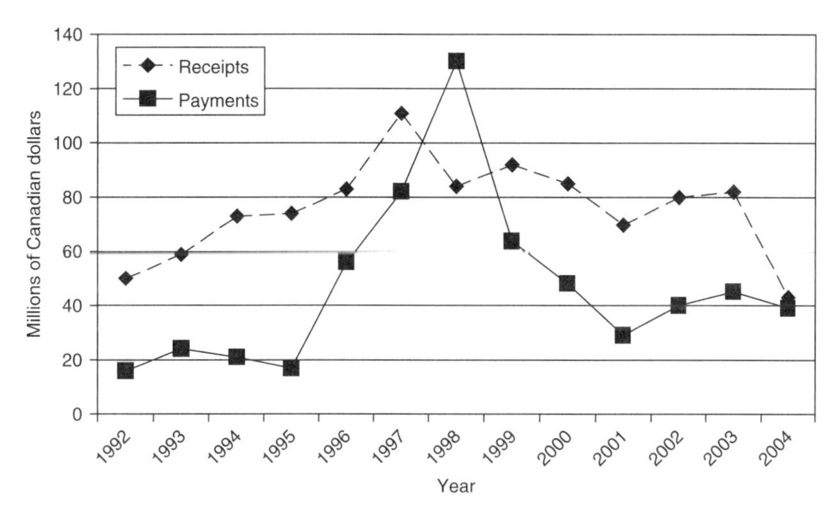

Source: Adapted from data extracted from CANSIM Table 376-0032 ('International transactions in services, transportation by category, annual dollars', special tabulations) by Statistics Canada staff, 28 February 2006.

Figure 5.5 Payments and receipts for Canada–US air transportation services

Table 5.6 Outstanding critical issues identified in 2005

Issue identified by the Canadian government	Considerations in evaluating options
Fifth freedom and seventh freedom rights	Prior to the 2005 Air Services Agreement, fifth freedom rights were quite limited (US–Gander and beyond, Canada–San Juan and beyond, and Canada–Honolulu–Australasia) and none of Canada's bilateral agreements included seventh freedom rights (for all cargo or passenger service). In 56 of the US's, Open Skies Agreements, the US has exchanged seventh freedom rights for all-cargo and not passenger air service (US State Department, 2006).
Pricing	Under the 1995 Air Services Agreement, both countries have the right to match the price of a flight carrying third country traffic with a direct flight, but not to offer a price that is lower or conditions that are more permissive without special permission.
Restrictions on flight numbering	Canadian flights to a third country with a stopover in the US require two separate flight numbers, a disadvantage in marketing the service.
Co-terminalization	Under the 1995 Air Services Agreement, co-terminalization was not permitted for large aircraft used for all-cargo courier operations. This required Fedex or UPS to contract with a Canadian courier operator for 'beyond' services.
Charters	At this time, there was very little Canada–US transborder charter business because of regulatory discrepancies.
Wet leasing	The US precludes the use of wet-leased aircraft, while Canada allows it on a case-by-case basis. This can be ironic if a Canadian company wants to wet-lease US aircraft for service into the US, because there are no Canadian aircraft available.

Note: This is a summary of the principal issues from a Canadian perspective. Further elaboration of most is available from Transport Canada (2005c).

and seventh freedom rights, pricing, restrictions on flight numbering, co-terminalization, charter issues, wet leasing, and code-sharing. In addition, stakeholders thought it important that Canadian officials explore the restrictions imposed by the *Fly America Act*.

Perhaps most significant was the progress made in early 2005 as part of the trilateral *Security and Prosperity Partnership of North America* (SPP). Its *Report to Leaders* dedicated a section to air transportation expansion with five specific initiatives as part of the package. Most important of these commitments, the three leaders agreed to explore opportunities to expand air transportation on a bilateral and *trilateral* basis (SPP, 2005, p. 24). They established a timeline of identifying issues towards pursuing a trilateral agreement by the end of 2006. The other four initiatives were (1) expansion of North American airspace capacity by implementing a Reduced Vertical Separation Minimum in January of 2005; (2) agreement to a consultation process to establish a compatible North American fractional ownership regulatory regime for business aviation (including fractionally owned aircrafts) to fly freely in and between all three countries with a timeline for implementation in 2006; (3) a strategy to improve aviation safety and air navigation, with targets for implementation in 2005; and (4) negotiation of a *Memorandum of Cooperation on a Mexico–US Bilateral Aviation Safety Agreement* by the end of 2006.

In September 2005, the *US–Mexico Aviation Agreement* was signed in Mexico City. While not an 'Open Skies' agreement according to the US State Department (2006), the agreement does liberalize the US–Mexico relationship further. Most important, from the point of view of market liberalization, an unlimited number of scheduled all-cargo carriers will be able to fly between the US and Mexico, a substantial change from the previous treaty, which only permitted five cargo carriers from each country to operate scheduled services to the other (US Department of Transportation, 2005a).

On 11 November, 2005 the US and Canada reached an Open Skies Agreement, scheduled to come into effect 5 September, 2006. The announcement noted a speedy negotiation (US Department of Transportation, 2005b): 'Today's agreement, reached after three days of talks in Washington, builds on the liberalized accord reached in 1995 between the two countries [and]will make Canada the United States' 73rd Open-Skies partner.' Finally, part of the agreement included extending fifth freedom rights to Canadian and US cargo and passenger air carriers. It also extended seventh freedom rights for all-cargo services between another partner's territory and third countries. Furthermore, it granted greater pricing freedom by allowing US and Canadian airlines to 'offer the lowest prices for services between the other partner's territory and a third country' (Canadian Airports Council, 2005). The key features are identified in Box 5.2.

The Canadian Press (2005) concluded that no high-level appetite in either country exists for completely open skies (cabotage). The new agreement has two possible benefits for Canadians; it will, through the availability of these

BOX 5.2 TERMS OF THE 2005 CANADA–US OPEN SKIES AGREEMENT

Under the new agreement US and Canadian airplanes will be permitted to:

1. Pick up passenger and/or all-cargo traffic in the other partner's territory and carry it to a third country as part of a service to or from their home territory.
2. Operate stand-alone all-cargo services between the other partner's territory and third countries.
3. Offer the lowest prices for services between the other partner's territory and a third country.

Source: Flying the Open Skies, www.tc.gc.ca/mediaroom/releases/nat/2005/05-h225e.htm, Ottawa: Transport Canada, 2005. Reproduced with the permission of the Minister of Public Works and Government Services Canada, 2007.

fifth freedom opportunities, enable Canadian cities that believe they are underserved in services to Europe (for example, Edmonton, AB, and Halifax) to see potentially more services from flights originating in the US. Second, new opportunities for air cargo may result in better access if, as suggested in the *Edmonton Journal* (The Canadian Press, 2005), US operators coming from Houston to Edmonton will now be able to continue on to the oil sands of Fort McMurray, AB or the diamond mines of the Northwest Territories. Furthermore, the Open Skies Agreement 'largely opened up routes between Canada and the US but fell short of liberalizing express cargo services' (anonymous, 2005a, p. 1).

Has security been an issue for the industry? One carrier, in informal discussions, noted that

> Security requirements have not damaged the market but airlines have had to increase the services provided. Open packages and spot checks [are needed]. Many Europeans use explosive detection systems or hyperbaric chambers for security assessment. I believe officials should move to the French approach: if you are licensed by the security agency, you as freight forwarder can inspect, put through the X-Ray machine and then palletize. The carrier then accepts for transport without re-inspection. Dogs are better than machines! For [our company] security has had a significant operational impact and added to costs, both managerial and operational. I cannot say it has damaged the business but it has had both monetary and personnel impacts.

To conclude, the 1995 Agreement was more restrictive than the agreements that the US subsequently signed with other countries. While the 2005 amendments put Canada on a level playing field with other US aviation agreements, it did not advance the relationship well beyond those with other countries, and it did not move the situation dramatically closer to the common aviation area proposed by the Canada Transportation Act Review Panel. As noted by Button (1998), the US Open Skies approach is a 'political marketing device' to open foreign markets where US operators would have an advantage while protecting the domestic market from full competition. It would eventually take a change of government and the Harper Conservative's Blue Sky policy released on 27 November, 2006 for Canada to move closer to US international air policy. It is clear from the discussion in this section of the report that many scholars believe all three NAFTA countries still have much further to go in liberalizing the air transportation services regulatory environment.

WHAT DOES THE AIR CARGO INDUSTRY NEED?

The primary focus of global airline regulation has been the passenger transport sub-sector. What was good for the passenger business was imposed on the freight business. In spite of this, the air cargo business has grown, fuelled by e-commerce, the desire of those willing to pay to have their purchases faster, and by just-in-time and agile global supply networks. In 2004, the global air cargo industry was forecasted to grow at a rate of 6.2 per cent between 2004 and 2023 (Boeing, 2004, p. 4). The North American market (Canada and the US) accounted, in 2003, for 14.3 per cent of that global market in tonne-kilometres and 22.6 per cent in pure tonnage terms (Boeing, 2004, p. 17). Of that, the US domestic market takes more than the lion's share (93.6 per cent) and the air express sector accounts for 60.9 per cent of that, leaving 19.3 per cent for scheduled freight.[21]

Boeing (2004, pp. 18, 22) highlights the severe imbalance on the Canada/US transborder traffic, noting that the dominant leg (northbound) grew rapidly after the 1995 agreement but the southbound remained flat. It does project that the transborder market will grow 7.5 per cent from 2003 to 2013, faster than either domestic market.

If the air cargo tonnage data for Canadian air carriers over the period from before the 1995 air service bilateral to the present day is examined (Table 5.7), air cargo tonnage carried by Canadian air carriers has grown from 1995 to 2000, with each year generating positive growth, but the pattern of overall growth is very inconsistent. When drilled down to examine the pattern of growth in just the transborder segment, the pattern bears no resemblance to overall growth, but does exhibit a higher rate

Table 5.7 Volume of goods carried by Canadian air carriers by sector, 1993–2004 (metric tonnes)

Year	Transborder	Total	Transborder share	Transborder growth	Total growth
1993	68 617	624 561	11.0%		
1994	59 758	653 444	9.1%	−12.9%	4.6%
1995	81 203	692 579	11.7%	35.9%	6.0%
1996	72 100	707 858	10.2%	−11.2%	2.2%
1997	77 387	789 146	9.8%	7.3%	11.5%
1998	94 176	822 025	11.5%	21.7%	4.2%
1999	93 261	832 987	11.2%	−1.0%	1.3%
2000	100 481	845 809	11.9%	7.7%	1.5%
2001	82 201	789 625	10.4%	−18.2%	−6.6%
2002	C	786 607			−0.4%
2003	C	662 612			−15.8%
2004P	C	693 798			4.7%

Note: C = data are confidential.

Source: Adapted from data in Transport Canada (2006), Table A9-11: 'Volume of goods carried by Canadian air carriers by sector, 1993–2004', Statistics Canada, *Canadian Civil Aviation* (Catalogue 51-206), *Aviation Service Bulletin*, (Catalogue 51-004), and special tabulations for revised data; *Transportation in Canada 2005 Annual Report Addendum*, Ottawa: Public Works and Government Services Canada. Reproduced with the permission of the Minister of Public Works and Government Services Canada, 2007.

of growth in the year of the agreement. Within NAFTA, the state of California is a dominant player, both inbound and outbound (Table 5.8), reflecting its importance in computer software, film and agricultural industries, all significant users of air cargo services.

According to Crockatt (2005, p. 8), the intra-North American air cargo market, the largest both domestically and internationally, contains few exclusive freight airlines. Air cargo in both Canada and Mexico does not have the volume of the US industry, and the Mexican industry is dependent on the US for the export of manufactured goods from the *maquiladora* sector. The air cargo industry in North America is more mature in comparison to elsewhere in the world. As a result, the major players in North America have well-established networks, and the industry growth rate is modest in comparison to other regions.

With the move towards air liberalization, there are both positive and negative public responses. Crockatt (2005, p. 4) points out that there are those who conclude that liberalization will have a positive impact on the growth of the economy, while others foresee that too much liberalization will result

Table 5.8 Air cargo activity in North America 2005

Weight of exports by air (short tons)			
From US State	**To Canada**	**To Mexico**	**US–NAFTA**
All US States	**123 593**	**39 769**	**163 362**
California	32 694	10 787	43 481
Texas	23 218	5 574	28 792
Illinois	9 692	3 795	13 487
Ohio	10 647	2 367	13 015
New York	9 472	3 150	12 622
Weight of imports by air (short tons)			
To US state	**From Canada**	**From Mexico**	**US–NAFTA**
All US States	**75 334**	**70 926**	**146 260**
California	13 225	11 465	24 690
Texas	8 656	6 274	14 930
Florida	2 651	11 697	14 348
Michigan	3 583	6 730	10 313
New York	5 130	3 133	8 264

Source: Selected data from US Department of Transportation, Research and Innovative Technology Administration (2006), Table A-4, p. 20.

in a negative impact on some carriers and economies. He concludes that 'a balanced approach is required that is responsive to both market forces and regional and national economic situations'.

CONCLUSIONS

At this point, it is quite obvious that the political environment in which air and marine services within the NAFTA region are provided is a charged one. While sometimes the NAFTA countries make decisions trilaterally, and sometimes bilaterally, most often decisions are taken domestically and without regard for the larger NAFTA picture, as is evident from the Government Accountability Office (US GAO, 2005) report on short sea shipping already discussed. The supranational institutions are weak, lack sufficient autonomy and are under-funded or just not there. The mindset of most politicians and companies in the marine and air sectors still seems to reflect a protectionist self-interest that fails to see the benefits of greater liberalization. The argument that a more integrated and cohesive transport network will improve North America's global competitiveness has not been bought by the air and marine sectors.

The existence of cabotage rules is a key foundation underpinning air and marine market structure. Not all development of short sea shipping in North America may be hindered by cabotage regulation. Large parts of the current market – the Gulf of Mexico, Great Lakes, East Coast or West Coast routes – operate under a foreign flag in a shuttle network configuration. Altering cabotage rules is not a high priority for the transport industry as a whole. Marine carriers are currently focused more on security issues and the high cost of fuel, with most seeking to maintain protection of their existing market. This is no wonder as they have invested heavily and have that investment to protect, but all this implies is that regulatory change needs to be phased in.

Furthermore, there has not been an investigation of the impact of a NAFTA flag option or adoption of mutual recognition. The necessary research for making policy changes to the existing environment is therefore not complete. Political will does not seem to exist in the Bush Administration to address this and, without the largest player able to see the opportunities for all players in the market, the discussion will not gain traction in the near future.

Canadian, American and Mexican maritime transport interests are politically divergent, but the *Memorandum of Cooperation* does provide a limited institution through which maritime issues can be addressed, albeit only as a sharing of experience. The three governments recommitted to this in April 2006, when they signed a *Declaration* in Vancouver at the North American Marine Conference to form a steering committee to facilitate the aims of the MOC, and further specify areas of cooperation. The key beneficiaries of a discussion on short sea shipping will be the manufacturers, suppliers and retailers trying to get global freight to local markets; they have no venue to voice their concerns but they do have the clout to raise issues under a continental gateway strategy.

As for air, there is still some way to go in liberalizing the North American air cargo market. International regulation of air cargo from the beginning has been driven by the requirements of the passenger transport aspect of the business; air cargo has been the stepchild of the passenger business. There is widespread recognition that the needs of the industry sectors differ, but it is only in the last decade that there have been calls for much more liberal regimes for air cargo. The progressive liberalization of air cargo was a high priority at the ICAO at the turn of the millennium, and comprised Agenda Item 27 at the 35th Assembly of the ICAO Economic Commission. While the case was made that the current bilateral system aggravates overcapacity (International Air Cargo Association, 2003) and it has been argued that liberalization of air cargo would open opportunity for secondary airports and alleviate congestion at primary hubs (Airports

Council International, 2003), the Assembly concluded that the prospect of achieving a global and comprehensive multilateral agreement did not exist.

Informal discussions with one cargo operator resulted in this explanation of the access issue:

> You have to have a good analysis of what opportunities are possible. The new agreement will allow a Canadian carrier to pick up in Miami and fly to Venezuela but only if the carrier also has rights with Venezuela. Therefore, the carrier needs to have 5th freedom rights with the third country. Therefore, it is a question of how many 5th freedom rights the US has versus how many Canada has. Every country has a different level of arrangements, some more open (example: UK and Germany) than others. Then you need to have enough equipment to take advantage of the opportunity; therefore exploitation of the opportunity is conditional on equipment access.

Governments moved more slowly to ease access than the cargo owners liked. From a Canadian perspective, Canada lagged behind other countries in signing 'open access' agreements, and this raises the question as to whether the absence of a more liberal Canadian international air policy has now left the country's air cargo operators at a serious and perhaps unrecoverable disadvantage by protecting access for too long. The continental air industry was probably in much better shape to weather the buffeting of industry restructuring in the latter part of the 1990s than it has been in this century.

POSTSCRIPT

In addition to the agreement with the US, Canada has signed 'open skies agreements' with the United Kingdom (21 April 2007) and Ireland (30 April 2007) since this chapter was completed.

NOTES

1. Only US marine carriers were contacted; in the case of air, the chapter relies on secondary sources and only one informal and unstructured interview.
2. Cabotage rules are found in many shipping markets; they require the use of a national flag vessel to carry cargo between two national ports. In the EU, with market liberalization, cabotage rules apply within the EU but not at the national level, so a Greek flag vessel is allowed to carry cargoes between two ports in Italy but a Panamanian flag vessel could not.
3. Hodgson and Brooks (2004) note that the latter adds significantly to the capital cost of the vessel, but that these costs are often not eligible for bank loans and so raise the equity necessary for the investment to unreasonably high levels, thereby providing a disincentive for fleet renewal.

4. Ballast legs are those segments of the overall trading pattern where the vessel does not carry cargo but must remain empty or partly empty (for example, travel in ballast).
5. Many states also provide varying degrees of relief from income tax for seafarers.
6. The unrestricted movement of ships from one sector to the other is in sharp contrast to the separation between the sectors imposed by Canada's implementation of its international shipping corporation tax regime (Brooks and Hodgson, 2005).
7. This is not intended to be inflammatory. It is a statement of fact that other developed countries have assessed their regulatory climate for domestic shipping and made adjustments to reflect the modern reality of trade and transport in the twenty-first century; Canada and the US have essentially retained their post-World War II policies for far too long.
8. It is now called *Memorandum of Cooperation on Sharing Short Sea Shipping Information and Experience between the Transportation Authorities of Canada, Mexico and the United States of America*.
9. The question was: Europe has increasingly eliminated the rules governing access to transport markets within Europe, reduced restrictions on European transport businesses, and harmonized the business environment (standards, taxation, labour and immigration, and so on) applying to transportation services within Europe. Would you want to see more of this type of regulatory reform within North America? Why? Why not?
10. This question was: If a second round of NAFTA negotiations were to be in the preparation stage today, what would you want to see on the table in terms of transportation or logistics elements? (Please develop a list of your top priorities and explain why.)
11. While some argue that the official name of this is the Harbor Maintenance Fee, and that it is not a tax, recent legislation introduced in the US specifically uses the word 'Tax' in the legislation, public speakers always refer to the HMT, not to the HMF, and so like popular use of brand names like Kleenex and Xerox for generic purposes, the HMT has become a tax through common usage, and so this is the term used here.
12. Examples given included the congested Highway 401 that services Ontario–Michigan transborder trade.
13. On 12 February, 2007, Congresswoman Stephanie Jones introduced the *Great Lakes Short Sea Shipping Enhancement Act of 2007* (H.R. 981) to exempt the tax for Great Lakes container and trailer cargoes. Shortly after, on 26 March 2007, Congressman David Weldon introduced H.R. 1701 (the *Blue Water Highway Act of 2007*) to waive the tax for containers and trailers between US mainland ports. Neither of these bills do anything for shallow draft vessels. Meanwhile, Congressman Cummings on 13 March introduced the *Short Sea Shipping Promotion Act of 2007* (H.R. 1499), which proposed to exempt Great Lakes cargo from HMT but, like H.R. 981, ignored other NAFTA short sea opportunities.
14. An excellent explanation of the freedoms and how they work may be found at the ICAO website at www.icao.int/cgi/goto_m.pl?/icao/en/search_icao.html.
15. The US has established, at a number of Canada's largest airports, US customs and immigration facilities; at these facilities, travellers bound for the US are 'precleared' for arrival at a US domestic airport without international arrivals facilities, such as Reagan National Airport in Washington, DC.
16. This Act was later replaced by the *Canada Transportation Act* in 1996.
17. The practice of serving more than one point in the territory of the other party on a single flight.
18. Reproduced with the permission of the Minister of Public Works and Government Services Canada, 2007.
19. The point Button makes is that, in both cases, the ownership restrictions deter rescuers from determining what investment is most efficient and optimal for the circumstances.
20. In the US, the *Federal Aviation Act of 1958*, section 101, limits foreign ownership of airlines to no more than 25 per cent of the voting interest. In Canada, the same 25 per cent limit on foreign ownership applies through the *Canada Transportation Act of 1996*, although there have been calls to change the ownership provisions (PWGSC, 2001). In Europe, the limit on foreign ownership is less restrictive at 49 per cent but present nonetheless.
21. The remainder is chartered freight and mail.

6. The 'undefended' Northern Border and perimeter security

> While there are a number of political hurdles that would have to be overcome, . . . it may also be time to begin to explore the idea of a North American Customs Zone or some type of perimeter concept from the security perspective to help meet security/trade facilitation goals. (Phillips, 2005)

INTRODUCTION

The Northern border has been heralded as 'the longest undefended border in the world'. In the aftermath of the 11 September, 2001 terrorist attacks, there was considerable discussion within Canada about whether Canada's interests would be best served by pushing out the boundaries for greater physical and/or economic security to the continental boundaries of North America. In particular, Canadian trade interests were extremely concerned that there not be a repeat of the perceived border shutdown that occurred in the three or four days following the attacks. The primary interest of the day was whether or not *NAFTA* provided an institutional framework (often called NAFTA Plus) that could be used to address US security concerns. Suddenly, on that September day, Americans saw the border with Canada as vulnerable, and Canadians became painfully aware that the nature of the relationship had changed.

This chapter examines the issue of security and the concept of a security perimeter, both before the defining date of 11 September, 2001 and after. It begins with a discussion of security concerns before, relying on secondary sources and the discussions of security as tied to infrastructure and border investment. It then moves to explore the idea of a common perimeter as discussed in the first three years after the defining date, first from an American perspective and then from a Canadian one. This leads to a review of studies already done on the impact security has had on Canada–US transportation and the economic problem of cargo delay. At this point, the chapter departs on what appears to be a tangent – the growing regional interest in trade and the rise of regional trade groups as a response to the inability of national governments to effect change at the speed desired by businesses and local governments. If a secure perimeter were achieved, perhaps continental corridors and gateways would be more effective and greater velocity in business supply chains would yield greater competitiveness for transborder firms. It is clear by the end of the chapter that there is an underlying tension between businesses and citizens on one hand and national governments (and their security advisors) on the other. The product of this tension is the growing interest in corridor development, with or without support from the federal political institutions within the region.

BEFORE 11 SEPTEMBER, 2001

> The decision to maintain a North American security perimeter and pursue a North American economic space was decided many years ago, based on agreements ranging from the NATO and NORAD to the auto pact and NAFTA. (Hart, 2003, p. 434)

Cross-border collaboration on issues of common interest has been a feature of the post-World War II relationship between Canada and the United States. While the two countries have had a common perimeter for national defense through the North American Aerospace Defense Command (NORAD), defence has not been the only area of 'common management'. As noted in Chapter 1, water management in the Great Lakes basin has also benefited from bilateral cooperation. *The Canada–United States Great Lakes Water Quality Agreement* is the main instrument to manage the relationship, with the International Joint Commission providing the guidance on implementation. Findlay and Telford (2006) believed that the arrangements for water management provide a model for smaller scale cooperation between the two governments but considered it a somewhat flawed model, noting problems of political interference in post-election periods.

Another illustration of cooperation that is working are the NAFTA arrangements for environmental cooperation, the North American Agreement on Environmental Cooperation (NAAEC) and its Commission for Environmental Cooperation (CEC). Kirton and Richardson (2006) noted the success of the CEC in its efforts to promote sustainable development,[1] and concluded that it provides a good model for regulatory integration and continental cooperation in spite of trilateral regulatory incongruence.

Coupled with the *NAFTA* itself, all of these imply that there was already a formal defence arrangement and an informal 'perimeter', and that there already existed some outward push to move the US border away from its political boundaries prior to the events of September 2001. However, they also indicate that the perimeter is not as strong as it could be were the two (Canada and the US) or the three (with Mexico) countries to desire further strengthening of the continental boundaries.

Cooperation in border management has a long history. For example, the US Customs Service developed the Land Border Carrier Initiative Program (LBCIP) in 1995.[2] Under this agreement, a land carrier agreed to increase its security measures at its place of business and on vehicles used to transport cargo from Mexico (US Department of Justice, 2002). The program was extended to Canada, and in October 1999, the Canada–US Partnership Forum (CUSP) was launched. CUSP was viewed by the US Department of Justice (2002) as a model program and was mandated to identify emerging issues and long-term trends, consult with government agencies with respect to progress in cross-border cooperation, promote dialogue (among the various levels of government on both sides of the border including border communities and stakeholders) to achieve a common vision for border cooperation, and report on the state of the border.

Perhaps nothing signals the closeness of the Canada–US relationship more strongly than the ironic fact that on 11 September, 2001, it was a Canadian at the helm of NORAD when the military jets were scrambled at the time of the attacks on the US.

'SECURITY TRUMPS TRADE': US PERSPECTIVES ON PERIMETER SECURITY

Paul Celluci, then US Ambassador to Canada, in his book, *Unquiet Diplomacy*, reported that he talked to Canadians about the need for a common security perimeter for the first five months of his appointment to Canada, prior to the events of September 2001. In his words, a common perimeter was 'never about walling off North America from the rest of the world' (Celluci, 2005, p. 84). To continue:

> My own goal was to establish a more coordinated approach to border security. I got the chance to argue the case when I was invited to brief the immigration sub-committee of the United States Senate. . . . My presentation to the committee was that we needed to make the land borders both more secure and at the same time more open, and we needed to create a security perimeter, a zone of confidence, around North America. (Celluci, 2005, p. 95)

In the first two years after 11 September, 2001, the US was very focused on understanding its trading relationships as it became increasingly concerned that freight networks could be used to import a weapon of mass destruction. As a result, the US government established a *Data Management Improvement Act* (DMIA) Task Force in order to begin the process of targeting security efforts to those means most likely to be used by terrorists.

The DMIA Task Force initially reported to Congress through the Department of Justice (2002), but by its second year was reporting to Congress through the recently created US Department of Homeland Security (2003). The reports of the DMIA Task Force on perceptions of border security, and with respect to perimeter clearance, could not be more clear on their view of the Canada–US border: '[The] borders are "shared" between these neighbors and should not be unilaterally managed' (US Department of Justice, 2002, p. 61). This sentiment was accompanied by the conclusion that joint cooperation, information-sharing and policy-making were required, and the report called for a further study of how border facilitation might be supported by 'moving the border outward'. The first priority was seen as public protection while the second was economic security for the US and its trading partners.

Perhaps the most vocal American on border management in the two years after the terrorist attacks was Stephen Flynn, broadly considered a fear-monger by citizens in all three countries. Flynn (2003) proposed that Americans adopt a two-border policy: the border with Mexico being hardened and the one with Canada being opened.[3] Flynn supported moving the 'border' back by engaging in effective targeting through anomaly detection and pre-screening to identify low-risk players. He also concluded that the Mexican drayage system for the immediate Mexico–US border move is less secure than continental long-haul operations by its very nature; poorly paid drivers who sit in congested traffic with the prospect of an empty backhaul make excellent prey for the criminal element.[4] It is clear that Flynn was supportive of special lanes for pre-approved (for example, FAST) drivers. After 9/11, he determined that the Northern Border came under intense scrutiny and became a convenient political target. It was also clear in those first few months that the US treated its two NAFTA colleagues differently.

It was not until Paul Celluci's speech to the Economic Club of Toronto on 25 March 2003 that the phrase that reverberated with Canadians – 'Security trumps trade' – was first delivered. True White House thinking was finally clear to Canadians; the zone of confidence or security perimeter had higher priority than US economic interests. As Pierre Pettigrew (2002), Canada's Minister for International Trade, focused on security issues as an opportunity to gain traction for principles of mutual recognition and greater harmonization in Canada–US trade, the US entered the War in Iraq in 2003, unsupported by Canada,[5] and had clearly chosen security as its highest order priority. It was a low point for Canada–US relations.

Over the years, the primary concern that is repeatedly raised from the American perspective is the wide gap in philosophy between the two countries when it comes to immigration and to refugee policy. Hart (2003) believed that, until this issue is addressed by both countries, Americans will continue to view the Canadian–US border as far too porous and that Canada is 'unwilling or unable to do what needs to be done to ensure a secure North American perimeter' (Hart, 2003, p. 437). Perhaps they have a concern; after all, Canadians like Stoffman (2002), Bissett (2002) and McMahon (2001) have been quite outspoken about the gaps in Canada's immigration and refugee policies and therefore acknowledge why Americans may view Canada as a conduit for global terrorists.[6]

Tanguay and Thierren (2004) expressed their concerns about joint border security policies as a prisoners' dilemma. Because increased border security provides public benefits, it is possible for one country to be a free rider, letting the other pay for increased security. They assumed that both Canada and the US are potential targets, and concluded from a prisoners' dilemma perspective that this means that both countries are better off increasing border security but each may under-invest, expecting the other to pay. In the final analysis, Tanguay and Thierren (2004, p. 95) concluded that a common security perimeter 'may be a good alternative'.[7] Will the Americans ever really accept such a system in which they will be required to pay the predominant share of the financial costs to securing the border and, perhaps, appear to be taking care of Canada? No. One could argue that it is Canada that receives the public benefits of such investment; this may explain why discussion of the 'zone of confidence' has disappeared from US political rhetoric.

CANADIAN PERSPECTIVES ON PERIMETER SECURITY

> Canadians do seem ready for almost any level of co-operation between the two governments. An Ipsos-Reid poll released last week found that 70 per cent supported jointly manned border posts, and 85 per cent endorsed 'making the types of changes that are required to create a joint North American security perimeter.' Also, 81 per cent said the two countries should adopt 'common entry controls' in treating refugees and immigrants. (Beltrame, 2001, p. 23)

Beltrame's article, published in mid-October 2001, captured the immediate Canadian reaction to the terrorist attacks of September that year; Canadians were shocked by the events and willing to work with the US to protect North America, including a willingness to share information deemed necessary to create a secure perimeter around the continent. Beltrame (2001) also noted in those early days that it was likely that Canada would be required to cede significant sovereignty to the US. Many Canadians believed that a much closer and more formal political arrangement between the two countries was now just a matter of time. McMahon (2001, np) noted: 'If long-term enemies like France and Germany can establish a common perimeter around Europe, surely long-term friends like Canada and the United States can establish one in North America.'

While the logic of McMahon's (2001) statement resonated well with many Canadians, others in Canada like the Council of Canadians feared it would mean ceding sovereignty to a neighbour they view as being too powerful. McMahon noted that in the immediate aftermath of the terrorist attacks, the Prime Minister of Canada delivered a message that a common security perimeter was not envisioned by Canada; however, it was not more than a few weeks before discussion about what might be done about physical security for the two countries was being conducted at the highest levels. Shortly after the event, the Canadian government instituted legislation similar to that of the US's anti-terrorist legislation. From this point, the floodgates of debate were open and discussion by the media and political pundits was under way. The concept of 'Fortress North America' had re-emerged.[8]

In the months that followed the attacks, many Canadians began to view the situation as an opportunity to reduce the real and potential negative economic impacts on Canadian trade with the US if the US strengthened its border security and reduced access to Canadian companies. The two countries signed a *30-Point Smart Border Declaration and Action Plan* on 12 December 2001; it included many projects that could be incorporated into a 'perimeter clearance' process, such as the agreement to station customs inspectors at each other's seaports for targeted maritime container inspections. As the US failed to exploit Canadian endorsement of the concept in any grand way in the first year after the attacks, initial interest in a common external boundary turned to concern about Canadian sovereignty and the opportunity to rethink the Canada–US relationship slowly seemed to evaporate.

In spite of the 30-point plan, transnational trade became sluggish. According to McMahon et al. (2003), authors of the Fraser Institute's 2003 trade survey, 72 per cent of Canadian exporters faced unofficial trade barriers, up from 45 per cent in 2002. Furthermore, not only were border effects more prominent, 8 per cent of Canadian firms faced sufficient buy-national policies in the US that they withdrew from the US market. The survey also noted that 96 per cent of Canadian exporters believed that Canada–US relations had worsened over the previous months and two-thirds believed it had damaged their ability to sell to the US. A fundamental question remains unanswered: how much re-sourcing of US purchases to domestic suppliers has happened since September 2001? While it remains difficult to separate loss of business from the post-2001 economic slowdown in the US from the impact of security and rising US protectionist sentiment, these findings indicate that border security regulations affected Canadian companies negatively. Canada's share of exports to the US market continues to decline from its high in 2000.

The forums for and forms of these discussions attempted to engage Canadians in contemplating their future within the North American political and economic space. The Canadian Institute of Strategic Studies in 2002 and the Institute for Research on Public Policy in 2004 held major conferences addressing the secure perimeter issue. The C.D. Howe Institute held a series of workshops and published a series of Border Papers. The sheer volume of research at this time illustrates the traction the issue held with academics and think tanks alike. A synopsis of some of the key viewpoints is presented in Table 6.1, and any reader anxious to understand more is well advised to begin with these selected papers.

Canadian citizens were not really engaged in the discussion of possibilities as they had been during the election campaign over the *Canada–US Trade Agreement*, perhaps because the economy was in a recession and their minds were otherwise preoccupied (health care had become a number one priority). While Canadians had long ago learned to live as a mouse next to (Pierre Trudeau's) elephant, perhaps few knew that their economic future (and the way that health care would eventually be paid for) was not entirely their own to determine, having placed too many economic eggs in the American basket over the previous 15 years. Trade dependence and security in combination meant that transport network integration was needed just at a time or just because US security concerns had become dominant. It is interesting to note that the debate raged over the nature and extent of the 'bargain' to be struck with the US, when the US was focused on the War on Terror and not those elements of interest to Canada. Furthermore, there seemed to be no Canadian interest in examining the role Mexico played in US thinking,[9] but it appeared to be widely assumed that Mexico had no relevance to the discussion. In short, it appeared to those outside inner political circles that Canadian academics were mostly talking to themselves.

Goldfarb and Robson (2003) of the C.D. Howe Institute struck a chord with their research examining Canada's vulnerability to the new trade relationship and security regime. Appropriately entitled *Risky Business*, their report called on the Canadian government to unequivocally announce that securing a free flow of goods across the border was an integral part of Canada's 'efforts to enhance North American physical and economic security'. Developing a matrix of vulnerability by region, commodity traded and jobs associated, they found that border disruptions have the potential to affect 45 per cent of Canadian exports, 390 000 jobs and C$3.7 billion of Canadian investment. The 'thickening' of the border, to use their words, could deprive Canada of the advantages that were gained from trade liberalization. What they did not do was examine the impact on trade in services and, in particular, trade in transportation services, other than examining transit time (for which they found mixed and 'contaminated' evidence).

Table 6.1 A synopsis of perimeter discussions in Canada

Source (and type)	Key proposition(s)
McMahon (2001) (Think tank commentary)	'The central sovereign duty a government owes its citizens is sound security and economic policy.'
Roussel (2002) (Conference presentation)	He presented four scenarios for a North American security perimeter: 1) a formal security perimeter (e.g., a comprehensive treaty like Schengen); 2) an informal or limited security perimeter (such as one featuring sectoral memoranda of understanding like the 2001 *Smart Border Declaration*); 3) a multilateral security perimeter, which could be formal or informal (e.g., NATO); and 4) coordinated national policies (e.g., a unilateral perimeter with no obvious cooperation). He concluded that the second would prevail because it was the easiest, although not the most efficient option for Canada (in his view the first of the four).
Dobson (2002) (Think tank commentary)	Canada's security agenda needs to include a proactive approach to immigration (including Canada's refugee policy), border security and defence. Her options included a customs union, a common market, or a 'strategic bargain' that mixed and matched components of interest to Americans. It would also require Canada to address a number of barriers to trade and support the development of a common competition policy. She never uses the phrase 'security perimeter'.
Gotlieb (2003) (Newspaper editorial)	This former Canadian ambassador to the US endorsed Dobson's position (as a 'grand bargain') and further developed the concept of a North American Community of Law, which was subsequently adopted by the Council on Foreign Relations (2005).
Noble (2004) (Conference presentation)	Noble (2004) provided a series of options that detail the requirements of physical and economic security. His vision of security had two platforms – (1) physical security and (2) physical and economic security; he did not consider economic security without physical security. The first platform had 11 'options' and the second an additional six; the tenth and eleventh options on the first platform were ones with a perimeter focus (Box 6.1).
Hart (2003), Hart and Dymond (2005) and Dymond and Hart (2005), Hart (2006)	These informative articles focus on the full range of issues in the Canada–US relationship. The two from 2005 are solid descriptors of the potential paths forward (focusing in particular on customs union and regulatory convergence). The style of relationship – described as adhocery by this

Table 6.1 (continued)

Source (and type)	Key proposition(s)
	time – is seen as a major problem in resolving the outstanding integrative issues between the two countries. These articles are also descriptive of how Americans see Canadians, for example, as unwilling to address their security concerns. The 2006 article deals specifically about regulatory convergence, and is discussed in Chapter 7.
Conference Board (2003) (Think tank commentary)	This briefing presents the notion that the 'big idea' (or the 'grand bargain') of Canada–US relations will be both unlikely to succeed and not in Canada's best interests. It even concludes that the concept is, by this time, already 'stillborn'. It calls for a comprehensive vision that involves mutual commitment between the two countries, and an approach of resolving individual issues in the context of a clear strategic vision as the path to maintaining a distinct identity in a more integrated continental economy.
Goldfarb (2003) (Think tank commentary)	Goldfarb (2003) did not consider a customs union from the perspective of services, only goods, and so the impact on transport equipment was considered, but not the impact on transportation services. This marked a critical juncture in the Canadian discussion of a customs union as opposed to a stronger external boundary.

Noble (2004) argued that physical security is very different from economic security, with Canada interested in the latter and the US focused on the former. This can be considered fact, not fiction or perception. In developing his 17 options for North America (Box 6.1), he laid out the variety of political paths available. We can only conclude that if an agenda of improving the competitiveness of the continent is even to begin to gain traction, Canada must really address US concerns about physical security. As already noted in Chapter 1, the last serious debate Canadians (at the grass roots level) had about 'who we are and where we want our country to go' was the highly charged one during the election campaign prior to Brian Mulroney's second term, when Canadians went to the polls on the issue of the *Canada–US Trade Agreement*. Without a solid signal that Canadian citizens understand the priority Americans place on their personal safety, and given the agenda of the Bush administration to place security at the top of all its international priorities, it appears that in the 'are you for us or against us?' question that accompanies the US view of the world, the security perimeter disappeared from US rhetoric.

BOX 6.1 JOHN NOBLE'S OPTIONS FOR NORTH AMERICA

Eleven Options for Physical Security

1. Maintain the status quo in defense/security/immigration/refugee policies and in the level of cooperation including the incrementalist approach built into the Smart Border plans;
2. Refuse to participate in BMD;
3. Participate in BMD with or without further cooperation with NORTHCOM;
4. Significant increase in Canadian defense budget;
5. Amend the administration of Canadian refugee and visitor visa policies to reduce the security threat;
6. Agree on common policies for temporary visas and refugee/asylum policies;
7. Formally develop the concentric ring approach to North American security;
8. Adopt a Schengen-type approach for free labour mobility within North America and common entry procedures for non-North Americans;
9. Support the American doctrine of unilateral pre-emption;
10. Adopt a perimeter approach for defense purposes only;
11. Adopt a perimeter approach for all kinds of threats.

For Physical and Economic Security

1. Maintain the status quo as provided in NAFTA;
2. Negotiate a common external tariff to eliminate rules of origin;
3. Negotiate a full customs union with a common trade policy;
4. Negotiate elements of a customs union and a common market (Dobson);
5. Negotiate a common market with full mobility of labour;
6. Negotiate a new agreement designed to deal with deeper integration with the necessary institutional backdrop to support them. (Dymond-Hart/CCEO/Dobson/Gotlieb, etc.)

Note: The 11 options for physical security are from pages 48–9 of the paper while the six options for physical and economic security are from page 51.

Source: Noble (2004).

Is a customs union the answer? There is a substantial volume of research on the Canadian side of the border that looks at a customs union as one possible solution to border issues. The Conference Board of Canada (2004) concluded that it would provide limited benefit and still not resolve the challenges arising from other border barriers. Perhaps the best consolidation of ideas on the debate is found at the Policy Research Initiative, North American Linkages website.[10] The June 2004 publication of its findings investigated these issues, such as the benefits of a common external application of most favoured nation (MFN) tariffs, the elimination of the rules of origin, and the reduction in regulatory restrictions and regulatory convergence. Kunimoto and Sawchuk (2004) concluded that MFN tariffs will often attract a lower cost than possible under *NAFTA*, which has higher compliance costs. However, in implementation, both Canada and the US would have to create a common directive for tariffs to be levied on third party countries, as well as a revenue sharing agreement for its product. Ghosh and Rao (2004) found that eliminating the NAFTA rules or origin, which Kunimoto and Sawchuk (2004) identified as being the most restrictive of 17 international trade agreements, would increase Canada's GDP by 1 per cent, and Canadian exports to the US by 19.2 per cent. They also concluded that, from the US perspective, it would also be a win–win situation, as US GDP would improve (albeit only by 0.1 per cent) and US exports to Canada would increase by 25 per cent. Ndayisenga (2004) noted that Canada lags both the US and the OECD in the rate of decline in regulatory restrictiveness, and that Canada's transport industry is much more restricted than is the US industry.

From a transport perspective, Noble's (2004) approach went much further than really necessary for an efficient and effective bilateral or trilateral transport network; it may be that integrating the services that make trade happen is logistically (pardon the pun) more realistic. Thus while the customs union mooted by Dobson (2002), Goldfarb (2003) and Dymond and Hart (2005) or an entirely new agreement within North America, as proposed by the Council on Foreign Relations (2005), would resolve the existing impediments to transport efficiency, it is not clear that the security perimeter proposed by the last is practicable. It is likely that the idea of a customs union is reaching much too far for the US political situation. Perhaps it is also overkill from a transportation efficiency point of view. What is needed here is a base hit. North Americans do not need to get a home run for immeasurable improvements; using a baseball analogy, we can win using a series of base hits, a primary one being regulatory convergence in transportation regulation. As indicated by Pamela Wallin (2006), it is often far easier to get incremental change to troublesome non-tariff barriers than to get acceptance (let alone implementation) of a grand vision for North America.

It appears that Canada's economy is more vulnerable to US security actions, with a greater impact on the Canadian economy than on that of the US (Goldfarb and Robson, 2003). Canadian manufacturers in the auto industry have been particularly hard hit, as geographically close production facilities bear the brunt of the costs when even temporary border delays slow shipments between plants. Hufbauer and Schott (2004) concluded that the sources of Canadian competitive advantage in manufacturing trade seem more vulnerable to security interruptions than those of Mexican competitive advantage, as cheaper labour drove US investments in Mexican *maquiladoras*. The vulnerability that can be addressed is the one of cargo delay.

THE PROBLEM OF CARGO DELAY

Just-in-time systems developed in the 1990s were, by the turn of the millennium, so finely tuned that more than a few minutes of delay at the Ontario–Michigan border moved the level of uncertainty too high for many tightly integrated supply chain operations to tolerate. One only has to note the impact on the automobile manufacturing industry of the terrorist attacks on production activities on 12 and 13 September. Very few North Americans forget the *Time* magazine picture of long lines of trucks (rumoured to have exceeded 30 kilometres) waiting in southern Ontario to gain access to the US on the 11th, or the press reports on 12 September that both General Motors and DaimlerChrysler idled some factories due to lack of component parts (Madore, 2001). Plant closures by Ford followed later in the week and were attributed to transportation problems at the border delaying parts deliveries (anonymous, 2001). The impact was felt all the way to the Carolinas and Mexico.

How much security is the most effective? This is, to use a game show analogy, the 64 thousand dollar question. US border management principles, as reported by Congressional Research Services (2004), enshrine the concept that the facilitation of the movements of people and goods at the border must be balanced with security concerns. The need to efficiently and accurately identify, inspect and intervene is clearly at the fore. The targeting of risky passengers, cargo, and transport personnel and equipment is recognized as a complex and multi-stage process. The greater the number of inspections and the more thorough the inspections, the greater the incidence and impact of border delay will be. However, as was seen above, the message today is still one of security as the primary priority.

While the public often confuses screening with inspection and uses the terms interchangeably, inspection is physical while screening may involve the querying of databases with or without the physical presence of the container, trailer or other conveyance of goods being screened. This is a particularly important distinction if trade facilitation processes are to be implemented and costs minimized, as the judicious use of computer databases can be fast and cost-effective while physical inspection can be timely and expensive. As regulatory demands impose more inspection, border delay grows exponentially. In the modern trading world, trade facilitation demands greater use of screening and more effective targeting for inspection so that both economic and security needs are met.

Prior to the terrorist attacks, Trickey (2001) suggested that the Canada–US border resulted in an average 6 per cent increase in the cost of Canadian manufactured goods, at a time when no tariffs were being collected on Canadian and American-made goods. Small et al. (1999) concluded that the cost of highway delay to motor carriers is very high, estimating it to be between US$144.22 and US$192.83 per hour. Belzer (2003, p. 25), in looking at one border crossing only, the Ambassador Bridge, estimated the cost of delay in 2000 at between US$135.6 million and US$180.6 million for truck trips from Canada to the US alone. He also noted that the cost of budgeted border delay time was 'staggering', at between US$37.1 and US$49.4 million (Belzer, 2003, p. 30). Border delay at some border crossings was clearly problematic before security concerns made it worse.

Studies undertaken since September 2001 have continued to sound the alarm bell on delay. Lepofsky et al. (2003) undertook a detailed study to examine border crossing times (travel time, processing time and delay time) in 2001. The Northern Border processing times were lower and had less variability than those on the Southern Border. Six of the seven border crossing points[11] were surveyed prior to 11 September and, from the data collected for both inbound and outbound crossings, they concluded that, with the exception of Blaine, WA, and the Ambassador Bridge crossing between Michigan and Ontario, it took longer to cross into the US than it did to leave. They also found that US-inbound traffic demonstrated greater variability in total time (crossing time plus processing time) without regard to volume. Belzer (2003, p. 24) found that, after the terrorist attacks, waits on the Canadian side at the Ambassador Bridge also became longer.

The initial Lepofsky et al. (2003) study was followed up in October 2002, and the authors found that more personnel had been deployed at some crossings to handle the volume as security procedures lengthened the processing time. They noted that, because the government was unable to move quickly enough to get the necessary border infrastructure investment approvals, the bridge owners made infrastructure investments at the Ambassador Bridge with private funds. The research, however, did not report the statistical variance that security measures, even with new personnel, incurred as this would have provided a clearer picture of the impact of new security requirements.

Industry Canada's Lean Logistics Technology Roadmap project (Industry Canada, 2004) found that only 18 per cent of Canadian manufacturing companies were unaffected by border delays; 82 per cent experienced increased wait times and therefore increased delivery times and 61 per cent claimed that border delays had a 'noticeable financial impact'. Almost 60 per cent of companies indicated that additional border time was in excess of one hour longer. If we use the truck cost of delay estimated by Small et al., (1999) there is also a noticeable impact on the cost of goods at destination from US border security policies.

After the defining day, the cost of the border has increased and is comprised of more than just the cost of delay; to it must now be added the increase in the cost of uncertainty. There have been a few studies that have examined the border impacts of security requirements in depth. Of these, the series by US academics Taylor et al. (2003, 2004a, 2004b), Canadian trucking interests (DAMF Consultants et al., 2005) and the Ontario Chamber of Commerce (OCC, 2004, 2005) are best known, and will be discussed next.

Taylor et al. (2003) attempted to quantify the cost of the border between Canada and the US and estimated that cost at 2.7 per cent of total 2001 US–Canada trade in goods (US$382.0 billion). Their research found that waiting issues were not so prominent. Taylor et al. (2004a) reported that actual border transit times were not dramatically longer than they were pre-9/11, but that there was greater uncertainty over the border-crossing time. They also concluded that the media's reporting on the need to 'secure' the border may have led US buyers to think twice about using sourcing in Canada.

Perhaps more interesting was the Taylor et al. (2004a) finding that cross-border trucking freight rates were considerably higher[12] than for similar US domestic moves reflecting border transit times, uncertainty about this cost, as well as the costs of border-related information systems support and administrative processes. In short, every surcharge or imposed fee for delay or uncertainty strengthens the economic argument for domestic sourcing and erodes any gains from trade liberalization. Taylor et al. (2004a, p. 295) concluded that the transit time and uncertainty costs of the border ranged from a minimum of US$2.52 billion to a maximum of US$5.27 billion, with a most likely estimate of US$4.01 billion, which represented slightly more than 1 per cent of total US–Canada trade in 2001, and 1.58 per cent of all truck-borne trade. These estimates did not include costs relating to duties, customs administration, or brokerage fees.

On the other hand, DAMF Consultants et al. (2005) narrowed their large research study to investigate the costs of compliance with the *Trade Act of 2002* and US security programs (C-TPAT, FAST, and so on) on the Canadian trucking industry. They estimated that US security measures have added considerably to the border crossing time (and therefore costs), between one hour and one and a half hours to the average transit time for trucks crossing the US border. The reason for the roughness of this estimate is that only about half the carriers who experienced an increase in waiting time could actually provide an estimate of it, which was approximately one hour with a range from 15 minutes to three hours (and there was significant variance by gateway).

DAMF found that truck delay accounted for the biggest component of the costs, but this cost was to some extent mitigated by the ability of the industry to impose offsetting surcharges (see Table 6.2). They also concluded that US security measures are exacerbating the driver shortage for transborder traffic and promoting a slight shift from LTL to TL movements, speculating that it may be because the LTL carriers, with multiple shipments, face more onerous US border clearance procedures. The carriers they interviewed did not see any noticeable shift in modal choice as a result of security measures.

The Ontario Chamber of Commerce study (OCC, 2004) found that border delays are costing the Canadian and US economies over C$13.6 billion annually with more than one-third of that cost being borne by Ontario. They noted that automotive manufacturers have, because of delay

Table 6.2 Impact of border delay

Cost impact item	**Annual minimum cost ($ millions)**	**Annual maximum cost ($ millions)**
Truck delay	231.0	433.0
Driver compliance	3.4	6.8
C-TPAT compliance	5.0	10.0
Computer systems	2.5	5.0
Administration	14.0	28.0
Cost impact sub-total	**255.9**	**482.8**
Less: Border surcharges	77.0	77.0
Net cost impact	**178.9**	**405.8**

Source: DAMF Consultants et al. (2005), *Final Report: The Cumulative Impact of US Import Compliance Programs at the Canada/US Land Border on the Canadian Trucking Industry*, www.tc.gc.ca/pol/EN/Report/BorderStudy/Main.htm, Ottawa: Transport Canada, p. ES-3. Reproduced with the permission of the Minister of Public Works and Government Services Canada, 2007.

uncertainty, had to increase inventory at a cost of C$1 million *per hour*. The study further concludes that in the Detroit–Windsor corridor alone, delays will result in a loss of 70 000 Canadian jobs by 2030. This study also found that it is the southbound move that is particularly difficult. The OCC (2005) study examined the impact of delay on the US economy and concluded that, without improvement, the border effect would be a cost of 91 194 jobs by 2030. Both OCC studies build on the work of Taylor et al., and other transnational regional studies, including transportation productivity studies. In other words, delay is an economic problem for both countries. As Canada is a larger market for US exports than all of the EU, but the US economy is 10 times larger, the border effect hits the Canadian economy harder, and that of Ontario the hardest.

These findings, when considered in conjunction with those of Belzer (2003) and Taylor et al. (2003, 2004a) raise doubts about the ability of Canadian manufacturing and distribution suppliers to compete against US domestic supply over the long term, and particularly in the face of a rising Canadian dollar. Belzer (2003) called for infrastructure investment (in a tunnel) to alleviate border pressure at Detroit–Windsor, arguing that the economic health of the region was at stake, as manufacturers and distributors would begin to make relocation decisions. As a result of their research, Taylor et al. (2003, 2004a) argued that an external perimeter would allow for most of the border costs to be saved, and that could be accomplished by maintaining border controls at the first point of entry to the two countries. Canada has, however, a far greater incentive to create such a perimeter because of its dependence on trade with the US, whereas the US is much less dependent on Canada.

What is particularly compelling about the security perimeter argument is that the use of Canadian and Mexican gateways could, in addition to resolving border woes associated with NAFTA trade, also alleviate the US of the necessity of making substantial port investments. The reduction in the need for internal border controls in a continental security perimeter improves North American competitiveness in a global trading environment. Given the asymmetry of the relationship, the US would be likely to dominate any security regulations applicable to the continental perimeter. This, however, requires a level of trust among the three that may just not be possible.

CORRIDOR DEVELOPMENT AND REGIONAL GOVERNANCE

While there is a large amount of planning, geography and political science literature on borders and border effects (for example McCarthy, 2003 and

Newman, 2006), the issue of a security perimeter (or the less formal zone of confidence) must be set against the concept that regional cooperative agreements and forums to discuss them provide an alternative means of resolving issues within the North American economic space. This is particularly relevant given the nature of bottom-up politics in the US. Furthermore, Proulx (2004) noted that the policies that governments put into place to facilitate such regional relationships are vital to their growth and economic development. This has been a well-discussed issue, growing out of the literature on regional cooperation in Europe and more lately in North America. This section will examine, first, whether there are lessons to be learned from Europe and, second, whether there are success stories to be found within the North American economic space.

Blatter (2001) compared four cross-border regions – two with strong asymmetries (France, Germany and Switzerland – the upper Rhine Valley – in Europe, and US and Mexico in North America) with two with low asymmetries (the Lake Constance Region of Europe and the US and Canada in North America). In the case of the former, he used the Californias (the San Diego–Tijuana region) and in the case of the latter, he used Cascadia (the Vancouver, BC/Seattle, WA/Portland, OR corridor).[13] He viewed regional cross-border cooperation as political institution-building, noting that the US–Mexico relationship is one of utilitarian exchange and the US–Canada relationship is one of ideological coalition-building. He reported that, in border regions, 'transnational integration and domestic decentralization/regionalization are challenging the dominance of national administrations in governing cross-border regions' (Blatter, 2001, p. 181). He described why he believed these cross-border groupings would not be successful in challenging national administrations, using the example of the Californias:

> The Californias (the San Diego–Tijuana region) is a primary example of a polity that is highly integrated in a very selective way (only by many public–private networks for economic development) and shows a high degree of material flows. Nevertheless, all attempts to widen this selective path of micro-integration into a more comprehensive political region (including identity facilitating institutions) failed. Neither on the US nor on the Mexican side has the idea of a common identity of this cross-border metropolis gained enough support to overcome long-standing negative attitudes. (Blatter, 2001, p. 199)

Blatter argued that Europe has a more multi-layered approach that involves the merging of political institutions on multiple levels, and, although it is not a perfect system, it provided a platform from which future economic integration could begin. In North America, he believed, there is more focus on the flow of goods and services within a region, but it lacks the formal political structures to support it. He argued that both Europe and North America are moving toward an era of ever-increasing cross-border integration, but that the multi-level governance approach of Europe is the stronger one.

Many view regional groupings as growing logically out of shared values. The issue of North America's underlying cultural values and regional affinities is not a new topic. In addition to the work of Michael Adams (2003) discussed in Chapter 1, the Canadian government has looked at the regional lens more recently through the Policy Research Initiative North American Linkages research program (Policy Research Initiative, 2006). Boucher (2005) examined the socio-cultural values, concluding that regions are distinctly different and that Canadian regions have more in common with northern US regions than they may have with each other, while northern US regions are more aligned with other US regions than they are with Canadian regions. While it may be comforting for regional groups of Canadians to look south, this implies that northern US states are also looking south! Most important, however, is that Boucher found that there is no statistically significant relationship between socio-cultural values and trade linkages. In other words, while we may think that economic integration will lead to a loss of cultural identity, they are unrelated. Trade is, therefore, about shared interests, not shared values, and Canadians have little to fear from this socio-cultural perspective. This answered the question raised by Fry (2004) about whether regional groupings (through sub-national governments) would erode what is in the national interest.[14] The Policy Research Institute (2006) concluded that transportation is a serious barrier to the development of cross-border regional linkages between Canada and the US. What is of interest from the perspective of transportation is the way the shared interests are addressed in regional cross-border organizations and associations, as examined by Abgrall (2005).

Abgrall (2005) looked at four regional groups – west, east, prairie/plains and Great Lakes/Ontario – to explore the nature and effectiveness of Canada–US regional cross-border organizations. He explored the level of integration and noted that three main themes emerge from these regional cooperation initiatives – economic development, security and the environment. He concluded that the west offers the most complex system of linkages, both formal and informal types, citing the Pacific North West Economic Region (PNWER) as a very dynamic organization. He concluded that PNWER and the Conference of New England Governors and Eastern Canadian Premiers (NEG/ECP) organization were the two major ones in Canada, reporting that while attempts have been made to copy the PNWER approach elsewhere, the model has not been successfully implemented in the other regions.[15]

Briefly looking at the other regions, Abgrall (2005) concluded that the Prairie/Plains area is far less dynamic that the other regions, due in large part to the greater reliance on agriculture for economic success. He reported that there is relatively little cross-border communication, and the organizations that do exist are neither powerful nor exercise a great deal of influence over the players on either side of the border. Because Abgrall drew this conclusion by only looking at the similarities between two regions and the level of reliance necessary and valuable to economic prosperity, he has missed perhaps one of the strongest transportation-focused entities that will determine the future potential of the region, North America's SuperCorridor Coalition, Inc.[16]

Abgrall (2005) also looked at the Great Lakes–Ontario region, which he defined as including Ontario and the states south of the Great Lakes, as well as the trade corridor between Quebec and New York. This is, after all, the region that defines the Canada–US economic relationship. He noted that there is a high level of integration and interdependence based on specialization, but there also is an absence of strong and dominant cross-border organizations. He concluded that this might be because cross-border relationships are more likely to develop at land borders than at marine borders. While this may be true, the largest land crossings on the Northern Border take place in this region, and it is here that the most vocal Canadian businesses reside.

Abgrall also concluded that there is far less emphasis on transborder cooperation in Eastern Canada, which he concluded is due to the New England Governors/Eastern Canadian Premiers (NEG/ECP) organization acting more like an organization to work with other organizations than a facilitator of trade. He noted that this organization was also developed earlier than those in other regions, at a time when the idea of free trade was not solidified. The Atlantic Institute for Market Studies (AIMS) would disagree with such a dismissal of focus on the east coast; it has been a strong supporter of Atlantica, the International Northeast Region (AINER),[17] a regional grouping of business interests that seeks to improve the economic fortunes of the eastern continent. Within the region, there are 23 truck border crossings, including 11 major truck gateways accounting for more than 43 per cent of the total 2000 Northern Border truck crossings, and seven major rail crossings for United States/Canada trade (AIMS, 2004). The AIMS premise is that economic development within Atlantica is limited by border geography and the congestion that occurs in attempting to cross the Hudson River to join the rest of North America. Perhaps more important to firms in the region is the fact that to go in a relatively straight line from Halifax, NS to Buffalo, NY, you must cross the border five times (see Figure 6.1 for the hypothetical route that would be

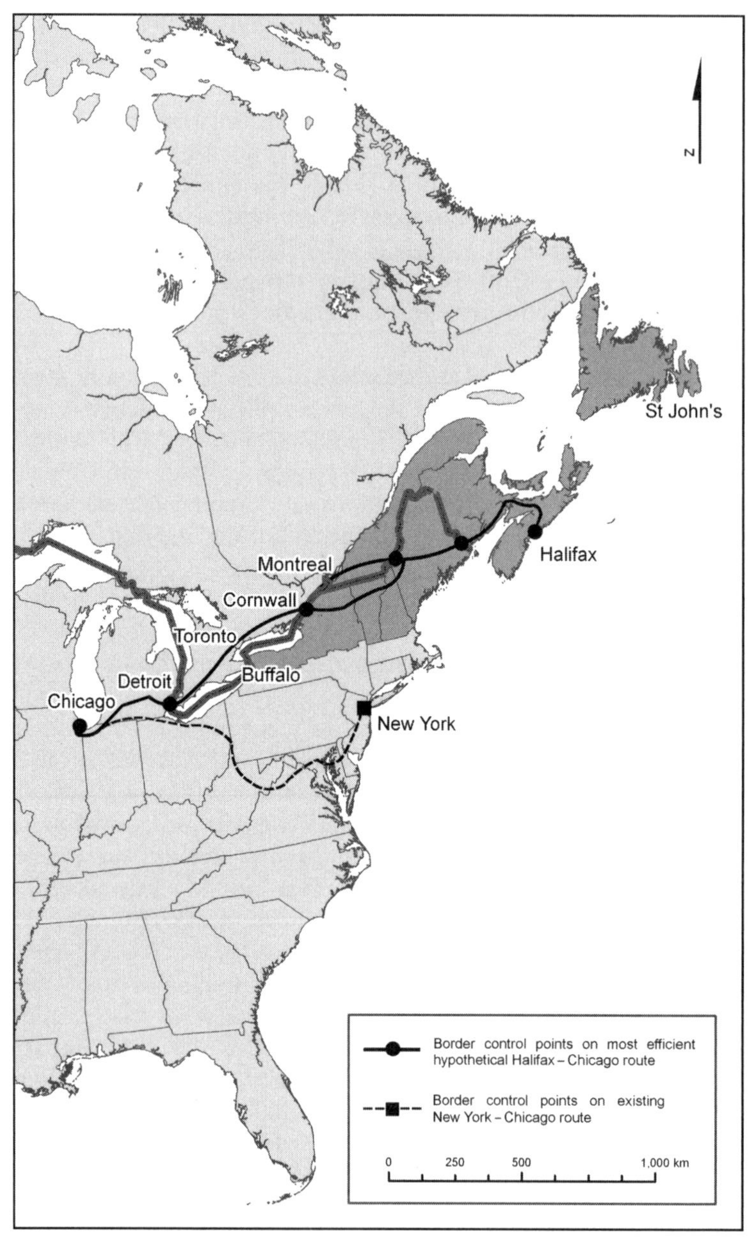

Source: Atlantic Institute of Market Studies (2004). Used with permission. Cartography: Dalhousie GIS Centre

Figure 6.1 The Atlantica international northeast region

more efficient if it were realized). While the history of the region has strong trading relationships going back to before the War of Independence, the Northern Border and security delay seriously damages the established business and cultural connections that draw these provinces and states together. It has been reported by one Atlantic Canadian agricultural producer, who declined to be named, that it lost business in Quebec because the border delays caused by crossing the border twice between Atlantic Canada and Quebec (i.e. taking the route through Maine rather than around Maine) imposed too many costs and too much delay in getting the product to market. Transportation is a strong element of the NEG/ECP relationship.

By focusing on the NEG/MPP grouping, Abgrall (2005) has missed the strongest policy forum in the region. The Council of State Governments Eastern Region Conference is held annually and provides a committee structure and institutional processes to deal with Canada–US regional issues.[18] Juneau (2004) would argue that Abgrall (2005) has neglected a significant fifth regional grouping by subsuming the Quebec–New York Corridor, one of the oldest bi-national transportation corridors, within the Ontario–Great Lakes group. This corridor has a regional focus on further integration in technology, information transfer and education, and in future energy. He concluded that the primary reason for the success of the corridor is its focus on business efficiency. Perhaps more interesting from the point of view of this book is that one of the purposes of the Quebec–New York Corridor is to 'promote commerce and industry throughout the corridor to serve a global marketplace' (Juneau, 2004, p. 2).

While Abgrall (2005) noted that the Cascadia region is the strongest of the Canada–US cross-border regional groups, Blatter made it clear that this success was still not as powerful as those found in Europe. Perhaps even more compelling is the conclusion by Artibse (2004) that long-standing political differences and competing visions of the future will challenge the move towards harmonization. As states and provinces have jurisdiction over many regulations that can act as barriers or impediments to trade, achieving the regional economic agenda will be difficult. He concluded that while PNWER's mandate is to liberalize trade, it must work within the confines of what its participating governments control and regulate. For example, PNWER does not have the jurisdictional right to liberalize trade rules that are under national jurisdiction. What seems to have been missed in all of these discussions about trade is that many transport regulations are made and implemented at the state level, and it is within the power of the state to make local changes in harmony with neighbouring states. Clarke (2000, np) would agree:

> Not all Cascadia organizations put transportation as their top priority. But by promoting a policy paradigm emphasizing regional and transnational arrangements as the appropriate solution to global competition, the Cascadia free marketeers effectively 'de-mobilized' the collective action possible around alternative paradigms advocating bioregionalism and citistate politics . . .

Each of these economic regions seems to have come late to the concept that transportation corridors and their development are critical to trade facilitation and economic development. Both the PNWER, and its International Mobility and Trade Corridor (IMTC) Project, and Atlantica with its championing of infrastructure projects on the eastern continent, are evidence of a changing perspective on the continent. Perhaps most interesting is the renewed interest in short sea research as both of these economic regions struggle with road congestion on one of their corridors, the I-5 and I-95 respectively.

Konrad and Nicol (2004) examined the changes that have occurred along the US–Canada border post-9/11, specifically how cross-border regions have changed. The changes that have occurred post-9/11 were steps that had been needed prior to the events but might have taken much longer to design and implement otherwise. The result is a more technologically-driven system, better equipped to facilitate trade while increasing security between the two nations.

> The reinvented border is much more than a stronger boundary between Canada and its powerful and often isolationist neighbor. The reinvented border lies at the core of a new definition of cross-border regions, regions that are both expedient transfer places between countries and expressions of trans-national community. In this sense the cross-border regions between Canada and the United States are a part of a global phenomenon and one of the world's most important proving grounds for transnational development. (Konrad and Nicol, 2004, p. 43)

Boychuk and VanNijnatten (2004) found that, after 1995, there are indications that convergence may be occurring at the state–province level that is not evident at the national level. Given the strong dominance of regional trading patterns found in most Canada–US trade in Chapter 3, it could be speculated that regional groupings and corridor trade are driving some of the concern in favour of regulatory convergence. It has always been supposed that economists at the national level see the benefits of reduced trade irritants in the form of regulatory differences, but it is also a grass roots issue in some cases. Witness the regional concerns about the impact of the Western Hemisphere Travel Initiative at the Council of State Governments Eastern Region Conference 2007 in Quebec City – the *Resolution Urging the Congress of the United States to Postpone Implementation of the Western*

Hemisphere Travel Initiative Land Border Rules was widely supported. Likewise there was regional interest in a bi-national scope to address short sea shipping by opening current legislative activities to ports in Canada and the US. However, in response to the question of addressing industry standards in Chapter 4, one trucking company had clearly expressed their concern about the balcanization of standards. Currently in trucking there are too many sets of standards.

Regional groups, both political and non-governmental, have strengthened their presence and raised the question about their future role within North America: will the role of regions grow more important in the relationship or will they be eclipsed by the rise of cities and a cities-driven agenda? Gibbins (2006) has argued that the urbanization of North America has prompted a need in both Canada and the US for a discussion on the appropriate role for cities, concluding that Canada's struggle with federal–provincial relations is not unlike the US struggle with states' rights. For the purposes of this and the next chapter, the role for cities will be left for another time.

CONCLUSIONS

One major result of the *Canada–US Trade Agreement* and the *NAFTA* is that trade flows in between Canada and the US have grown to dominate, and Canada's former East–West internal trade has diminished. While the agreements have led to greater economic integration in many sectors (cattle, energy, auto production come to mind), the development of regional trade patterns has been clear. This has also created an even higher level of interdependence between the two countries that has not been accompanied by an equivalent investment in transport and border infrastructure.

Both Canada and the US have recognized that there are at least two components of border activities, those related to trade (and originally tariff collection) that are of an economic nature (which may also include a component of immigration policy), and those related to maintaining physical security, which in addition to being concerned about goods which may pose a biological, chemical, nuclear or radiological threat also has an immigration component (the possible admission of terrorists). Thus economic security and physical security are closely intertwined. The reality is that border cooperation in terms of the Container Security Initiative and in terms of information-sharing are well advanced. As already noted in Chapter 3, there has been a conscious effort through such programs as C-TPAT (and its Canadian equivalent PIP), FAST and NEXUS (and its Canadian equivalent CANPASS) to ensure that physical security procedures are expedited so that economic security is not jeopardized. In addition, there has been a concerted effort to identify those aspects of the clearance process that can be satisfied away from the border and reduce the potential for delay in the transport chain. However, security requirements have triggered a paradigm shift; just-in-time systems were built around the expectation of reliable delivery times (that can no longer be guaranteed), and the business community has not yet found a new business model that confers greater competitive advantage.

Whatever the choice of terminology, a 'security perimeter' or the less offensive 'zone of confidence', Canada and Mexico are now faced with a go-forward situation that is clearly two bilateral relationships with a trading partner who holds the dominant position and appears to be less willing to focus on border issues than even to tackle domestic issues like social security (the primary focus of the Bush administration immediately after the 2004 election). However, the ability to pay for social security benefits or medical care is dependent on a future vibrant economy, one that is clearly interdependent on the fortunes of its two closest neighbours, a fact apparently lost in the Bush administration's climate of fear.

The US and Canada have had a long history of agreements that have predominantly dealt with security issues. If implemented today, would a secure perimeter be a new version of the older model or would it be an entirely new creation? At the moment, neither seems likely. Whatever the nature of political discussions, it will be a significantly difficult process to form such a relationship between the US and Canada without Mexico being involved, yet Mexico has a host of financial, social and political issues that would require major change for the country to be in a position to implement improvements with their two NAFTA partners.

Where does the US perspective of trade corridors under the *Intermodal Surface Transportation Efficiency Act* and more lately under *SAFETEA-LU* legislation come into play? If border investment continues to be driven by congressional budget earmarks and side-tracked by parochial concerns, global competitiveness will not have the profile required to reclaim, for the NAFTA partners, the potential for global economic leadership. The frustration of Washington bureaucrats with their own inability to allocate funds because of state-controlled spending of the highway trust funds on other than trade-supporting infrastructure is clear. Canada is not seen as any better. There is a perception in Washington transportation circles that Canadian politicians and departments are all about announcements and failure to follow up with allocating the funds needed to execute the promise. This perception has been dampened of late as the Harper government found funds to make the Vancouver Gateway a stronger presence in west coast–Asia trade. The transportation system factors that need to be considered in improving continental competitiveness are the focus of Chapter 7.

In sum, the terrorist acts have promoted a reconsideration of the security perimeter of the Cold War's Fortress North America. It has also shifted the focus from NAFTA implementation to a new trilateral agreement, the *Security and Prosperity Partnership for North America*, which reflects the strong US interest in security over trade.

NOTES

1. In particular, Kirton and Richardson (2006) noted that the complexity of the Sound Management of Chemicals program shows that the *two* nations can work together to formulate and execute very complex systems.
2. The LBCIP was eventually replaced after the terrorist acts of 2001 with the current voluntary program, the Customs–Trade Partnership Against Terrorism.
3. Flynn noted that a closed border is tantamount to a self-imposed embargo. If this happens, the terrorists 'win'. The victim has implemented action against itself.
4. Flynn recognized that a hardened border gives rise to unintended consequences; while it appears logical to have tighter controls, tighter security provides incentives to criminal elements to make informal arrangements and to prey on low-paid security staff. Andreas (2003) noted that, prior to the terrorist attacks, US border enforcement policy was a failure due to the unintended consequences as described by Flynn (2003) – more sophisticated transnational crime and smuggling groups had emerged along the Southern Border.
5. The Canadian view was that Canada was fully committed in Afghanistan, was incapable of expending further resources, and did not see UN support for this US initiative. Americans perceived Canada choosing its relationship with the UN as more important than its relationship with the US. The deteriorating relationship was perceived to be the product of poor communication of Canada's position to the Bush administration.
6. On the other hand, Green (2004) has concluded from his study of Canadian and US immigration policy (through three waves beginning in 1870) that immigration is a matter in which Canada must maintain its sovereign role. Canada's ability to withstand structural adjustment in the economy because of its immigration policy, which is tied to the labour market situation, has left it far better off economically as a result, while the US continues to struggle with the inflow of undocumented workers and a backlash socially. Stoffman (2002) would argue that this may have been true at one time, but that the system is now broken and Canadian immigration is less tied to labour skills than perceived by the Canadian citizen.
7. The free-rider problem between Canada and the US has often been illustrated by the so-called 'peace dividend' that Canada has enjoyed from its military relationship with the US since World War II.
8. The phrase 'Fortress North America' had emerged during World War II when Canada and the US contemplated the possibility that the rest of the world might fall to the Axis powers and they would be left to defend the continent. It first re-emerged during the Cold War, when concern about the rising tide of communism led the US to consider renewing earlier isolationist policies. The option faded from discussion with the formation of NATO.
9. Only one Canadian study seems to have addressed the role of Mexico – Goldfarb (2005). She concluded that because Mexican and Canadian priorities are so different, they should look for areas where mutual cooperation advances joint interests, such as mutual recognition of education credentials, expansion of the Canadian guest worker program, withholding taxes, and crime prevention. She did not examine the concept of regulatory convergence in transportation regulation or border management approaches.
10. The Government of Canada under Human Resources and Social Development Canada established the Policy Research Initiative in its efforts to grapple with the direction

Canada could take on a number of social issues. Its website can be found at http://policyresearch.gc.ca.

11. The six were four on the Northern Border – Blaine, WA; Blue Water Bridge, MI; Ambassador Bridge, MI; and the Peace Bridge, NY – and two on the Southern Border – Otay Mesa, CA and Zaragoza Bridge, TX. The one surveyed in October 2001 was the World Trade Bridge, TX.
12. They noted the discrepancies between sources on this point, with differential rates cited as between 10 per cent and 35 per cent higher, depending on the source. They also reported that several carriers charge a border-crossing premium and/or for 'wait time' at the border.
13. There is not a common definition of the Cascadian region. Membership in the Pacific Northwest Economic Region (PNWER) is generally the proxy; currently, it is a public–private sector organization made up of representatives from five US states and three provinces: Alaska, Alberta, British Columbia, Idaho, Montana, Oregon, Washington and the Yukon. Artibse (2004) noted that Cascadia is really a subset of PNWER and comprises just British Columbia, Oregon, and Washington.
14. Fry (2004) argued that sub-national governments, through regional cross-border activities and the power conferred by cooperative action, have a significant potential to shape the nature of economic integration in North America.
15. It is important to note that Abgrall (2005) only looked at cross-border regions through a Canadian lens, thereby missing those with a stronger US perspective.
16. NASCO, Inc. is a non-profit organization along the mid-continent trade and transportation corridor that aims to develop an international, integrated and secure, multimodal transportation system between Canada, the US and Mexico. It desires to secure global access to the continent through its participating ports and transport network partners. By building, for example, a strong relationship with Mexican container terminals, NASCO can secure business for Kansas City's SmartPort. For more information on NASCO, visit its website at www.nascocorridor.com.
17. Atlantica is a region broadly composed of the four Atlantic Canadian provinces, the south shore of the Province of Quebec, the northern tier of the New England states and upstate New York. These territories have a number of characteristics in common – similar demographics, diversity and migration; a shared history; and interrelated transport issues.
18. Such groups are able to develop policy positions on transnational issues and bring state and provincial governments together to develop positions on issues of regional importance that they do not feel have received the attention of the national governments that they deserve. At the 2007 conference, the Western Hemisphere Travel Initiative and short sea shipping were both up for discussion and resolution as part of the Economic Development/International committee's efforts rather than as part of the Transportation committee efforts www.csg.org/policy/infra/default.aspx.

7. A secure North American transportation network for the 21st century?

> The borders are among the most prominent bottlenecks in the freight system. . . . A single continental network would have greater effective capacity than the sum of its parts. (TRB, 2003, p. 33)

INTRODUCTION

While the NAFTA negotiators envisaged growth in trade arising from liberalization, they failed to consider the sheer impact of volume growth on the borders or on transport infrastructure in general. Investments in border personnel or physical infrastructure were minimal, and such commitments remained entirely under the purview of each national government or local (regional) planning agency. The capacity of border infrastructure to handle the growth in trade proved to be inadequate and bottlenecks resulted. This problem is particularly obvious on the Southern Border, where the substantial efficiency gains from open access strangled the trade flow.[1]The ability of the existing infrastructure to not only handle NAFTA-generated trade but also the tremendous growth in continental imports arising from globalization, trade liberalization and the outsourcing of North American manufacturing to other parts of the world (but particularly to Asia) was certainly not contemplated during the *NAFTA* negotiations.

Trade and transportation are two pillars of a vibrant global trading community of which the area governed by *NAFTA* is part. Globalization and the specialization of manufacturing have been encouraged by a deregulated transport system whose costs have been driven down by technology (larger ships and a levelling of knowledge of logistics options via the Internet), improved telecommunications globally, and a functioning, effective global financial network. The bottlenecks in the current global trading system are, for the most part, landside, that is, at the beginning or end of the international supply chain. The infrastructure and border processing systems of North America are more late twentieth century than twenty-first. Without significant improvement in developing a seamless continental transport network, North America's global competitiveness is at stake. (As Limao and Venables (2001) discovered, as transport costs go up, they have a greater impact on transport volumes, explaining why countries with more inefficient transport markets have less trade; in North America, transport costs did go down until the past two years.)

Opinions on the effect of *NAFTA* on North American trade are divided. On one hand, Acharya et al. (2003, p. 62) argued that the depreciation of the Canadian dollar coupled with a buoyant US economy were primarily responsible for the dramatic rise in Canadian exports to the US post-NAFTA. On the other hand, Sawchuk and Sydor (2003) argued that there was a considerable increase in intra-industry trade in the 1990s, drawing on their assessment of two-way trade in auto parts and finished vehicles, computers, and textiles and apparel. In contrast to Acharya et al. (2003), they concluded that there was a rise in intra-firm trade, noting that, in 1998, one-third of all Canada's trade was movement between parent and affiliate, while one-quarter of Mexico's trade was between parent and affiliate. They also expected that advances in telecommunications, information technology and transportation would promote foreign sourcing, and encourage greater intra-firm and intra-industry trade. Davidson (2004) determined that increased trade between Canada and the US resulted because of global trade restructuring. Friedman (2005) argued that the 'flat' world would create the opportunities of the twenty-first century.

It is true that reduced tariffs between North American countries increased outsourcing, but this was a wider, global phenomenon as trade liberalization initiatives had similar impacts elsewhere. In the end, Mexico was only a temporary beneficiary of *NAFTA*; as the world became 'flat', China replaced Mexico as a major source of US manufacturing inputs and US consumer goods imports. Canadian companies sourced very little other than auto parts and household appliances from Mexico, and so did not switch input sources in the same way as US multinationals. Outsourcing and global supply chain development is considerably easier today than it was in the 1980s when internalization theory was widely adopted following the work of Buckley and Casson (1976) and Rugman (1981). The twenty-first century is all about global supply chains, collaboration, and adding value through intellectual capital (Dunning, 1997), yet borders, security and infrastructure gaps may limit the competitive potential of North American companies this decade and beyond.

Trade liberalization and its product, economic integration, are argued to be the key factors in improving productivity and, hence, competitiveness. The global competitive position of a country, therefore, reflects its willingness to reduce protective tariffs, improve inefficient transport systems, and reduce administrative burdens among other things. It is clear from Chapter 1 that the global competitive position of North America has deteriorated, reflecting its difficulties in maintaining its position in global trade and transport. When the World Economic Forum released its *Global Competitiveness Report 2006–2007* (World Economic Forum, 2006), the accompanying press releases were quite blunt. The US was concluded to have a dominant position because of innovation capacity and a high quality system of higher education. However, it was deemed to be vulnerable to those now ahead of it in the competitiveness rankings (Table 7.1), and it has fallen from first to sixth in only one year. There was no press release issued for Canada, whose rank at 16th left much to be desired (by Canadians). Mexico, at 58th, moved up one position, and now ranks behind Chile (at 27th), Costa Rica (53rd), and is equal to Panama, which has moved up rapidly from 65th the year before.

As a key input to competitiveness, the current regulatory climate can be repaired. The OECD (Koyama and Golub, 2006) recently ranked Canada as one of the more restrictive OECD countries in terms of barriers to foreign personnel, operational freedom and foreign ownership. In the three sectors of the transport industry they examined (air, maritime and road), Canada scored much more poorly than the US and even the OECD average. In short, all three countries in North America need to make improvements in both the transport infrastructure and the regulatory environment.

The North American Free Trade Agreement was a trade agreement, not an instrument of larger scope, such as the border-minimizing initiative of the European Single Market. While *NAFTA* contained numerous clauses to reduce tariffs and otherwise implement a new North American trading

Table 7.1 Competitiveness of the NAFTA countries

Country/economy	2006 rank	2006 score	2005 rank
Switzerland	1	5.81	4
Finland	2	5.76	2
Sweden	3	5.74	7
Denmark	4	5.70	3
Singapore	5	5.63	5
United States	6	5.61	1
Canada	16	5.37	13
Chile	27	4.85	27
Costa Rica	53	4.25	56
Mexico	58	4.18	59

Source: World Economic Forum (2006).

relationship, its impact has been diminished by the mere fact that the trade in services provisions did not include all transportation services. As noted in Chapters 2 and 5, some transportation services were included (primarily trucking), while others were specifically excluded (marine and air). Consistent regulatory principles were not a feature of the new regulatory environment. Furthermore, the trucking elements of *NAFTA* were not fully implemented and, while the agreement gives the governments the mandate to complete implementation, they did not choose to do so (described in Chapter 2).

Regulatory reform of the rail sector in Canada, undertaken in the *Canada Transportation Act of 1996*, was very effective in helping the industry become more profitable. Shulman and Shea (2000) concluded that future productivity improvements in the Canadian rail system would have to come from increasing rail density and service quality. A similar conclusion could be drawn about the US system. In both Canada and the US, rail productivity improvements were considerable in the post-9/11 period.[2] Mexico, as well, has worked hard to reform its rail industry. As a result, the North American rail system is healthier than it has been in a long time, and the network is as integrated as is possible without M&As at the Class 1 level.

Chapter 5 documented the state of regulation in both air and marine modes. In the air sector, which addressed many of its concerns through the *Canada–US Open Skies Agreement of 1995* and the more recent 2005 agreement, there is still work to be done. However, this heavily regulated sector operates outside the institutional framework that *NAFTA* provides, and therefore needs greater political willingness to liberalize if it is to achieve additional efficiencies. The marine sector, although forgotten by *NAFTA*, has a new mechanism for discussion in the form of the *Memorandum of Cooperation*.

The importance of the border and the 'border effect' cannot be dismissed. Beginning with McCallum's (1995) finding of a significant border effect in Canada–US trade, Helliwell (1998) concluded that trade integration had not proceeded as far in North America as in Europe. Furthermore, he found the border effect for service industries to be much higher than for goods manufacturers. His 2002 book (Helliwell, 2002) suggested that economists and gravity models have underestimated the role of less quantifiable cross-border costs, such as currency risks and non-tariff barriers (such as equipment standards), and have ignored intangible social factors, like cultural affinities (that may explain the Canada–US bi-national trading patterns).

It has been argued that removing much of the border effect could improve trade on the continent; it should be argued that to remove the border effect, or go some way to minimizing it, would enable better coordinated planning to optimize the use of continental gateways and to enhance the security of the continent. 'Security' and 'prosperity' require intelligent, principled planning and a less protectionist mindset on the part of policy-makers. A customs union or political union is not a necessary first step in dealing with existing non-tariff barriers in transportation services; regulatory convergence can be. Deeper integration is really a company-level phenomenon with two antecedents – a public policy environment that removes non-tariff barriers as well as tariff barriers, and ready access to efficient financial, transportation and communications networks. Transportation services are a key element of both; fixing the transport policy environment, so that services optimize the usage of continental network and supply chain systems, will serve trading interests well on a global scale.

While outstanding issues vary by mode, there are some common themes across the modes. The issues fall mainly into four broad categories: (1) those that may be ameliorated through physical infrastructure investment; (2) those that may be resolved through better information and data sharing; (3) those that may require changes to the security environment; and (4) those that are of a 'softer nature', that arise from differences in regulations, governance or institutions (and may therefore be addressed by mutual political will). The next four sections will explore these cross-cutting themes, so that they may be addressed in a coherent way on a go-forward basis. After these four specific themes are addressed, the chapter will close by examining the progress made under the *SPP*, along with the achievements of the North American Competitiveness Council (NACC),[3] to draw conclusions about what might be added to their agendas from a transportation perspective.

INFRASTRUCTURE AND BORDER INVESTMENT

European transport infrastructure policy is focused on making better use of existing capacity. The overall Common Transport Policy in Europe is generally supportive of intermodal transport, and using market mechanisms and planning to resolve bottlenecks and implement entwined policies in the areas of sustainability, environment and energy. Furthermore, the European approach focuses on making the Trans-European Networks function better. In North America, infrastructure investment and using new technologies to improve border efficiency or, better yet, extract greater capacity out of existing infrastructure seem to be the preferred options.

> Further investments in border infrastructure, both physical and technological, are greatly needed to improve the speed, safety, and security with which cargo moves throughout our three countries. (US Department of Justice, 2002, p. 150)

> Since 1989, with the advent of first the Canada–US Free Trade Agreement and then the North American Free Trade Agreement, the volume of traffic at our land borders has increased significantly. . . . Yet investment in port facilities and border and transportation infrastructure has increased only minimally relative to the growth in trade. (US Department of Justice, 2002, p. 156)

Due to the rapid growth in Canada–US trade prior to September 2001, there was considerable pressure building on the infrastructure at land borders. The need to manage the border effectively was recognized early and reinforced in the year after the terrorist attacks: '[T]he borders are "shared" between these neighbors and should not be unilaterally managed' (US Department of Justice, 2002, p. 61). Park (2003, p. 356) reported 'delays ranging from 30 to 90 minutes are routine at most southern Ontario border crossings. The Ambassador Bridge in Detroit routinely reports delays, ranging from four to six hours'. Most importantly, there is the issue of lost productivity in the truck transport market. '[D]rivers spend between 33 and 43 hours per week waiting – unpaid – while technically on duty. . . . This excessive waiting time represents a US$1.5 billion productivity loss' (Park, 2003, p. 355). The case for investment, or revising business processes, is strong.

In 2000, before security concerns became paramount, the US began to deal with Canada and Mexico much more separately than they had previously. Evidence of this was the formation of two separate bilateral organizations, one for each border; on the Northern Border, the Transportation Border Working Group (TBWG) was formed, while on the Southern Border, the US–Mexico Joint Working Committee was tasked with addressing border infrastructure issues. The mandate of the TBWG is to improve the safe, secure and efficient movement of passengers and trade across the border, and to provide a means of 'advancing border transportation initiatives of common interest, consistent with the broader Canada–US border management agenda' (IBI Group, 2004, p. 7).[4]

In its formative year, the TBWG undertook to create a compendium on border infrastructure needs, which was published in 2003 (Federal Highway Administration Transportation Border Working Group, 2003). The *Compendium* identified 224 infrastructure projects needed, at a total cost of US$13.4 billion. The majority of these, 55 per cent, were at border crossings but only accounted for 13 per cent of the investment dollar total. Corridor improvements accounted for 27 per cent of the projects but 75 per cent of the investment dollars. The majority of these corridor improvements were located in just four provinces/states: Michigan, New York, Ontario and New Brunswick. What is particularly interesting about the *Compendium* is its conclusion: the investment dollars needed comprise the value of a mere 10 days' worth of trade between the two countries.

Most important, the TBWG really only has a mandate for planning and discourse; it has no spending authority. Neither government has downloaded a spending authority to address bilateral infrastructure investment needs that both countries recognize as being needed.

Brown et al. (2005) investigated how transportation infrastructure investments are funded in Canada, and how they are governed. They noted the multi-jurisdictional nature of transportation regulation, concluded that Canada is facing an infrastructure challenge, and recommended that policy-makers must make greater use of a variety of available approaches to funding. Robson (2007, p. 3) noted that the problem is not really a funding one:

> While political and project risks are inevitable, diversification and participation by myriad smaller investors can mitigate their effects. Securitized infrastructure could help close the gap between Canadian retirement savers looking for good opportunities, and the infrastructure repairs and expansions that need their support.

Particularly acute for both Canada and the US is the challenge of the busiest border crossing point, the privately-owned Ambassador Bridge (Fitch and Muller, 2004). This key piece of border infrastructure is a chokepoint in Canada–US trade, and a delay in investment enhances its monopoly returns. A key priority for future investment is a competing option for this border crossing, so as to minimize the 'border effect' and improve the fortunes of carriers and cargo interests in both countries. Given that both Ontario and Michigan recognized the importance of resolving the crossing issue, they announced, on 14 November 2005, a four-way partnership between the two states (with the support of their respective federal governments) to address the infrastructure planning problem (Transport Canada, 2005g).

Recently, there have been significant investments in infrastructure in both Canada and the US, driven more by global trading needs than by continental ones. The Asia–Pacific Gateway and Corridor Initiative (Government of Canada, 2006a) committed C$591 million for investment in British Columbia, including its commitment of C$30 million in the new container terminal at Prince Rupert, BC. A further C$233.5 million is promised for future investments to improve the flow of international trade through Canada's West Coast. The 2007 Budget has, in addition to the funds noted above, committed C$2.1 billion to gateways and corridors (with a national gateway and trade corridor policy framework to 'guide' the government's investment decisions) and a new border crossing at Windsor–Detroit (Government of Canada, 2006b).

Large-scale infrastructure investments in the US have resulted, or are in development, from similar motivation. The first example is the Alameda

Corridor, which opened in 2002. It was a US$2.4 billion project that enabled the quick movement of marine containers inland and away from the congested port facilities at Los Angeles and Long Beach, CA; it expanded the capacity of the ports to service global trade requirements (Alameda Corridor Transportation Authority, 2006). The capital program included US$400 million in government loans and the issuance of revenue bonds as part of the total funding package (Hahn, 2002).

A second example is currently under way; the Port Authority of New York and New Jersey has a capital program that includes dredging harbour channels and constructing on-dock rail facilities and rail connections for its marine terminals. The dredging program includes US$882 million in the federal government funding as part of a total expenditure plan for 'efficient goods movement' over 2006–2015 of US$2.1 billion of its own funds and US$3.8 billion in spending by other government agencies or from federal grants (Port Authority of New York and New Jersey, 2006).

A third example is a mega-project in response to current growth in Asian opportunities; the Heartland Corridor rail line expansion from Virginia to Ohio will support the Port of Norfolk's (VA) efforts to service its hinterland by making the shortest route to Chicago accessible to doublestack trains. This US$309 million project includes earmarked federal funding of US$140.4 million from the federal government, and some state-level funds as well as funds from the Norfolk Southern Railway (Federal Highway Administration, nd, a).

A fourth large project is not really about global trade but does have continental congestion-alleviating impact. All Class 1 Canadian and US rail networks meet in Chicago, and CREATE – a combination of rail and highway improvements in Chicago – is intended to improve rail intermodal terminal operations and interline transfers. At an estimated cost of US$1.5 billion, the project is stalled (as all funding is not yet in place) (Federal Highway Administration, nd, b).

Finally, there are two major greenfield projects – the new container terminal at Prince Rupert (already noted) and the new container terminal for Maersk's APM Terminals in Norfolk, both opening in the fall of 2007. These investments are substantial, and are less about the North American continental trade and more about global supply chains opportunities.

Shortly after President Calderón assumed power in Mexico, he too announced large-scale infrastructure investments; most of those announced were aimed at improving Mexico's domestic transportation network, its gateway potential to access the continent, and to build its attractiveness as a location for foreign investment targeting participation in North American supply chains.[5]

Not all infrastructure investment requirements today are at border. Lack of corridor investment may also cause bottlenecks in international trade flows; the Maine Border Crossings map developed by the Federal Highway Administration, Office of Operations (2005) shows strong traffic volumes as far south as Virginia (from a crossing that is not in the top 5)!

Investment in rail infrastructure is also a continuing and contentious issue; five years ago, Ritchie (2002) noted:

> Today's railway industry operates largely on the last-improved alignments of the early 1900s, reflecting the earth-moving technology of those times. And it operates on the number of main tracks, or fewer, that were built at that time. While the industry has metaphorically repaved its old 2-lane road many times since with better materials, underneath it is still the original 2-lane road.

Today, the North American rail network is running close to capacity. Railways have been willing to enter into co-production agreements to improve service options and infrastructure capacity on the North American rail network. Cairns (2006) provided a number of illustrations of these, including directional running, haulage rights, rationalization of duplicate but underutilized facilities, and noted that these business agreements have been accepted by both Canadian and US competition authorities.

The silo nature of transportation regulation and financial support has meant that governments assume that if there is insufficient capacity, the demand can be handled by another mode; this is no longer true. There is only so much extra capacity railways can extract through co-production agreements. The position of the Association of American Railroads (2005, p. 4) is that the funding the US government provides under its Corridors and Borders Program is 'woefully inadequate'. Such a position makes clear that rail is becoming increasingly concerned about insufficient financing for the US freight system as a network in general!

As solving infrastructure problems unilaterally does little to address border bottlenecks, there is a strong need for bi-national and trilateral solutions to border infrastructure issues. While a bi-national border infrastructure investment agency was seen by carriers (in Chapter 4) to be a key priority, it is highly unlikely that such an institution will be developed.

To conclude, finding the funding for border investment is a challenge of jurisdictions and vision. During the early months of this research, there was a perception in transportation circles in Washington that Canadian politicians and departments were all about announcements and failed to follow up with allocating the funds needed to execute the promise.[6] In Ottawa, the development of a Border Infrastructure Fund (first announced in August 2002), the commitment to fund a new border crossing at Detroit–Windsor, and the 2007 budget support for the Asia-Pacific Gateway and Corridor Initiative are viewed as more than just announcements.

At that time, there was also palpable frustration in Washington with US inability to allocate substantial funds because of state-controlled spending of the gas tax on other than trade-supporting infrastructure.[7] While border control and border infrastructure are clearly within the purview of federal entities on both sides of the border, this jurisdictional paralysis is the very reason why the regional groupings emerging, such as the PNWER (in Cascadia) or NEGACP (in Atlantica), are so important to resolving the issues, both infrastructure and, in some cases, regulatory as well.[8]

An increase in trade volume does not necessarily require an equivalent increase in transport infrastructure. What is required is a systematic approach to infrastructure planning so that trade flows are managed efficiently, and congestion does not extract too great a delay cost, so that the gains from freer trade are not lost to transport inefficiency. The two border working groups have been revitalized under the *Security and Prosperity Partnership*; the question now becomes: will this be enough to generate appropriate border and corridor investment from a continental perspective?

THE INFORMATION CHALLENGE

It is a simple fact that no one really knows how much moves by what mode. The transportation flows of international crude oil, and many dry bulk commodities, are relatively easy to capture because vessel loading and unloading statistics are straightforward to collect and report. In spite of commodity flow survey data collected by the Bureau of Transportation Statistics every five years in the US, the data are incomplete; even less is known about traffic in Canada and Mexico. The problems of data capture for planning purposes, in particular infrastructure investment, are well documented by the US General Accounting Office (2004). The National Research Council (2005) investigation into international trade on the US highway network concluded that the available data did not permit determination of traffic levels and that diesel fuel data, as a model input, would produce unreliable results.

The relationship between supply and demand for intermodal containers is also not well understood, because of inadequate data for understanding the demands of this mode on the transport system. To illustrate, Brooks et al. (2006), when assessing freight flows for east coast short sea services, found only southbound data for the competing truck mode, as northbound international data were unavailable. According to Villa (2006, p. 15), it is also a substantial problem on the Southern Border; he noted that 'the paucity of information (traffic volumes by category of laden or unladen, FAST, non-FAST, total crossing time, origin–destination, commodity, etc.) makes planning an expensive exercise'. Furthermore, he concluded that every land border crossing has different problems, that inter-agency coordination and communication is informal, and that there is significant variability, therefore, between efficiency levels at the various border crossings. Villa's findings on the Southern Border are entirely consistent with the comments received from all the stakeholders interviewed in the course of the research reported in this book. Border-crossing inefficiency is not just a product of infrastructure investment, but also one of information availability, quality and processes.

It is difficult to develop new logistics systems for continental transport management if the planners do not know what moves where or why. Network optimization requires a solid understanding of buyer decision processes, route options and total logistics costs by route. The recent work by Chow (2007) goes some way to understanding these issues for continental gateway decision-making for goods travelling from Shanghai to Toronto or by extension to Chicago. C-TPAT and other security programs could allow governments to collect the data needed to truly understand the markets and the players. Because better security management demands more and timely data collection, the opportunity for better transport planning on the continent is a potential collateral benefit of the new security environment.

The creation of cross-departmental cross-national information forums could go some way towards addressing the dilemma that those who collect the data are not those who use it for transport planning purposes. The US has begun its own cross-departmental approach, creating the International Trade Data System (ITDS) under the guidance of the Bureau of Customs and Border Protection. ITDS was conceived in 1993, but remains a US-only initiative, isolated from Canada and Mexico. While the three countries have cooperated, for example, in collecting data and publishing data, they have not taken the next significant step of developing a common, multilateral data warehouse.

With the new security emphasis on border operations, opportunities to mitigate the loss of data, or its absence, exist. Information technology is so much more advanced than when *NAFTA* was signed that the large questions can be addressed if the data gaps can be filled. Future research is needed to optimize the prospects of a NAFTA data warehouse. While the Security and Prosperity Partnership (2006) noted 'completed' progress on the development of a statistics interchange for North American transportation statistics, such information has not yet filtered down to regional and site-specific policy-makers.

The information challenge is not just about information for infrastructure planning and for security purposes. The ability of good information management supports trade and travel efficiency objectives. The recommendations of US Department of Justice (2002, p. 60) with respect to the US relationship with Canada on the Northern border could not be clearer:

> Finally, the Subcommittee strongly believes that registered border-crossers [including truckers] should have to **enroll only once, carry only one card, and have that card usable at all POEs [ports of entry]: land, sea, or air**. The entry/exit system should be capable of recording, reading, and matching multiple biometrics. . . . The Subcommittee would also suggest that current and proposed USCS programs for registering truck drivers be integrated with the NEXUS programs and the entry/exit system, with the goal of using common technology in the cards and the readers, and allowing integration of the databases.
>
> Without segregating this [low risk passenger and commercial] traffic and expediting its processing, increases in cross-border traffic predicted in the near future will, on their own, create gridlock. . . . With only two-lane access to inspection plazas at many POEs, pre-cleared traffic simply would not be able to get to their dedicated lanes . . .

The TBWG has focused some of its efforts on developing a standard border Intelligent Transportation System architecture to facilitate the movement of goods and people, a group to examine border data, and another to examine border wait times. Although it was noted in Chapter 2 that the number of truck crossings at Blaine had deteriorated since 2001, the border congestion in the Cascadia region, and the high proportion of trips by a small number of companies, made it a good site for pilot work on the use of technology to expedite crossings (Whatcom Council of Governments, undated). It remains to figure out how the implementation of information management systems can be expedited. North Americans have had 15 years to solve some of the information issues, but the pace of change is still glacial.

On the Southern Border, Bomba et al. (2005) found significant problems in data exchange between US and Mexican authorities. The roll-out of security programs left those Mexicans participating in security programs unable to see any benefit from participation. They concluded that the immediate future allows time to repair the problems, and that there should be disincentives that encourage program participation. There would probably be, according to Villa (2006), significant improvement in gains for Mexican companies if security program problems can be addressed.

The focus on security has a significant benefit for planning – it enhances the potential for capturing missing data. As advance notification requirements in support of targeted screening have shown, the border is not the only data capture point. Voluntary security programs have altered the meaning of the word 'border'. Through the CSI (Container Security Initiative), security personnel are now located in other countries, far from the border, and the border has been rolled back to more 'secure' locations, closer to the source of the goods. The border is now a psychological as well as physical boundary between markets, and, as was seen in Chapter 6, some political boundaries have become significant irritants for pro-trade regional forums. Intelligent transportation systems can minimize the irritants, but only if implemented evenly at all significant border crossings and with accompanying inter-agency coordination.

The Automated Commercial Environment (or ACE) is currently being rolled out along the Northern Border; this process incorporates electronic filing of documents and is a process improvement from border management and security perspectives. It has the potential to speed border crossing time while meeting security needs. The American Transportation Research Institute (2007) study found that the border crossing was smoother with the ACE Truck e-Manifest, but that some companies found initial start-up costs to be considerable. They concluded that the e-Manifest 'has the potential to provide net operational benefits for medium and large carriers'. In terms of efforts to improve administrative burden, address border delay and maintain security vigilance, this electronic document filing system should be seen as a positive move towards streamlining administrative procedures and addressing security concerns through advance notification.

A critical component in any activities to ensure a more effective and efficient border operation, therefore, involves not only identifying those aspects of the customs clearance process that can be eliminated, or at least satisfied away from the border, but developing a plan to do so. Such border reform is not just relegated to emerging economies;[9] transport costs and efficiency are major determinants of global competitiveness. Administrative reform is a critical component to trade facilitation and must include the reform of transportation as well as trade documents. A review of the World Bank (2006) *Doing Business* database illustrates that the administrative burden faced by Mexican companies is, in part, the key problem they confront in improving competitiveness and efficiency. Mexican companies must complete twice the number of documents to import or export than do Canadian companies. While Canada and the US have a much lower administrative burden than Mexico, that burden is still greater than found, for example, in either Denmark or Hong Kong.

The Federal Highway Administration found that border-crossing delay was less predictable than delay on urban highways and so embarked on developing the data needed to address the problem. The resulting simulation, Border Wizard, developed by the General Services Administration, and used by the Federal Highway Administration and Customs and Border Protection in the early part of this decade, provided useful input for planning at the local level; a number of border crossings in North America were simulated to assess incremental changes that would help improve their efficiency. With this exception, and the traditional tool of traffic counts, currently available, regularly collected data do not meet the needs of planners. The North American governments have an opportunity to fix the problem through better information management but need to solve the information gaps together. Intelligent Transport Systems, Global Positioning Systems and Geographic Information Systems offer the means to the end, so the impediments can be concluded to be political.

SECURITY CONSIDERATIONS

> [E]conomic integration has outpaced the capacity of institutions, policies and infrastructure to manage the sharply increased volumes of trade, giving rise to concerns about the physical border even prior to the terrorist attacks of September 11, 2001. (Conference Board of Canada, 2005, p. 1)

Security regulations have been found to be substantial factors in a less efficient transport network. DAMF Consultants (2005) noted their impact on trucking operators. Brooks et al. (2006) and Cambridge Systematics Inc. (2007) concluded that security considerations were a significant impediment to the development of short sea shipping alternatives to land transport on the corridors paralleling the east and west coasts of North America, respectively. This supported Ward's (2005) argument that, as a result of security requirements, marine cargo was induced to switch to truck on the congested Ambassador Bridge between Ontario and Michigan. The advance notification requirements are particularly onerous for marine containers originating on the continent.

There are two sides to this coin. Security may be seen as a threat to trade growth or as an opportunity to improve efficiency. In other words, if security regulations are part of a broader move towards either mutual recognition or regulatory convergence within the jurisdiction of the *NAFTA*, the end result could make the continent as a whole more competitive globally. Improved access to US markets from Mexico could allow Mexico to improve its competitiveness against other low-cost manufacturing locales, such as Eastern Europe, Brazil and Southeast Asia. Such improved access may be had through new technologies applied to resolve immigration or equipment security issues. If the conclusions of the Alliance for Security and Trade (anonymous, 2004) that a 20 per cent increase in border delay would cost 375 000 jobs are even close to reality, imagine how many jobs could be created by more efficient borders, or the implementation of a continental security perimeter.[10]

For the positive impacts, cooperative relationships have evolved to support the development of new technologies (such as biometrics and VACIS scanning) and programs to streamline border processing. Programs like FAST and C-TPAT may have been driven by security concerns, but might have developed anyway under the mounting pressure to address border bottlenecks without investing in expensive infrastructure. On the other hand, while these programs to resolve problems developed, the research reported in Chapters 3 and 4 leaves no doubt that industry believes many of the benefits promised have not been delivered. FAST, for example, is not useful if the access ramp to the expedited lane remains blocked by congestion, and traffic is not moving at normal speed because of inadequate investment in near-border infrastructure.

On the other hand, over the past few years, most of the regulatory requirements administered at the border involve matters secondary to the primary objective of maintaining a secure border. For example, the US Department of Agriculture has used the threat of bio-terrorism as a non-tariff barrier and, most recently, imposed new Animal and Plant Health Inspection Service (APHIS) fees for inspections but without substantially increasing hours of operation to handle the activity.[11]

Freight is like the blood of the economy. Like water, it will flow along the best route given tradeoffs of cost, transit time and reliability. However, regulatory irritants, administrative burden, and inadequate infrastructure investment can clog the arteries of the continent. North America's decline in global competitiveness is an obvious symptom that needs to be addressed if prosperity is to be maintained; security can be part of the problem or part of the solution. Continental security, if implemented effectively, can streamline business processes and have efficiency effects, as was seen in Chapter 3 by the cargo owners and in Chapter 4 by the carriers. Technology exists to assist cargo providers and carriers offer a more secure continent. This means that security is intricately tied to not only how well the three countries manage the investment decisions but also the information challenges.

REGULATORY DIVERGENCE, INSTITUTIONS AND GOVERNANCE

According to Phillips (2005), the rail industry responded rapidly to the 11 September, 2001 attacks. It established four alert levels with specific actions to thwart terrorist threats, created task forces to address key issues, established a 24/7 railroad security operations centre, and shared data with authorities. Under the April 2003 *Rail Declaration of Principles*, US Customs and Border Protection installed VACIS and radiation detection machines along the US–Canada border to screen cargo entering the US by rail, starting with the nine border crossings that accounted for 90 per cent of rail traffic entering the US from Canada. On a go-forward basis, Phillips noted that there are four principles of importance to the North American rail industry: (1) security enhancement without impeding trade; (2) modal equity; (3) harmonization of the information requirements by the relevant NAFTA agencies; and (4) use of risk management approaches in all future regulations. She presented a vision of NAFTA regulatory convergence as a key feature in any future trilateral negotiations. Is regulatory convergence possible? This is the fourth key element that needs to be put in place.

To this point, the book has not examined the relative merits of mutual recognition as opposed to regulatory harmonization, and it does not intend to do so. Such a debate is better left to the economists and political scientists who specialize in this. The Government of Canada Standing Committee on Foreign Relations and International Trade (2002) attempted to evaluate the relative merits of the different options.[12] *NAFTA*, while engaging in some mutual recognition in areas such as certification of professionals, focused its transportation agenda on standards harmonization attempts through the relevant committees detailed in Chapter 2. These committees have only picked the low-lying fruit.

Take the vehicle size and weight issue facing the North American trucking industry, for example. This topic has been flagged as very protectionist and parochial. Although its study took place almost a decade after the *NAFTA* was signed, the TEA-21-mandated Committee reviewing equipment standards for commercial motor vehicles in the US did not, in the entirety of its chapter on conclusions and recommendations, consider the impact of *NAFTA* or the efforts of the Land Transportation Standards Subcommittee on the topic to be worthy of mention (Transportation Research Board, 2002). On the other hand, the Government of Canada Standing Committee on Foreign Relations and International Trade (2002) concluded, in Recommendation 30, that Canada should move towards encouraging mutual recognition in general, as Canada and the US have been unable to reach common policies or harmonization of standards. Is this to be a one-sided effort? With the principle of mutual recognition, such US blindness to supra-national considerations would have less impact, but such an approach is wishful thinking.

On the other hand, there is no reason not to have the two governments agree on two transnational jurisdictions based on climate; where 'freeze–thaw' cycles lead to significant pavement damage from longer, heavier vehicles, a more restrictive regime would apply. Such a two-tier geographical standard would, as concluded by some carriers in Chapter 4, lead to 'balkanization' of standards. However, such a principles-based approach would find favour in the north–south (Canada–US) regional groupings discussed in Chapter 6; moreover, as the more southerly US regions would have higher standards, it would be easier to bring Mexicans (with no standards) on board. The key solution is to take a principles-based approach and a phased-in timetable to protect existing fleet investment.[13]

At a University of Ottawa conference on 4 November 2005, Michael Hart indicated that any resolution to Canada–US disharmony and any path towards regulatory convergence are dependent on scholars taking the time to do the investigative research on areas that hold promise for regulatory cooperation.

> The institutional gap is filled by inspired ad hocery. The interconnected natures of the Canadian and American economies virtually require Canadian and US officials to work closely together to manage and implement a vast array of similar, but not identical, regulatory regimes from food safety to refugee determinations. (Hart and Dymond, 2005, p. 5)

While Hart (2000) mooted the idea of a customs union with a single set of rules before the age of terrorism, a customs union is insufficient to address key pro-integration issues from a transport network perspective – immigration, equipment regulation, and safety and security standards. As he noted more recently (Hart, 2006), all three governments have agreed, under the *Security and Prosperity Partnership*, to establish a Regulatory Cooperation Framework by 2007, in order to encourage the reduction in red tape that hampers trade. He concluded, however, that progress on regulatory convergence has been glacial.[14] His suggestion of a bilateral commission for transportation issues might make progress faster, particularly as the US will move forward on its own and at its own pace on the trucking relationship with Mexico.

As for the institutions for progress, many scholars believe *NAFTA* is not the appropriate instrument to make further progress. MacDonald (2004, p. 40) for example, believed that the agreement 'failed to build a public constituency for North American integration'. The problem is less one of forums for developing solutions but more one of political will 'to get the job done' and the ability to bring state governments onside. This requires grass roots support, and neither Canada nor the US has worked to build that support. Haynal (2004, p. 36) argued that *NAFTA*, as 'a trade agreement with a few adornments, is not the right tool for building subsidiarity or managing regulatory obsolescence'. Furthermore, making changes to the *NAFTA* will be just about impossible from a political perspective; Congress is not in favour of opening up the agreement and progress on implementing the original deal was stalled until recently, when Secretary Peters announced the Mexican trucking pilot project (Peters and Hill, 2007).

The dilemma with respect to the institutions of North America could not be better expressed than by Pastor (2001, p. 2):

> What's wrong with NAFTA is not what it did but what it omitted. . . . [I]n the absence of a compelling vision to define a modern regional entity, and lacking institutions to translate that vision into policies, the old patterns of behavior among the three governments remained. This meant that the US penchant for unilateralism and the Canadian and Mexican preference for bilateralism have trumped NAFTA's promise of a novel trilateral partnership.

Hufbauer and Schott (2005) concluded that NAFTA's institutional framework was so 'skeletal' that it impeded achievement of its objectives, in part due to the advisory nature of its working committees. Biersteker (2003, p. 54) seems to have captured the key sentiment of the US's NAFTA trading partners towards the issue of governance:

> First, it is striking, although not terribly surprising, to note how much scholars writing from both Canada and Mexico share a common perception of asymmetrical interdependence with the United States. Accompanying this perception is the common conviction that it is they who must adapt. The Mexican predicament – 'so far from God and so close to the United States' – seems increasingly to be shared by colleagues north of the US border, as indicated when Peter Andreas refers to Pierre Elliot Trudeau's comment about 'sleeping with an elephant.' . . . further moves toward integration and policy harmonization in North America need to be accompanied by a greater institutionalization of governance in the region.

Such sentiments suggest the need for new institutions, and for governments to recommit to resolving outstanding issues. While Appendices 7.1 and 7.2 illustrate that there are many trilateral and bilateral institutions with a mandate to deal with these issues, the problem is really one of execution; the track records of the various NAFTA Working Groups are mixed, and so they have, in many cases, failed to reach consensus on the advice they are to provide.

There is a preference within Canada to deal with the US on a bilateral basis. All parties need to recommit to the use of the trilateral institutions in light of declining global competitiveness for all three NAFTA partners. The question is then whether or not the *SPP* offers a more effective solution to (a) shared security concerns and (b) resolving the current 'border effects' problem caused by regulatory discrepancies and border infrastructure deficits. It is encouraging that the NACC list of recommendations (2007, p. 22) to the leaders includes the following: 'Re-engage the Land Transport Standards Subcommittee/Transportation Consultative Group (LTSS/TCG) to continue the dialogue involving the public and private sectors.'

Politically, both Canada and Mexico must recognize that the US will only cooperate in its own way. The US political system, devised in the 1700s (with its horse-trading negotiation style), remains somewhat trapped in the old ways of doing things. Therefore, as noted by Gotlieb (2005), when dealing with the US, it is better to be narrower in scope as single-issue interests are more likely to be successful. This will only work, however, if there is a strategic vision for the future of the continent.

INDUSTRY AS A PARTNER

> The American Trucking Associations (ATA), the Canadian Trucking Alliance (CTA), and the Camara Nacional del Autotransporte de Carga (CANACAR) have jointly worked with our countries' respective customs, immigration, and various other federal agencies to develop not only the necessary physical infrastructure to improve the movement of trade, but also technologies that can facilitate the clearance process at land border POEs. Such projects include the North American Trade Automation Prototype (NATAP), NAFTA's access and investment trucking provisions, the easing of 'cabotage' rules for the utilization of foreign equipment and the International Trade Data System (ITDS). (US Department of Justice, 2002, p. 150)

It is not just the large industry associations that have worked with governments to help bring efficiencies to the transportation system. There are a number of transborder groups and alliances, like the Border Trade Alliance (founded in 1986), that have focused on issues on trade and economic development. Such organizations inevitably bring transportation issues to the attention of governments. In fact, one of the more outspoken industry associations on border delay, the Ontario Chamber of Commerce, has refocused its efforts recently on infrastructure and border facilitation (OCC, 2006, 2007a, 2007b); that is, they have made their advocacy work more about the solution than about the problem.

In the wake of the *SPP* in 2005, North American businesses were keen to be involved in the next steps of building security and prosperity for the continent. Hosted by UPS in Louisville, KY, a number of key North American companies began to talk about what should be next. A public–private dialogue initiated by the Council of the Americas made three recommendations of relevance here (Council of the Americas, 2006); they were:

> As currently formulated, the SPP promotes regulatory coordination, not necessarily harmonization. In lieu of a common regulatory system, SPP seeks agreement on basic principles and mutual recognition of standards.
>
> Both the public and private sectors have a role in strengthening North American supply chains. Elimination of the NAFTA certificate was strongly advised, as was establishment of a North American competitiveness council.
>
> Shared and/or compatible infrastructure in areas such as customs operations, border security, energy, health, and particularly transportation, is highly conducive to North American competitiveness and security.

Furthermore, the meeting in Louisville concluded that:

> North American integration issues . . . must be approached from the bottom, up. To that end, participants stressed an essential third leg of political support in addition to federal governments and the private sector for a North American agenda: leadership from state/provincial and local leaders.

These conclusions align with those of Chapter 6: regional and local groups have a key role to play in the development of solutions to transportation problems within the North American economic space.

The North American Competitiveness Council provides a mechanism for industry to have input into the dialogue between the leaders. In its first report to the leaders of the three governments (NACC, 2007), it made 51 recommendations in three key areas, two of which are outstanding issues for the transportation network: (1) border-crossing facilitation, and (2) standards and regulatory cooperation. Aligned with this research are several longer-term recommendations supportive of the freer movement of goods, as presented by Stewart-Patterson (2007, np) are: 'elimination of duplicate screening, conversion from paper to electronic processing, coordinated regulatory requirements, . . . a comprehensive North American customs clearance system, a common system for transmitting import and export information, [and] . . . simplified customs processes.'

After years of what appears to be a stalled focus on transportation within North America, there has been considerable recognition of what needs to happen next by both the *SPP* process and the North American Competitiveness Council. This is very promising. However, the wish list of issues for discussion among the three as reported in SPP (2005) should only be seen as a beginning. The key transportation components are itemized in Appendix 7.3, along with the progress made by the summer of 2006 (SPP, 2006); a glaring absence is the truck driver shortage (currently being experienced in both Canada and the US), and the concurrent unanswered question about whether changes to immigration might provide a solution. This list, to some extent, looks to be assembled based on work under way; the items where progress is delayed need new champions and the pace needs to be accelerated.

Furthermore, citizens perceive both the *SPP* and the NACC, like *NAFTA* was seen at the time, as taking place behind closed doors. While the SPP process has not been as transparent as many North Americans would like, it does appear that the combination of political and commercial interests is working to indicate that future progress (in helping the three countries address the outstanding transportation issues) is possible.

COMMENTS AND CONCLUSIONS

According to Dunning (1997), as protectionism declines, the role of the state in developing commercial infrastructure (both regulatory and physical) grows ever more important to national prosperity. This means that the regulatory challenge for North America must be to address the irritants, and those regulations where harmonization has not occurred. As noted by McCallum (1995), the 'innocuous' border shared between Canada and the US has a decisive effect on trade flows, and borders do matter.

However, there is a question about the pace of change. Vernon (2001) noted that public support in OECD countries for open markets is on the decline as interest groups are prepared to sacrifice the open borders desired by traders for environmental reasons, among others. The events of the last six years have illustrated that the US public is prepared to harden its borders for security reasons; fear is a powerful motivator. While the *SPP* provides for a dialogue on border issues and regulatory convergence, and the North American Competitiveness Council provides a feedback loop from the business community to policy-makers, it appears that transportation issues, other than perhaps infrastructure, are not as high on the political agenda as the industry needs. The most important element of the *SPP* to keep in mind is its momentum; it must be able to deliver on the promises *NAFTA* was not able to deliver. North Americans need more progress, and faster, not the pace of the last decade. One key element is to deliver a secure and efficient transport network for freight in the immediate future, not a century from now.

Beatty (2002) described the Canada–US relationship as one in which, because of past lifestyle similarities, common defence arrangements through NORAD, and many joint cooperative institutions (as already noted in Chapter 6), Canadians fear the associated benign neglect of American politicians and bureaucrats. He concluded that because Americans focus their energies on those areas where their strategic interests are under threat, there are some grounds for Canadian concern about the alignment of interests. The existing political and security environment in North America has done little to assuage those fears, and Canada has found it difficult to engage US attention on border and transport issues from the positive perspective of promoting a pro-competitive outward-looking network. This, therefore, raises the question about whether Canada moves bilaterally and seeks to address outstanding transport issues through the TBWG process, or is more inclusive by supporting Mexican participation in addressing continental transportation infrastructure gaps and regulatory divergence via the trilateral SPP process. The answer depends on whether the transport network, and perhaps the political situation, is seen as a bilateral one or a trilateral one.

The liberalization provided by the *NAFTA* was the extension of the Canadian trade agreement to Mexico. Therefore, the future from a Canadian perspective cannot be divorced morally from Canada's relationship with Mexico. By treating the region as two bilateral relationships, the US has signalled that there is a pecking order in the North American household. Given the continuing inequality of many modern marriages, Canada's role is that of the first wife, one of greater but diminishing standing than Mexico's position of the mistress who, herself, is being replaced by the Chinese beauty in the other room. Canada cannot assume that her future is assured; in fact, the challenge is one of maintaining position or status in the face of the Asian challenge. To use a phase from an article in *The Economist* (anonymous, 2005c), Canada's 'passion for bronze' may be realized.

What is Mexico's future with respect to transportation? According to Eaton (2004, p. 59), it is clear: 'Mexico has the opportunity to use the creation of a secure transportation system as a comparative advantage in the global search for investment.' Like Canada, Mexico provides access points to the extensive North American consumer market. Eaton believed that if Mexico could align its interests to adopt C-TPAT and Container Security Initiatives, it could serve as a critical link in global supply chains. He saw that manufacturers were reconsidering, in light of growing port congestion and international transport bottlenecks, their overly long Pacific supply chains. For Mexico to play in the new gateway and corridor game, it would have to develop a more competitive transport system. The vision in Canada is very similar. The opportunities for Canadian ports and trade corridors to play a larger role in servicing the US economy is being taken seriously. The largest impediment to Canada's role as a gateway to North America is continuing border wait times, the uncertainty about delay in border processing, and the continuing regulatory divergence that impacts operations of continental transport suppliers. Both borders, while very different, have much in common. Canada's future is not morally divorced from Mexico's future.

Hufbauer and Schott (2004, p. 5) argued that Canada's agenda must include the Mexicans, but for another reason:

> Canadians must bear in mind that Republicans and Democrats alike energetically court the fastest-growing ethnic block – the Hispanic vote – in presidential, congressional and statehouse races. But neither Republicans nor Democrats compete for the Canadian vote. NAFTA politics in the United States are thus far more sensitive to Mexico than Canada.

Biersteker (2003) sees the same outcome but for different reasons. From his perspective, the traditional way to gain progress is for Canada first to establish the rules, and then to seek extension to Mexico. This is how progress started in the two forgotten modes – marine and air – with the short sea *Memorandum* and the 1995 Open Skies agreement. This was also true in the development of the 'smart border' rules, in the establishment of the border working groups, and, most obvious of all, in the sequencing of *CUSTA* then *NAFTA*.

Although Mexico is seen by many in the world as a failing state (Hart, 2003), it seeks to bring its informal economy into its formal one, and to improve transparency and living standards; without this, Mexican emigration to the US will continue to be problematic. As a result, the NAFTA partners need to make any changes a 'win' for Mexico in order for it to be a win for all. Both Canada and Mexico need to see transportation liberalization and investment in transportation services infrastructure as an important component of their plans for participation in future growth in the North American economic region.

The only perspective for North Americans in a globalized world must be a continental one. However, regulatory control of the most important transport operations is at the state/provincial level, in the case of the most dominant mode trucking, or 50 years out of date, in the case of the marine mode. As the groundswell of environmental concerns in North America gains traction, the three governments have a limited time to fix the 'softer' concerns as well as the infrastructure.

All three countries are in need of a new vision of North America, one that puts forward trilateral institutions. Vision is a matter of both desire and direction. For most North Americans, the desire for 'succeeding together' seems weak. Even for those with desire, the direction is a subject for debate. Should the end be sought by means of a common perimeter or greater cooperation, with incremental steps that 'chip away' at regulatory irritants? The cooperative route still requires delivery on the existing promise.

It is important to consider Biersteker's approach. Mexico had a much longer road to travel in its liberalization and reform plans. It is up to the US and Canada to work together to bring Mexico into prosperity just as northern Europe has helped Spain and Portugal. The *SPP* and the North American Competitiveness Council provide forums for dialogue and working groups to enable both internal North American adjustment and external efforts to deal with globalization impacts and continental security efforts. The past has shown that Canada–US agreements can be extended to Mexico successfully as was the case with both *NAFTA* and the *Memorandum of Co-operation on Short Sea Shipping*. There is room for both bilateral and trilateral agendas and activities in the North American economic space.

The time for turf battles has passed. The rest of the world is quickly removing remaining non-tariff barriers in their efforts to streamline processes and improve trade efficiency. North Americans must see the trade-facilitating aspects of convergence in equipment regulation or immigration as part of a larger security and prosperity agenda. Mexico continues to look north to both countries for support; both Canada and the US need to see Mexico as part of the solution, not part of the problem. Greater security can come from developing a continental approach, through a series of trilateral institutions.

Progress on competitiveness needs an even greater commitment on streamlining the transportation system and the management of borders than the current SPP process or even the NACC envisage. The transportation regulatory climate remains firmly entrenched in the mid-1990s, while Europe has proceeded to liberalize its trade in transportation services and develop continental networks. The administrative burden on transborder flows needs streamlining. The 'age of terrorism' is a given for the foreseeable future; the industry sees security as a competitive necessity. From a transportation network perspective, the system needs to be evaluated continentally, not nationally, if a secure and efficient transportation network for the twenty-first century is to be realized.

APPENDIX 7.1 CANADA'S KEY TRANSPORT-RELATED TRILATERAL NAFTA INSTITUTIONAL RELATIONSHIPS

NAFTA Land Transportation Standards Subcommittee Transportation Consultative Working Group # 1 (LTSS # 1) – Cross Border Operations and Facilitation
NAFTA Land Transportation Standards Subcommittee Working Group # 2 – vehicle weight and dimension (VW&D) harmonization
North American Aviation Trilateral (NAAT)
Tri-national Technical Safety Committee (Canada, US and Mexico) and Steering Committee
NAFTA-LTSS Transportation Consultative Group (TCG) Working Group # 2 (rail safety and economic issues)
NAFTA – TCG 5 (Marine Policy and Safety issues)

Note: This table excludes Canada's multilateral relationships where trilateral transport issues may be discussed, e.g., International Civil Aviation Organization, International Maritime Organisation, Organisation for Economic Cooperation and Development, and so on.

Source: Mouafo, D., N.P Morales and J. Heynen (2004), *Building Cross-Border Links: A Compendium of Canada US Government Collaboration*, Ottawa: Canada School of Public Service, http://dsp-psd.pwgsc.gc.ca/Collection/SC103-6-2004E.pdf, pp. 152–3. Reproduced with the permission of the Minister of Public Works and Government Services Canada, 2007.

APPENDIX 7.2 TRANSPORT CANADA'S KEY BILATERAL INSTITUTIONAL ARRANGEMENTS WITH THE US

Canada–US Transportation Border Working Group (TBWG)
Border Information Flow Architecture Working Group (BIFAWG)
Transport Canada National Civil Air Transportation System Shut Down Plan Development – Co-ordination with Federal Aviation Agency (FAA)
NASA Space Shuttle Emergency Landing Site Contingency Plan; Co-ordination with NASA and US Department of State and US Embassy
Bilateral Aviation Safety Agreement (2000)
Airport Pre-clearance Agreement
TC/FAA Regional Cross Borders Transportation Summit (annual event)
TC/FAA communications over issues concerning regional certification / transborder / commercial operations co-ordination
Canada–US Air Transport Agreement
North American Aerospace Surveillance Council (NAASC)
FAA Working Group on the US Standard for Terminal Instrument Procedures (TERPS)

Transportation Research Board, Freeway Operations Committee – exchange of technical information on Intelligent Transportation Systems (ITS)
ENTERPRISE Shared Pool Fund (Collaborative efforts to further develop and demonstrate ITS)
National Transportation Commission for ITS Protocol (NTCIP)
Canada–US Ontario–Michigan Bi-national Transportation Partnership
Ontario–Michigan Border Working Group (OMBWG)
Upper Midwest Freight Corridor Study, investigation of freight activities in corridor between Minnesota and Ohio[1]
Canadian–American Border Trade Alliance (Can/Am BTA)[2]
Canada–US Transportation Security Co-operation Group (with the TSA)
Bi-National Marine Security Compliance and Enforcement Working Group
Memorandum of Cooperation on Sharing Short Sea Shipping Information and Experience between the Transportation authorities of Canada, Mexico and the United States of America.
Joint Canada–US study on future infrastructure needs of the Great Lakes – St. Lawrence Seaway navigation system
International Mobility and Trade Corridor [Project] (IMTC) (1)

Notes:
1. A corridor-specific study group.
2. The Can/Am BTA is strictly a non-governmental private sector stakeholder advocacy organization

Source: Mouafo, D., N.P Morales and J. Heynen (2004), *Building Cross-Border Links: A Compendium of Canada US Government Collaboration*, Ottawa: Canada School of Public Service, http://dsp-psd.pwgsc.gc.ca/Collection/SC103-6-2004E.pdf, pp. 147–52. Reproduced with the permission of the Minister of Public Works and Government Services Canada, 2007.

APPENDIX 7.3 KEY ISSUES AND PROGRESS (AS OF AUGUST 2006) VIA THE SECURITY AND PROSPERITY PARTNERSHIP

Security and Prosperity Initiatives[1]	Progress[2]
Regulation of Land Modes – Road	
Recognize and harmonize North American motor carrier regulations and standards. Hold scoping meetings in 2005 and early 2006 to identify specific, potentially resolvable VWD issues.	Delayed
By 2010, recommend coordination methods and implement appropriate standards and administration adjustments.	On track
By the end of 2007, establish procedures for the electronic exchange of motor carrier safety data.	On track
By the end of 2007, develop a system of reciprocal recognition of motor carrier safety ratings.	On track

Work toward establishing an intermodal corridor work plan and a Memorandum of Cooperation and pilot project.	Delayed
Regulation of Land Modes – Rail	
Coordinate North American rail safety. Continue to conduct bi-annual senior management meetings to consider ways of promoting rail safety and facilitating cross-border flows of rail traffic.	On track
Examine rail safety regulations to identify opportunities for further harmonization by the end of 2006.	On track
Marine and Air Liberalization	
Enhance short sea shipping. Hold a continental Short Sea Shipping conference by spring 2006.	Completed
Implement the Memorandum of Cooperation by 2007.	On track
Develop a collaborative approach within 12 months (June 2006) in dealing with each country's flag vessels calling at one of the other countries' ports.	On track
Explore opportunities for expanding air transportation relations on a bilateral and trilateral basis.	On track
Address economic barriers to an open trilateral regime by identifying constraints at the national level and determining how they can be addressed, and reaching agreement on an equitable regime applying to all three countries.	On track
Work toward a Mexico–US Bilateral Aviation Safety Agreement (BASA).	On track
Reducing Border Effects	
Use new or enhanced mechanisms to support border planning, information sharing and communications. Revitalize the Canada–US Transportation Border Working Group and the US–Mexico Joint Working Committee on Transportation Planning by the end of 2005	Completed
. . . [D]evelop an implementation plan for priority infrastructure investments at key land border ports of entry by 2008.	Assumed to be ongoing
Track and analyze border trade and traffic flows using modern technologies. Maintain and update trinational data held in the North American Transportation Statistics Interchange. . . .	Completed
Assess the feasibility of further streamlining FAST processing at ports of entry (green lanes) within 18 months (December 2006).	Delayed
Develop and deploy an accurate system for measuring and reporting border transit times within 36 months (June 2008).	US–CN: Initiated US–MX: On track

Complete a review of our transportation and border facility needs and identify priorities within 24 months (June 2007), and;	On track
Then, in partnership with state and provincial partners, develop an implementation plan to prioritize future infrastructure investments by 2008.	On track
Amelioration of Cargo Security Effects	
Develop and expand upon our joint public–private partnerships to secure the supply chain of goods arriving in North America, and to expedite the movement of low-risk goods within North America. Develop targets to increase percentage of FAST/Expres [sic] shipments at agreed upon FAST/Expres [sic] locations, including joint marketing activities within 12 months (June 2006) and annually thereafter.	On track
Make compatible US–Canada requirements for participation in Customs–Trade Partnership Against Terrorism (C-TPAT) and Partnership in Protection (PIP) within 36 months (June 2008).	On track
Develop compatible standards, technologies and processes for intermodal supply chain security that emphasize risk management, a layered approach to supply chain security, and the expedited movement of low-risk commerce. Evaluate within 6 months (December 2005) and seek to expand within 18 months (December 2006) the use of E-manifest.	On track
Within 6 months (December 2005), initiate a five-year Canada–US program to work toward harmonization of automated commercial information systems, including advance interdepartmental reporting and the single window concept for other government departments' and agencies' requirements.	Completed
Develop and implement a US–Mexico cargo initiative that includes the implementation of the 24-hour rule, exchange of cargo manifest data, and joint security targeting.	On track
Develop appropriate linkages, including officer exchanges among Canadian, Mexican and US customs agencies, to ensure analysis of cargo data and appropriate sharing of information on high-risk shipments.	Initiated

Notes:

1. This table has selected elements, and parts of elements, to interpret the concept of progress under headings provided by the author. Some of the elements were already under way when the SPP (2005) was compiled and so are not listed, like the compendium on Canada–US border infrastructure requirements (Federal Highway Administration Transportation Border Working Group, 2003) and the use of *Border*

Wizard to evaluate Mexican border architecture. For a complete list and original order, please consult the original document.
2. The progress assessment is the political one reported in the source document.

Source: Security and Prosperity Partnership of North America (2006).

NOTES

1. See US International Trade Commission (2002), pp. 135–6 for a clear discussion on border effects.
2. Shulman and Shea (2000) noted that the reduction in operating costs in the latter parts of the 1990s had a major impact on the profitability of the Canadian rail service and agreed with the findings of Public Works and Government Services Canada (2001, p. 50) that Canada's Class 1 railroads were finally viable financially for the first time in decades.
3. The North American Competitiveness Council was officially launched on 15 June 2006 by the leaders of the three governments.
4. The TBWG had its first meeting in January 2002 and is mandated to meet twice a year.
5. The first step is a one-year study to identify projects of high impact in generating trade and economic growth (Field, 2007).
6. This view was widely held by those interviewed in the winter and spring of 2005.
7. This view was also widely held by those interviewed. In Canada, there has been a well-established recognition that public–private partnerships can be used to fund transport investment, while the US has been more reticent to take this approach. The success of the Alemeda Corridor project in California has prompted renewed interest in examining such arrangements, given the US's current financial circumstances.
8. The New England Governors and Maritime Premiers have been making progress on understanding the issues, and the Atlantic Provinces Chamber of Commerce, a Canadian NGO, recently appointed its president from Bangor, ME (US) to strengthen regional bilateral ties (Power, 2007).
9. Boardman (2006) focused partly on reducing transportation regulation 'behind the border' as part of the process for increasing global competitiveness of the countries emerging from the former communist states of eastern Europe.
10. The same group found that the US visit program would cost 1.4 million jobs in its 2005 study (Brezosky, 2005).
11. While APHIS fees have been in place to recover costs on agricultural exemptions, these fees were adjusted upwards in 2004 to recover the costs of 'increased inspection activity'. Canada has always enjoyed an exemption from the fees on Canadian goods being imported to the US. The US first proposed to remove the exemption effective 24 November, 2006 and, while implementation has been postponed twice, the fees were implemented effective 1 June, 2007.
12. The Committee's report presented the key arguments for several courses of action, including customs union, and its Chapter 4 is recommended reading.
13. As Table 4.1 indicated, truck fleets are generally replaced every 5.5 years so a phase-in period of six years is certainly a reasonable one.
14. Martin (2005), under the Policy Research Initiative, noted that transportation was on the list for regulatory cooperation but without any other details. The North American Competitiveness Council (2007) lauds the SPP for its progress on developing the framework and the 4-page framework document was posted on the US SPP website after the August 2007 Montebello summit. The principles are written in such a way as to leave a reader to conclude that cooperation will occur in the regulation of goods and through existing working groups, but transportation is not specifically identified as an area for further work.

References

Abgrall, J.-F. (2005), 'A survey of major cross-border organizations between Canada and the United States', Policy Research Initiative working paper series 009, Ottawa, published in *North American Linkages*.

Acharya, R., P. Sharma and S. Rao (2003), 'Canada–U.S. trade and foreign direct investment patterns', in R.G. Harris (ed.), *North American Linkages: Opportunities and Challenges for Canada*, Calgary, AB: University of Calgary Press, pp. 13–88.

Adams, M. (2003), *Fire and Ice: The United States, Canada and the Myth of Converging Values*, Toronto: Penguin Canada.

Airports Council International (2003), 'Air cargo liberalization (ATConf/5-WP/94)', presentation to Worldwide Air Transport Conference Challenges and Opportunities of Liberalization, March, Montreal, QC, accessed at www.icao.int, pp. 24–9 of conference report.

Alameda Corridor Transportation Authority (2006), 'Fact sheet, 2006', accessed at www.acta.org/newsroom_factsheet.htm.

American Transportation Research Institute (2007), 'ATRI research measures impact of ACE truck E-Manifest system on trucking operations', press release, 29 March, accessed at www.atri-online.org/news/.

American Trucking Associations (2005), 'American trucking trends 2004', accessed at www.truckline.com.

Andreas, P. (2003), 'A tale of two borders: The U.S.–Canada and U.S.–Mexico Lines after 9-11', in P. Andreas and T.J. Bierstekcr (eds), *The Rebordering of North America: Integration and Exclusion in a New Security Context*, New York & London: Routledge, pp. 1–23.

anonymous (2001), 'Transportation glitches prompt Ford closures', *Calgary Herald*, 15 September.

anonymous (2003), 'Combinatorial auction: a boon for small trucking companies?', accessed at www.its.berkley.edu/publications/ITSReviewon line/winter 2003, 2, 1.

anonymous (2004), 'New border security technology faces test', *NewsMax.com Wires*, 15 November.

anonymous (2005a), 'Airports could see route expansion under Canadian open skies', *Airports*, **22**(47), 1.

anonymous (2005b), 'The Americas: burghers beef over mad economics; Canada', *The Economist*, **376**(8433), 54.

anonymous (2005c), 'The perils of cool', *The Economist*, **377**(8455), 15–16.

Arnold, M. and J.G. Dickinson (2003), 'Cracking down on cross-border drug sales', *Medical Marketing and Media*, **38**(6), 34.

Artibse, A.F.J. (2004), 'Cascadian adventures: shared visions, strategic alliances, and ingrained barriers in a transborder region', in H. Nicol and I. Townsend-Gault (eds), *Holding the Line: Borders in a Global World*, Vancouver, BC: University of British Columbia Press, pp. 238–67.

Association of American Railroads (2005), *TEA-21 Reauthorization and Railroad Infrastructure Investment*, February, Washington, DC: Association of American Railroads.

Association of American Railroads (2006), 'Class 1 railroad statistics', accessed at www.aar.org/AboutTheIndustry/RailroadProfiles.asp.

Atlantic Institute for Market Studies (AIMS) (2004), 'AIMS on Atlantica: two countries, one region', Autumn, Atlantic Institute for Market Studies Halifax, NS, accessed at www.aims.ca/library/atlanticapart2.pdf.

Baker, J.A. III (2000), 'Present at the creation: the American side', in M.E. Kreinin (ed.), *Building a Partnership: The Canadian–United States Free Trade Agreement*, Ann Arbor, MI: Michigan State University Press, pp. 1–8.

Barzyk, F. (1996), 'Trucking in a borderless market: a profile of the Canadian trucking industry 1988–1994', *Canadian Transportation Research Forum Proceedings*, **1**, 24–41.

Beatty, P. (1999), 'Confident nations don't cower behind barriers: Canada reaps the multiple benefits of liberalized world trade agreements', *Plant*, **58**(18), 26.

Beatty, P. (2002), 'Canada in North America: isolation or integration?', in P. Hakim and R.E. Litan (eds), *The Future of North American Integration: Beyond NAFTA*, Washington, DC: Brookings Institution Press, pp. 31–71.

Beltrame, J. (2001), 'Fortress North America: how our world will change', *MacLean's*, **114**(42), 23–7.

Belzer, M.H. (2003), 'The jobs tunnel: the economic impact of adequate border crossing infrastructure', *Sound Science*, 3 November, Ann Arbor, MI, accessed at www.is.wayne.edu/mbelzer/.

Belzer, M.H., D. Rodriguez and S.A. Sedo (2002), 'Paying for safety: an economic analysis of the effect of compensation on truck driver safety', 10 September, accessed at www.is.wayne.edu/mbelzer/pubs/PayAndSafety_Report_020910.pdf.

Biersteker, T.J. (2003), 'The rebordering of North America: implications for conceptualizing borders after September 11', in P. Andreas and T.J. Biersteker (eds), *The Rebordering of North America: Integration and*

Exclusion in a New Security Context, New York & London: Routledge, pp. 153–65.

Bissett, J. (2002), 'Canada's asylum policy: a threat to American security?', May, Center for Immigration Studies background paper, Washington, DC, accessed 1 December, 2005 at www.cis.org/articles/2002/back402.html.

Blank, S. and M. Coiteux (2003), 'The state of North American integration', *International Management*, **8**(1), 1–7.

Blank, S. and J. Haar (1998), *Making NAFTA Work: US Firms and the New North American Environment*, Miami, FL: North-South Center Press.

Blatter, J.K. (2001), 'Debordering the world of states: towards a multi-level system in Europe and a multi-polity system in North America? Insights from border regions', *European Journal of International Relations*, **6**(7), 175–209.

Boardman, H.G. (2006), *From Disintegration to Reintegration: Eastern Europe and the Former Soviet Union in International Trade*, Washington, DC: The World Bank.

Boeing (2004), 'World air cargo forecast 2004/2005', accessed at www.boeing.com.

Bomba, M., J.C. Villa, W. Stockton and R. Harrison (2005), 'Current issues related to security and safety initiatives for Mexican truck carriers along the Texas–Mexico border' (5-9014-01-P7), June, University of Texas at Austin, Center for Transportation Research, Austin, TX.

Bonsor, N. (1995), 'Competition, regulation and efficiency in the Canadian railway and highway industries', in Filip Palda (ed.), *Essays in Canadian Surface Transportation*, Chapter 2, Vancouver, BC: The Fraser Institute.

Boucher, C. (2005), 'Toward North American or regional cross-border communities, a look at economic integration and socio-cultural values in Canada and the United States', Policy Research Initiative working paper series 002, Ottawa, published in *North American Linkages*.

Bowland, J. and D. McKnight (1996), 'Best practices in the North American trucking industry', *Canadian Transportation Research Forum Proceedings*, **1**, 11–23.

Boychuk, G.W. and D.L. VanNijnatten (2004), 'Economic integration and cross-border policy convergence: social and environmental policy in Canadian provinces and American states', Policy Research Initiative, Ottawa, *Horizons*, **7**(1), 55–60.

Brezosky, L. (2005), 'Study: new US visa program could cost millions of dollars, jobs', *The Daily Texan*, 20 January.

Brooks, M.R. (1994), 'The impact of NAFTA on transportation companies: a Canadian point of view', *Transport Reviews*, **14**(2), 105–17.

Brooks, M.R. (2006), 'The Jones Act under NAFTA and its effects on the Canadian shipbuilding industry', Atlantic Institute for Market

Studies, Halifax, NS, accessed at www.aims.ca/library/BrooksResearch.pdf.

Brooks, M.R. and K.J. Button (2007), 'Maritime container security: a cargo interest perspective', in K. Bichou, M. Bell and A. Evans (eds), *Port, Maritime and Supply Chain Security: Frameworks, Models and Applications*, London: Informa, pp. 221–36.

Brooks, M.R. and J.D. Frost (2004), 'Short sea shipping: a Canadian perspective', *Maritime Policy and Management*, **31**(4), 393–407.

Brooks, M.R. and J.R.F. Hodgson (2005), 'The fiscal treatment of shipping: a Canadian perspective on shipping policy', in K. Cullinane (ed.), *Shipping Economics: Research in Transportation Economics*, **12**, 143–71.

Brooks, M.R. and S. Kymlicka (2007), *Unfinished Business: A NAFTA Status Report*, Halifax, NS: Atlantic Institute for Market Studies.

Brooks, M.R. and P. Ritchie (2005), 'Trucking mergers & acquisitions in Canada and the US since NAFTA', *Transportation Journal*, **44**(3), 23–38.

Brooks, M.R., J.R.F. Hodgson and J.D. Frost (2006), 'Short sea shipping on the East Coast of North America: an analysis of opportunities and issues', project ACG-TPMI-AH08, Transport Canada, Dalhousie University, Halifax, NS, accessed at http://management.dal.ca/Research/ShortSea.php.

Brown, D., G. Hoover, A. Howatson and J. Schulman (2005), *Canada's Transportation Infrastructure Challenge: Strengthening the Foundations*, Toronto: The Conference Board of Canada.

Buckley, P.J. and M. Casson (1976), *The Future of the Multinational Enterprise*, New York: Holmes & Meier.

Burney, D.H. (2000), 'Present at the creation: the Canadian side', in M.E. Kreinin (ed.), *Building a Partnership: The Canadian–United States Free Trade Agreement*, East Lansing, MI: Michigan State University, pp. 9–18.

Button, K.J. (1998), *Opening U.S. Skies to Global Airline Competition*, 24 November, Washington, DC: Cato Institute.

Cairns, M. (2002), 'Rail perspective on international competition and transportation', presentation to the Canadian Transportation Research Forum Semi-Annual Meeting, Saskatoon, SK, 25 October.

Cairns, M. (2006), 'Overcoming rail infrastructure capacity constraints: implications for competition', Proceedings, Canadian Transportation Research Forum Annual Meeting, Quebec City, QC, May, pp. 327–43.

Cambridge Systematics Inc. (2005), 'Short sea and coastal shipping options: final report', report prepared for the I-95 Corridor Coalition, November.

Cambridge Systematics Inc. (2007), 'Cross border short sea shipping study: final report phase II', report prepared for the Whatcom Council of Governments, January, accessed at www.wcog.org/library/imtc/sss 2report.pdf.

Cameron, M.A. and B.W. Tomlin (2000), *The Making of NAFTA: How the Deal was Done*, New York: Cornell University Press.
Canadian Airports Council (2005), 'Canadian airports welcome open skies agreement', news release, 11 November, accessed 3 March 2006 at www.cacairports.ca/english/news/OpenSkiesAgreementNov05.pdf.
Canadian Press (2005), 'Canada, U.S. expand open skies agreement – with reservations', *Edmonton Journal*, November, B7.
Carlisle, T. (2003), 'Canada cools to U.S. drug flow; some online pharmacies aren't filling big orders due to fears of shortages', *Wall Street Journal*, New York, 26 December, A9.
Celluci, P. (2005), *Unquiet Diplomacy*, Toronto: Key Porter Books.
Chow, G. (2007), 'Collateral benefits of security and supply chain improvements at international gateways', presentation to the International Conference on Gateways and Corridors, Vancouver, 4 May.
Chow, G. and J. McRae (1990), 'Non-tariff barriers and the structure of the U.S.–Canadian (transborder) trucking industry', *Transportation Journal*, **30**(2), 4–21.
Chow, G., R. Gritta and T. Shank (1994), 'Financial performance of Canadian and US motor carriers', *Canadian Transportation Research Forum Proceedings*, **29**, 464–78.
Clarke, S.E. (2000), 'Regional and transnational discourse: the politics of ideas and economic development in Cascadia', *International Journal of Economic Development*, **2**(3).
Clausing, K.A. (2001), 'Trade creation and trade diversion in the Canada–United States free trade agreement', *Canadian Journal of Economics*, **34**(3), 677–96.
Coiteux, M. (2004), 'North American integration and the single currency?' in A. Rugman (ed.), *North American Economic and Financial Integration (Research in Global Strategic Management Vol. 10)*, Greenwich, CT: JAI Press (Elsevier), pp. 175–91.
Commission of the European Communities (1985), 'Completing the internal market', (COM [85] 310 Final), Brussels: Office for Official Publications of the European Communities.
Condon, B. and T. Sinha (2001), 'An analysis of an alliance: NAFTA trucking and the US insurance industry', *The Estey Centre Journal of International Law and Trade Policy*, **2**(2), 235–45.
Condon, B. and T. Sinha (2003), *Drawing Lines in Sand and Snow: Balancing Border Security and North American Economic Integration*, Armonk, NY: M.E. Sharpe.
Conference Board of Canada (2003), *Renewing the Relationship: Canada and the United States in the 21st Century*, Toronto: The Conference Board of Canada, February.

Conference Board of Canada (2004), *Performance and Potential 2004–05: How Can Canada Prosper in Tomorrow's World?*, Toronto: The Conference Board of Canada, February.

Conference Board of Canada (2005), *In Search of a New Equilibrium in the Canada–U.S. Relationship*, Toronto: The Conference Board of Canada, January.

Congressional Research Services (2004), 'Border and transportation security: overview of Congressional issues', CRS report to Congress RL32705, 17 December, Washington, DC.

Connecticut Department of Transportation (2001), *Container Barge Feeder Service Study*, March, Hartford, CT: Connecticut Department of Transportation.

Corsi, T. and J. Stowers (1991), 'Effects of a deregulated environment on motor carriers: a systematic, multi-segment analysis', *Transportation Journal*, **30**(3), 4–28.

Council of the Americas (2006), 'Findings of the public/private sector dialogue on the security and prosperity partnership of North America', Louisville, KY, 10–11 January, accessed at www.as-coa.org/files/PDF/grp_10_15.pdf.

Council on Foreign Relations, Inc. (2005), *Building a North American Community: Report of the Independent Task Force on the Future of North America*, Washington, DC: Council on Foreign Relations.

Crockatt, M. (2005), 'Air cargo: the view from 35,000 feet', presentation to the Pan-Am Partnership for Business Education Study Group meeting, Kansas City, MO, 13 October.

DAMF Consultants with L-P Tardif & Associates (2005), 'Final report: the cumulative impact of U.S. import compliance programs at the Canada/U.S. land border on the Canadian trucking industry', 24 May, Ottawa: Transport Canada.

Davidson, L. (2004), 'Regional integration of U.S. border states with Canada: evidence from U.S. state exports', in A. Rugman (ed.), *North American Economic and Financial Integration (Research in Global Strategic Management Vol. 10)*, Greenwich, CT: JAI Press (Elsevier), pp. 69–84.

Del Pilar Londoño, Maria (2006), *Institutional Arrangements that Affect Free Trade Agreements: Economic Rationality Versus Interest Groups*, Rotterdam: Erasmus Research Institute of Management.

Delgado, C.P., J. Prozzi and R. Harrison (2003), 'Opening the southern border to Mexican trucks will have a negative impact on the US transportation system: where is the evidence?', presentation 03-3522 to the Transportation Research Board Annual Meeting, January, Washington, DC.

Department of Foreign Affairs and International Trade (2004), 'Smart border action plan status report', 17 December, Department of Foreign Affairs and International Trade, Ottawa.
Dobson, W. (2002), *Shaping the Future of the North American Economic Space, A Framework for Action (Commentary No. 162)*, Toronto: C.D. Howe Institute.
Doganis, R. (2002), *Flying Off Course: The Economics of International Airlines*, London: Routledge.
Drennen, C. (2004), 'Trucking services under NAFTA', in A.M. Rugman (ed.), *North American Economic and Financial Integration (Research in Global Strategic Management, Volume 10)*, Oxford: Elsevier, pp. 263–82.
Dukert, J.M. (2004), 'The quiet reality of North American energy interdependence', Institute for Research on Public Policy working paper series no. 2004-09h, Montreal.
Dunning, J. (1997), *Alliance Capitalism and Global Business*, Routledge: New York.
Dymond, B. and M. Hart (2005), 'Policy implications of a Canada–US customs union', June, Policy Research Initiative, Ottawa, published in *North American Linkages*.
Eaton, D.W. (2004), 'Roads, trains and ports: integrating North American transport', *Policy Options*, **25**(6), 58–61.
Edmonson, R.G. (2003), 'Is this efficiency? Special report: Mexico trade and transportation', *The Journal of Commerce*, 14–20 April, pp. 14–18.
European Commission (2001), 'European transport policy for 2010: time to decide', White Paper, Luxembourg: Office for Official Publications of the European Communities.
External Affairs and International Trade Canada (1991), *Transportation services between Canada and Mexico*, Ottawa: External Affairs and International Trade Canada.
Federal Highway Administration (undated, a), 'PPP case studies: heartland corridor', accessed at www.fhwa.dot.gov/PPP/heartland.htm.
Federal Highway Administration (undated, b), 'PPP case studies: Chicago region environmental and transportation efficiency program' (CREATE), accessed at www.fhwa.dot.gov/PPP/create.htm.
Federal Highway Administration Transportation Border Working Group (2003), Border Infrastructure Compendium: 2003 and Beyond, December, Washington, DC: US Department of Transportation.
Federal Highway Administration, Office of Operations (2005), 'Freight flow maps: Maine border crossings', US Department of Transportation data accessed 2 April, at www.ops.fhwa.dot.gov/freight/freight_analysis/state_info/maine/pb_me.html.

Federal Motor Carrier Safety Administration (2005), 'Hours-of-service regulations – effective October 1, 2005', accessed 24 February, 2006 at www.fmcsa.dot.gov/rules-regulations/topics/hos/hos-2005.htm.

Federal Motor Carrier Safety Administration (2006), 'Summary statistics for US DoT active motor carriers', accessed 22 August at http://ai.fmcsa.dot.gov/international/border.asp.

Field, A.M. (2007), 'Laying groundwork', *Journal of Commerce*, 19 February, pp. 12–16.

Findlay, R. and P. Telford (2006), 'The international joint commission and the Great Lakes water quality agreement: lessons for Canada–United States regulatory co-operation', Policy Research Initiative working paper series 23, Ottawa, published in *North American Linkages, Pollution Probe.*

Finn, S. (2004), 'CN: a true success story', presentation to the PanAmerican Partnership Study Group, 15 November, Montreal.

Fitch, S. and J. Muller (2004), 'The troll under the bridge', *Forbes*, 15 November, accessed at www.forbes.com/forbes/2004/1115/134_print.html.

Flynn, S. (2003), 'The false conundrum: continental integration versus homeland security', in P. Andreas and T.J. Biersteker (eds), *The Rebordering of North America: Integration and Exclusion in a New Security Context*, New York and London: Routledge, pp. 110–27.

Friedman, T.L. (2005), *The World is Flat: A Brief History of the Twenty-first Century*, New York: Farrer, Strauss and Giroux.

Fry, E. (2004), 'The role of subnational governments in the governance of North America', Institute for Research on Public Policy working paper series no. 2004-09, pp. 30–37, Montreal, published in *Mapping the New North American Reality*.

Ghanem, Z. and P. Cross (2003), 'The import intensity of provincial exports', *Canadian Economic Observer*, Statistics Canada (11-010), **16**(6) (June), 3.1–3.6.

Ghosh, M. and S. Rao (2004), 'Possible economic impacts in Canada of a Canada–US customs union', Policy Research Initiative, Ottawa, June, pp. 32–4, published in *North American Linkages*.

Gibbins, R. (2006), 'Canadian federalism in an age of federalism: the case for a new national policy', in *Canada by Picasso: The Faces of Federalism – The 2006 CIBC Scholar-in-Residence Lecture*, Ottawa: The Conference Board of Canada, pp. 59–98.

Global Insight (2006), 'Four corridor case studies of short-sea shipping services: short-sea shipping business case analysis', report for the US Department of Transportation Office of the Secretary.

Globerman, S. and P. Storer (2004), 'Canada–U.S. economic integration following NAFTA', in A. Rugman (ed.), *North American Economic and*

Financial Integration (Research in Global Strategic Management Vol. 10), Greenwich, CT: JAI Press (Elsevier), pp. 17–45.

Goldfarb, D. (2003), *The Road to a Canada–U.S. Customs Union: Step-by-Step or in a Single Bound? (Commentary No. 184)*, June, Toronto: C.D. Howe Institute.

Goldfarb, D. (2005), *The Canada–Mexico Conundrum: Finding Common Ground (Backgrounder No. 91)*, Toronto: C.D. Howe Institute.

Goldfarb, D. and W.B.P. Robson (2003), *Risky Business: U.S. Border Security and the Threat to Canadian Exports (Commentary No. 177)*, March, Toronto: C.D. Howe Institute.

Gotlieb, A. (2003), 'A grand bargain is exactly what we need', *National Post*, 8 March.

Gotlieb, A. (2005), ' "A special relationship": Canada–U.S. trade in the 21st century', remarks for a trade corridors roundtable, 25 April, reprinted in M. Van Pelt and R. Kuykendall (eds), *Greenlighting Trade: A Trade Corridors Atlas*, Hamilton, ON: Work Research Foundation, pp. 61–71.

Government of Canada (1992a), 'Canadian objectives met in North American Free Trade Agreement', news release no. 65, 12 August.

Government of Canada (1992b), *The North American Free Trade Agreement: Overview and Description*, August, Ottawa: Government of Canada.

Government of Canada (2002), 'Canadian NAFTA resource manual', April, accessed 15 January, 2007 at www.tc.gc.ca/pol/nafta-alena/en/resource-manual/adobe/English.pdf.

Government of Canada (2006a), *Canada's Asia-Pacific Gateway and Corridor Initiative*, (TP14605), October, Ottawa: Government of Canada, accessed at www.tc.gc.ca/majorissues/APGCI/initiative.htm.

Government of Canada (2006b), 'Budget 2007: Chapter 5', October, Ottawa: Government of Canada, accessed at www.budget.gc.ca/2007/bp/bpc5be.html.

Government of Canada Standing Committee on Foreign Relations and International Trade (2002), 'Partners in North America: advancing Canada's relations with the United States and Mexico, third report', 37th Parliament (2nd session).

Green, A.G. (2004), 'Beyond harmonization: how US immigration rules would have worked in Canada', *Policy Matters*, **5**(4), 27.

Hahn, J. (2002), 'Oral testimony of the Honorable Janice Hahn, member, Los Angeles City Council Chairwoman, Alameda Corridor Transportation Authority to a joint hearing of the U.S. Senate Environment & Public Works Committee and Finance Committee', 25 September, accessed at www.acta.org/Releases/releases_092602.2.html.

Hart, M. (2000), 'Disarming the undefended border: Rationale for a Canada–U.S. customs union', in M.E. Kreinin (ed.), *Building a*

Partnership: The Canada–United States Free Trade Agreement, East Lansing, MI: Michigan State University Press, pp. 132–42.

Hart, M. (2003), 'Canada, the United States and deepening economic integration: next steps', in R.G. Harris (ed.), *North American Linkages: Opportunities and Challenges for Canada*, Calgary: University of Calgary Press, pp. 419–45.

Hart, M. (2006), *Steer or Drift? Taking Charge of Canada–US Regulatory Convergence (Commentary No. 229)*, March, Toronto: C.D. Howe Institute.

Hart, M. and W.A. Dymond (2001), *Common Borders, Shared Destinies: Canada, the United States and Deepening Integration*, Ottawa: Centre for Trade Policy and Law.

Hart, M. and W.A. Dymond (2005), *The Geography of Integration*, Ottawa: Institute for Research on Public Policy.

Hart, M., W.A. Dymond and C. Robertson (1994), *Decision at Midnight: Inside the Canada–US Free Trade Negotiations*, Vancouver, BC: University of British Columbia Press.

Haynal, G. (2004), 'The next plateau in North America: what's the big idea?', *Policy Options*, June–July, pp. 35–9, accessed at www.irpp.org.

Heads, J. (1992), 'Motor carrier and railway competition between Canada and the United States', in *Proceedings, Canadian Transportation Research Forum Annual Meeting*, pp. 1–14.

Heads, J., B. Prentice and M. Harvey (1991), *The Transborder Competitiveness of Canadian Trucking*, Winnipeg, MB: University of Manitoba Transport Institute.

Hejazi, W. and A.E. Safarian (2005), 'NAFTA effects and the level of development', *Journal of Business Research*, **58**(12), 1741–9.

Helliwell, J.F. (1998), *How Much Do National Borders Matter?*, Washington, DC: Brookings Institution.

Helliwell, J.F. (2002), *Globalization and Well-Being*, Vancouver, BC: University of British Columbia Press.

Hillberry, R.H. and C.A. McDaniel (2002), 'A decomposition of North American trade growth since NAFTA', US International Trade Commission Office of Economics working paper 2002-12-A, December, Washington, DC.

Hills, C. (1999), 'NAFTA: from the Yukon to the Yucatan', speech to Free Trade @ 10: A Conference on the 10th Anniversary of the Canada/United States Free Trade Agreement and the 5th Anniversary of the North American Free Trade Agreement, 4–5 June, Montreal, QC, accessed at www.freetradeat10.com.

Hilsenrath, J.E. and R. Buckman (2003), 'Factory employment is falling world-wide; study of 20 big economies finds 22 million jobs lost; even China shows decline', *Wall Street Journal*, 20 October, A2.
Hodgson, J.R.F. and M.R. Brooks (2004), *Canada's Maritime Cabotage Policy: A Report for Transport Canada*, Halifax, NS: Marine Affairs Program.
Hufbauer, G.C. and J.J. Schott (1993), *NAFTA: An Assessment*, October, Washington, DC: Institute for International Economics.
Hufbauer, G.C. and J.J. Schott (1998), 'North American economic integration: 25 years backward and forward, Canada in the 21st century', Industry Canada Research Publications Program paper no. 3, November.
Hufbauer, G.C. and J.J. Schott (2004), *The Prospects For Deeper North American Economic Integration: A U.S. Perspective*, Toronto: C.D. Howe Institute.
Hufbauer, G.C. and J.J. Schott (2005), *NAFTA Revisited: Achievements and Challenges*, Washington, DC: Institute for International Economics.
Hummels, D. (2006), 'Global trends in trade and transportation', proceedings of the European Conference of Ministers of Transport, 17th International Symposium, CD-ROM, October, Berlin.
Ibarra-Yunez, A. (2004), 'NAFTA as a vehicle for regulatory and institutional convergence in the North American region', '*Mapping the New North American Reality*', Institute for Research on Public Policy working paper series no. 2004-09, pp. 48–52, Montreal.
IBI Group (2004), *Transportation technology at the Washington–British Columbia International Border: Final Report*, November, Seattle, WA: Washington State Department of Transportation.
Industry Canada (2004), 'Canadian supply chain efficiency smart border study overview', April, accessed at http://strategis.gc.ca.
Industry Canada (2006), 'Trade data on-line', accessed 3 August at www.strategis.gc.ca/sc_mrkti/tdst/engdoc/tr_homep.html.
International Air Cargo Association (2003), 'The case for all-cargo liberalization', ATConf/5-WP/83, presentation to International Civil Aviation Organization Worldwide Air Transport Conference: Challenges and Opportunities of Liberalization, 24–29 March, Montreal, accessed at www.icao.int.
International Trade Canada (annual), 'Trade, investment and economic statistics', accessed 15 January 2007 at www.international.gc.ca/eet/.
Janda, R., T. Flouris and T.H. Oum (2005), 'International air transport policy issues for Canada: views from the Air Currents Conference of January 2004', *Canadian Journal of Administrative Sciences*, **22**(1), 73–91.

Jones, J. (1990), *A Comparison of Trucking Productivity in Canada and the United States, 1978–1988: Final Report*, October, Kingston, ON: Canadian Institute of Guided Ground Transport, Queen's University.

Juneau, A. (2004), 'Québec–New York trade corridors initiatives, *Mapping the New North American reality*', Institute for Research on Public Policy working paper series no. 2004-09, Montreal.

Karemera, D. and W.W. Koo (1994), 'Trade creation and diversion effects of the US–Canadian Free Trade Agreement', *Contemporary Economic Policy*, **12**(1), 12–23.

Kirton, J. and S. Richardson (2006), 'The Commission for Environmental Co-operation: Lessons for Canada–United States regulatory co-operation', Policy Research Initiative working paper series 24, Ottawa, published in *North American Linkages*.

Konrad, V. and H. Nicol (2004), 'Boundaries and corridors: rethinking the Canada–United States border', *Canadian–American Public Policy*, **60**, 1–51.

Koyama, T. and S. Golub (2006), 'OECD's FDI regulatory restrictiveness index: revision and extension to more economies', Organisation for Economic Co-operation and Development, Economics Department working paper no. 525, December, Paris.

KPMG (2001), 'The tax burden of Canadian railways: a comparison of other modes and industries', report for the Railway Association of Canada, 7 June.

Kunimoto, R. and G. Sawchuk (2004), 'Moving towards a customs union: a review of the evidence', *Horizons*, **7**(1), 23–31, Ottawa: Policy Research Initiative.

LaCroix, D., J. Bowland and F. Collins (1993), *Transportation Taxation and Competitiveness*, September, Ottawa: Transportation Association of Canada.

Lazar, F. (2003), *Turbulence in the Skies: Options for Making Canadian Airline Travel More Attractive*, Toronto: C.D. Howe Institute.

Lepofsky, M., D.R. Ellis and R.E.L. Davis (2003), 'Establishing benchmarks for international border crossing truck travel time', Proceedings, Canadian Transportation Research Forum, pp. 547–61.

Limao, N. and A.J. Venables (2001), 'Infrastructure, geographical disadvantage, transport costs, and trade,' *The World Bank Economic Review*, **15**(3), 451–79.

MacDonald, L. (2004), 'Civil society and North American integration, mapping the New North American reality', Institute for Research on Public Policy working paper 2004-09, pp. 38–42, Montreal.

Machalaba, D. and J. Millman (2004), 'Kansas City Southern to buy Mexican railroad', *Wall Street Journal*, 16 December, A9.

Madore, J.T. (2001), 'Terrorist attacks', *Newsday*, New York, 12 September.
MariNova Consulting Limited (2005), *Short Sea Shipping Market Study (TP14472E)*, September, Ottawa: Transportation Development Centre of Transport Canada.
Martin, J.K. (2005), 'North American regulatory co-operation: a results agenda', Policy Research Initiative symposium report, December, Ottawa.
McCallum, J. (1995), 'National borders matter: regional trade patterns in North America', *American Economic Review*, **85**(3), 615–23.
McCarthy, L. (2003), 'The good of many outweighs the good of one: regional cooperation instead of individual competition in the United States and Western Europe?', *Journal of Planning Education and Research*, **23**, 140–52.
McMahon, F. (2001), 'Perimeter puzzle', December, Fraser Institute, accessed 8 December, 2006 at http://oldfraser.lexi.net/publications/forum/2001/12/section_13.html.
McMahon, F., C. Curtis and A.O. Adegoke (2003), 'The unseen wall: The Fraser Institute's 2003 trade survey', Fraser Institute occasional paper 76, December, Vancouver, BC.
McNiven, J. (1999). 'Economic integration in the NAFTA zone: corporate strategy and public policy at the operating level', unpublished paper.
Mead, K.M. (2002), 'Implementation of commercial motor carrier safety requirements at the US–Mexico border', statement to Committee on Appropriations, Subcommittee on Transportation; Committee on Commerce, Science and Transportation, Subcommittee on Surface Transportation and Merchant Marine, United States Senate, US Department of Transportation, 27 June.
Mouafo, D., N.P. Morales and J. Heynen (2004), *Building Cross-Border Links: A Compendium of Canada–US Government Collaboration*, Ottawa: Canada School of Public Service, accessed 5 June 2007 at http://dsp-psd.pwgsc.gc.ca/Collection/SC103-6-2004E.pdf.
NAFTA Secretariat (2001), 'In the matter of cross-border trucking services, Case USA-Mex 98-2008-01, final report of the panel', 6 February, accessed at www.nafta-sec-alena.org/.
National Research Council (2005), *Measuring International Trade on US Highways*, Washington, DC: National Academies of Sciences.
Ndayisenga, F. (2004), 'Economic impacts of regulatory convergence between Canada and the United States', *Horizons*, **7**(1), 9–16.
Newman, D. (2006), 'The lines that continue to separate us: borders in our "borderless" world', *Progress in Human Geography*, **30**(2), 143–61.
Nix, F.P. (2003), 'Truck activity in Canada – a profile', Transport Canada, accessed at www.tc.gc.ca/pol/EN/Report/TruckActivity/Chapter 8.htm.

Nix, F.P., J. R. Billing and M. Delaquis (1998), 'Impact of size and weight regulations on trucks crossing the Canadian–U.S. border', in *Transportation Research Record 1613*, pp. 33–42.

Noble, J. (2004), 'Fortress America or fortress North America', paper prepared for the Institute for Research on Public Policy Conference on North American Integration: Migration, Trade and Security, 1–2 April.

North American Competitiveness Council (NACC) (2007), 'Building a secure and competitive North America: private sector priorities for the security and prosperity partnership of North America', report to leaders from the North American Competitiveness Council, 21 August, accessed 22 August 2007 at www.ceocouncil.ca/en/.

North American Transportation Statistics (2006), accessed at http://nats.sct.gob.mx/nats/.

Organisation for Economic Co-operation and Development (OECD) (1997), *The Future of International Air Transport Policy: Responding to Global Change*, Paris: OECD.

Organisation for Economic Co-operation and Development (OECD) (1999), *OECD Principles of Corporate Governance*, (SG/CG(99)5), Paris: OECD.

Organisation for Economic Co-operation and Development (OECD) (2005), *OECD in Figures*, OECD Observer 2005, Supplement 1, accessed 24 February 2006 at www.oecd.org.

Organisation for Economic Co-operation and Development (OECD) (2006), *OECD Factbook 2006 (Economic, Environmental and Social Statistics)*, Paris: OECD.

Ontario Chamber of Commerce (OCC) (2003), 'Borders task force: final report', report for Governing Council meeting, 22 November.

Ontario Chamber of Commerce (OCC) (2004), 'Cost of border delays to Ontario', May, accessed at http://occ.on.ca/Policy/Reports/121.

Ontario Chamber of Commerce (OCC) (2005), 'Cost of border delays to the United States economy', April, accessed at http://occ.on.ca/Policy/Reports/122.

Ontario Chamber of Commerce (2006), '2006 border policies', 10 October, accessed at http://occ.on.ca/Policy/Reports/255.

Ontario Chamber of Commerce (2007a), '2006 transportation infrastructure policies', 21 June, accessed at http://occ.on.ca/Policy/Reports/301.

Ontario Chamber of Commerce (2007b), '2007–2008 transportation infrastructure policies', Ontario Chamber of Commerce, 28 February, accessed at http://occ.on.ca/Policy/Reports/331.

Oum, T.H. (1998), 'Overview of regulatory changes in international air transport and Asian strategies towards the US open skies initiatives', *Journal of Air Transport Management*, **4**, 127–34.

Park, J. (2003), 'Not enough hours in a day', *Canadian Transportation Research Forum Proceedings*, **1**, 348–62.

Pastor, R.A. (2001), *Toward a North American Community: Lessons from the Old World for the New*, Washington, DC: Institute for International Economics.

Peters, M. and J. Hill (2007), 'Statement of The Honorable Mary E. Peters, Secretary of Transportation, and John H. Hill, Administrator of the Federal Motor Carrier Safety Administration, before the Senate Appropriations Subcommittee for Transportation, Housing and Urban Development, and Related Agencies', March 8, accessed at http://testimony.ost.dot.gov/test/peters 3.htm.

Pettigrew, P. (2002), 'The Canada we want in the North American we are building', speech for: 8th Annual Canadian–American Business Achievement Award and International Business Partnership Forum, accessed 13 November, 2006 at http://w01.international.gc.ca/minpub/Publication.aspx?isRedirect=True&FileSpec=/Min_Pub_Docs/105546.htm.

Phillips, K.B. (2005), 'CN – the rail perspective on future NAFTA issues', presentation to the Transportation Research Board 84th Annual Meeting, 12 January, Washington, DC.

Policy Research Institute (2006), 'The emergence of cross-border regions between Canada and the United States: roundtables synthesis report', in 'North American Linkages', May, Ottawa: Policy Research Institute.

Port Authority of New York and New Jersey (2006), 'The Port Authority strategic plan: transportation for regional prosperity' (2nd printing), August, accessed at www.panynj.gov/AbouttheportAuthority/InvestorRelations/strategic_plan_06.html.

Porter, R.B. (2000a), 'The negotiating process: a panel discussion', in M.E. Kreinin (ed.), *Building a Partnership: The Canada–United States Free Trade Agreement*, East Lansing, MI: Michigan State University Press, pp. 19–40.

Porter, R.B. (2000b), 'The successful quest for a Canada–United States free trade agreement', in M.E. Kreinin (ed.), *Building a Partnership: The Canada–United States Free Trade Agreement*, East Lansing, MI: Michigan State University Press, pp. xi–xix.

Power, B. (2007), 'Maine business to lead Atlantic business group', *The Chronicle-Herald* (Halifax, NS), 13 June, C1.

Prentice, B.E. and M. Ojah (2002), 'Transportation: bottlenecks and possibilities', in E.J. Chambers and P.H. Smith (eds), *NAFTA in the New Millennium*, Edmonton, AB: University of Alberta Press, pp. 331–53.

Proulx, P.-P. (2004), 'Economic regions in North America,' *Horizons*, **7**(1), 35–41.

Public Works and Government Services Canada (PWGSC) (2001), *Vision and Balance: Report of the Canada Transportation Act Review Panel*, June, Ottawa: Public Works and Government Services Canada.

Public Works and Government Services Canada (PWGSC) (2006), *Transportation in Canada 2006: Annual Report*, TP-13198E, Ottawa: Public Works and Government Services Canada, accessed at www.tc.gc.ca/pol/en/Report/anre2006/.

Retail Industry Leaders Association (2005), 'The Department of Homeland Security: promoting risk-based prioritization and management', written statement for the House Committee on Homeland Security, 13 April, accessed 12 May at www.retail-leaders.org.

Retail Industry Leaders Association (undated), 'Effective contingency planning is needed to keep commerce flowing in the event of a terrorist attack on the supply chain', accessed 12 May, 2005 at www.retail-leaders.org.

Ritchie, R.J. (2002), 'Remarks to the Conference Board of Canada 2002 Business Outlook Briefings', 8 April, Calgary, AB, accessed 24 February 2005 at www.cpr.ca.

Robson, W.B.P. (2007), *Found Money: Matching Canadians' Saving with their Infrastructure Needs*, 8 March, Toronto: C.D. Howe Institute.

Rosson, P.J. (2004), 'Buying and selling prescription drugs on the Internet: Canada–United States trade', *Journal of Electronic Commerce in Organizations*, **2**(4), 47–62.

Rothberg, P. (2003), 'North America Free Trade Agreement: truck safety considerations', in C.V. Anderson (ed.), *NAFTA Revisited*, New York: Nova Science Publishers, pp. 119–33.

Roussel, S. (2002), 'The blueprint of fortress North America', in D. Rudd and N. Furneaux (eds), *Fortress North America: What 'Continental Security' Means for Canada*, Toronto: The Canadian Institute of Strategic Studies, pp. 12–19.

Rugman, A.M. (1981), *Inside the Multinationals: The Economics of Internal Markets*, London: Croom Helm.

Sawchuk, G. and A. Sydor (2003), 'Canada–U.S. trade and foreign direct investment patterns', in R.G. Harris (ed.), *North American Linkages: Opportunities and Challenges for Canada*, Calgary: University of Calgary Press, pp. 117–80.

Schwanen, D. (1997), *Trading Up: The Impact of Increased Continental Integration on Trade, Investment and Jobs in Canada*, Toronto: C.D. Howe Institute.

Schwanen, D. (2004), 'Canada and free trade – 15 years on', *Policy Options*, (February), 65–70.

Security and Prosperity Partnership of North America (SPP) (2005), 'Report to leaders', June, accessed 13 March 2006 at www.spp.gov.

Security and Prosperity Partnership of North America (SPP) (2006), 'Report to leaders II', August, accessed at www.spp.gov/2006_report_to_leaders/.

Security and Prosperity Partnership of North America (SPP) (2007), 'Canada/United States/Mexico SPP Regulatory Cooperation Framework', August, accessed at www.spp.gov/pdf/spp_reg_coop_final.pdf.

Shulman, J. and A. Shea (2000), *Lower Rates and Improved Performance: Regulatory Reform of Freight Railways*, Toronto: Conference Board of Canada.

Small, K.A., R. Noland, X. Chu and D. Lewis (1999), *Valuation of Travel Time Savings and Predictability in Congested Conditions for Highway User-Cost Estimation*, NCHRP report no. 431, Washington, DC: Transportation Research Board.

Sparling, D. and J.A. Caswell (2006), 'Risking market integration without regulatory integration: the case of NAFTA and BSE', *Review of Agricultural Economics*, **28**(2), 212–28.

Springer, G.L. (2005), 'Integrating the Gulf of Mexico border', presentation to the Transportation Research Board, 12 January, Washington, DC.

Statistics Canada (2002), *Rail in Canada 2000*, (52-216-XIB), Ottawa: Statistics Canada.

Statistics Canada (2006), *Trucking in Canada 2004*, (53-222-XIE), Ottawa: Statistics Canada.

Stewart-Patterson, D. (2007), 'Building a secure and competitive North America', remarks to the I.E. Canada 16th Annual Conference, 23 April, Markham, ON, accessed at www.ceocouncil.ca/en/view/?document_id=567&type_id=3.

Stoffman, D. (2002), *Who Gets In: What's Wrong with Canada's Immigration Program and How to Fix It*, Toronto: Macfarlane Walter & Ross.

Studer, I. (2004), 'The North American auto industry, mapping the new North American reality', Institute for Research on Public Policy, working paper 2004-09, pp. 96–101, Montreal.

Tanguay, G.A. and M.-C. Thierren (2004), 'Protecting Canada and the U.S. against terrorism: a common security perimeter', in A.M. Rugman (ed.), *North American Economic and Financial Integration* (*Research in Global Strategic Management, Volume 10*), Oxford: Elsevier, pp. 85–96.

Taylor, J.C. and D.J. Closs (1993), 'Logistics implications of an integrated US–Canada market', *International Journal of Physical Distribution & Logistics Management*, **23**(1), 3–13.

Taylor, J.C., D.R. Robideaux and G.C. Jackson (2003), 'The U.S.–Canada border: costs attributable to the border and trade policy, and the implications for an external perimeter strategy', *Canadian Transportation Research Forum Proceedings*, 1, 228–42.

Taylor, J.C., D.R. Robideaux and G.C. Jackson (2004a), 'Costs of the U.S.–Canada border', in A.M. Rugman (ed.), *North American Economic and Financial Integration* (*Research in Global Strategic Management, Volume 10*), Oxford: Elsevier, pp. 283–98.

Taylor, J.C., D.R. Robideaux and G.C. Jackson (2004b), 'US–Canada transportation and logistics: border impacts and costs, causes and possible solutions', *Transportation Journal*, **43**(4), 5–21.

Terry, J.J. (1991), 'Investor's bloodbath in trucking – the deteriorated valuation of trucking company equity securities', in *Transportation Research Forum Proceedings of the 33rd Annual Meeting*, pp. 323–32.

Thibault, M., M.R. Brooks and K.J. Button (2006), 'The response of the US maritime industry to the new container security initiatives', *Transportation Journal*, **45**(1), 5–15.

Thompson, P. (2003), 'Online sales spark national controversy: delegates disagree on delivering drugs to Americans', *Canadian Pharmaceutical Journal*, **136**(6).

Toronto Stock Exchange Committee on Corporate Governance (1994), *Where Were the Directors? Guidelines for Improved Corporate Governance in Canada*, Toronto: Toronto Stock Exchange.

Transport Canada (1996), 'Federal Government releases progress report on open skies agreement', Transport Canada press release 34/96, 28 March, Ottawa.

Transport Canada (1997), *Transportation in Canada 1996 (TP13012)*, Ottawa: Public Works and Government Services Canada.

Transport Canada (1998), 'NAFTA plenary report 1998', accessed 8 January 2007 at www.tc.gc.ca/pol/nafta-alena/en/plenaries.htm.

Transport Canada (2000), *Transportation in Canada 1999 (TP13198)*, Ottawa: Public Works and Government Services Canada.

Transport Canada (2004), *Air Liberalization: A Review of Canada's Economic Regulatory Regime as it Affects the Canadian Air Industry*, Ottawa: Public Works and Government Services Canada, November.

Transport Canada (2005a), *Transportation in Canada 2004 (TP13198E)*, Ottawa: Public Works and Government Services Canada.

Transport Canada (2005b), 'Flying the "Open Skies" ', Transport Canada press release H225/05, 11 November, Ottawa.

Transport Canada (2005c), *Canada–United States Air Transport Agreement Consultation with Stakeholders*, May, Ottawa: Public Works and Government Services Canada.

Transport Canada (2005d), *Government Response to the Fourth (Interim) Report of the Standing Committee on Transport: Air Liberalization and the Canadian Airports System in Canada*, Ottawa: Public Works and Government Services Canada.

Transport Canada (2005e), speaking notes for Transport Minister Jean-C. Lapierre to the Annual General Meeting of the Air Transport Association of Canada, Montreal, QC, 7 November.

Transport Canada (2005f), 'Commercial vehicle drivers hours of service regulations, 2005', accessed 8 January 2007 at http://canadagazette.gc.ca/partII/2005/20051116/html/sor313-e.html.

Transport Canada (2005g), 'Border transportation partnership identifies central area of analysis for new Detroit–Windsor border crossing', Transport Canada press release H226/05, 14 November, Ottawa.

Transport Canada (2006), Transportation in Canada 2005: Annual Report, Ottawa: Public Works and Government Services Canada.

Transportation Research Board (TRB) (2002), *Regulation of Weights, Lengths, and Widths of Commercial Motor Vehicles (Special Report 267)*, Washington, DC: National Academy of Sciences Transportation Research Board.

Transportation Research Board (2003), *Freight Capacity for the 21st Century (Special Report 271)*, Washington, DC: National Academy of Sciences Transportation Research Board.

Trefler, D. (1999), 'The long and short of the Canada–U.S. free trade agreement', Industry Canada Perspectives on North American Free Trade Series, paper no. 6, Ottawa, September, accessed at http://strategis.ic.gc.ca/epic/internet/ineas-aes.nsf/en/ra01773e.html.

Trickey, M. (2001), 'The undefended border: economic concerns spur campaign to erase line between us and the U.S.', *The Montreal Gazette*, 4 August, A12.

UNCTAD (2006), *Review of Maritime Transport 2005*, Geneva: United Nations Conference on Trade and Development.

UNCTAD (undated), FDI/TNC database, accessed April 28, 2005 at www.unctad.org/Templates/Page.asp?intItemID=3137&lang=1.

United Nations (2000), *Monitoring Human Development: Enlarging People's Choices*, Geneva: United Nations, accessed 21 August 2006 at http://hdr.undp.org/reports.

United Nations (2005), 'Human development report 2005', Geneva: United Nations, accessed 21 August 2006 at http://hdr.undp.org/reports.

US Census Bureau (2006), 'US populations 1996–2005', accessed 29 April at www.census.gov/prod/2001pubs/statab/sec01.pdf.

US Department of Homeland Security (2003), 'Data Management Improvement Act (DMIA) task force: second annual report to Congress', December, Washington, DC: US Department of Homeland Security.

US Department of Justice (2002), *Data Management Improvement Act (DMIA) Task Force: First Annual Report to Congress*, December, Washington, DC: US Department of Justice.

US Department of Transportation (2005a), 'U.S., Mexico agree on expanded aviation services', 21 September, accessed 3 March, 2006 at www.dot.gov/affairs/dot13305.htm.

US Department of Transportation (2005b), 'United States, Canada reach open-skies aviation agreement', States News Service, November, accessed at www.dot.gov/affairs/dot16605.htm.

US Department of Transportation, Bureau of Transportation Statistics (2002), 'National transportation statistics 2002', Washington, DC, accessed at www.bts.gov/publications/national_transportation_statistics/2002/html/table_01_49.html.

US Department of Transportation, Research and Innovative Technology Administration (2005), 'US–North American trade and freight transportation highlights', June, Washington, DC.

US Department of Transportation, Research and Innovative Technology Administration (2006), 'North American Freight Transportation', June, Washington, DC: Bureau of Transportation Statistics.

US General Accounting Office (GAO) (2004), 'Freight transportation: strategies needed to address planning and financing limitations (GAO-04-165: report to the Committee on Environment and Public Works, US Senate)', December, Washington, DC, accessed at www.gao.gov.

US Government Accountability Office (GAO) (2005), *Short Sea Shipping Option Shows Importance of Systematic Approach to Public Investment Decisions (GAO-05-768)*, July, Washington, DC: Government Accountability Office.

US International Trade Commission (2002), *The Economic Effects of Significant U.S. Import Restraints: Third Update*, pub. 3519, Washington, DC: US International Trade Commission.

US State Department (2006), 'Open skies partners', accessed 28 February at www.state.gov/e/eb/rls/othr/2005/22281.htm.

US–Canada Power System Outage Task Force (2004), *Final Report on the August 14, 2003 Blackout in the United States and Canada: Causes and Recommendations*, April, Washington, DC: US Department of Energy and Natural Resources Canada.

Vernon, R.J. (2001), 'Big business and national governments: reshaping the compact in a globalizing economy', *Journal of International Business Studies*, **32**(3), 509–18.

Villa, J.C. (2006), 'Status of the U.S.–Mexico commercial border crossing process: analysis of recent studies and research', in *Transportation*

Research Record 1966, Transportation Research Board of the National Academies, Washington, DC: TRB, pp. 10–15.
Viscusi, W.K., J.M. Vernon and J. Harrington, Jr. (1996), *Economics of Regulation and Anti-Trust*, 2nd edn, Cambridge, MA: MIT University Press.
Wallin, P. (2006), unpublished comments on influencing policy makers at the North America Works II in Kansas City Conference, Kansas City, MO, 1 December.
Ward, G. (2005), 'Short sea shipping: view from the front line', presentation to the Transportation Research Board annual meeting, 12 January, Washington, DC.
WESTAC (1991), 'Canada–U.S. air industry: Debating "Open Skies"', Vancouver: Western Transportation Advisory Council.
WESTAC (1992), 'Canada's rail industry: developments and issues since 1980', Vancouver, BC: Western Transportation Advisory Council.
Whatcom Council of Governments (2004), 'Short sea shipping on the Canada–United States west coast', accessed at www.wcog.com/imtc/.
Whatcom Council of Governments (undated), 'Free and Secure Trade (FAST) program promotion', accessed at www.wcog.com.
Wilson, A. (2003), 'NAFTA's effect on Canada–U.S. trade and investment', in C.V. Anderson (ed.), *NAFTA Revisited*, New York: Nova Science Publishers, pp. 197–207.
World Bank (2006), 'Doing business' database, accessed 6 November at www.doingbusiness.org/ExploreTopics/TradingAcrossBorders.
World Economic Forum (2006), *Global Competitiveness Report 2006–2007*, A. López-Claros, M.E. Porter, X. Sala-i-Martin and K. Schwab (eds), Basingstoke: Palgrave MacMillan, accessed 13 November at www.weforum.org/en/initiatives/gcp/Global%20Competitiveness%20Report/index.htm.
World Shipping Council (WSC), The International Mass Retail Association, and the National Industrial Transportation League (2003), 'In-transit container security Enhancement' working paper, 9 September, accessed 12 May, 2005 at www.retail-leaders.org.
World Trade Organization (2004), *International Trade Statistics 2003*, Geneva: World Trade Organization.
World Trade Organization (2005), *International Trade Statistics 2004*, Geneva: World Trade Organization.
World Trade Organization (2006), 'International Trade Statistics trade database', accessed 24 July at http://stat.wto.org.
World Trade Organization (2007), *International Trade Statistics 2006*, Geneva: World Trade Organization.

Index